HOW TO PAINT YOUR CAR
REVISED & UPDATED

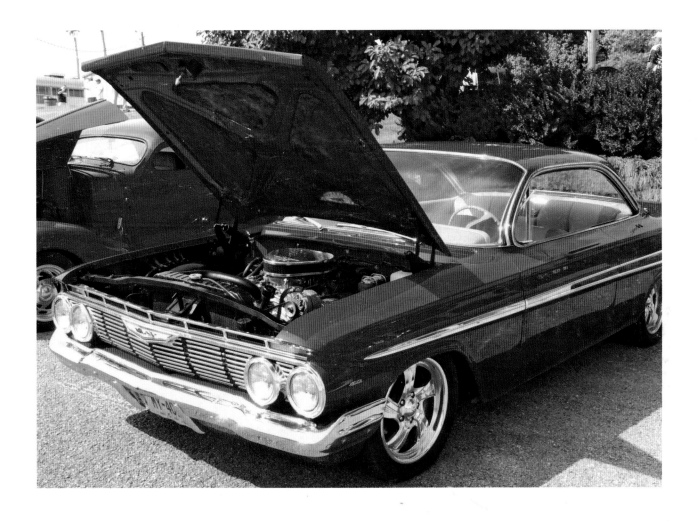

By Dennis W. Parks

motorbooks

Dedication

To my wife, Sandy, for putting up with me for all these years, and to Roger Ward,
for knowing the answers to most of life's questions.

First published in 2013 by Motorbooks, an imprint of MBI Publishing Company, 400 First Avenue North, Suite 400, Minneapolis, MN 55401 USA

Motorbooks titles are also available at discounts in bulk quantity for industrial or sales-promotional use. For details write to Special Sales Manager at MBI Publishing Company, 400 First Avenue North, Suite 400, Minneapolis, MN 55401 USA.

To find out more about our books, visit us online at www.motorbooks.com.

Editor: Jordan Wiklund
Design Manager: Brad Springer
Designer: Kim Winscher

Printed in China

ISBN-13: 978-0-7603-4388-3

Library of Congress Cataloging-in-Publication Data

Parks, Dennis, 1959-
  How to paint your car : updated & revised / by Dennis Parks. -- Second edition, revised & updated.
      pages cm -- (Motorbooks workshop)
  Summary: "Dennis Parks' updated edition of How To Paint Your Car features comprehensive guidance on every aspect of automotive painting and exterior upkeep. A verteran Motorbooks author, Parks walks readers through everything they need to know, from primer to paint, tools and materials, and much more"-- Provided by publisher.
  ISBN 978-0-7603-4388-3 (pbk.)
  1. Automobiles--Painting. I. Title.
TL255.2.P35 2013
629.2'6--dc23
                                    2012045325

Contents

Foreword

*H*ow To Paint Your Car is an informative, well-written book that will help the first-time painter, the novice hobbyist, or even the professional custom car painter. Whether painting for a business or as a hobbyist, there are many pitfalls to avoid, and the way you react can make or break a paint job. Paint products change so frequently that it is vitally important to read and understand the latest tech sheets for all the products you are using.

To the novice painter: always try to do the next job better than the one you just finished, and you're on your way. Remember that good taste and simplicity always work. Good luck.

Roger Ward
Automotive paint professional

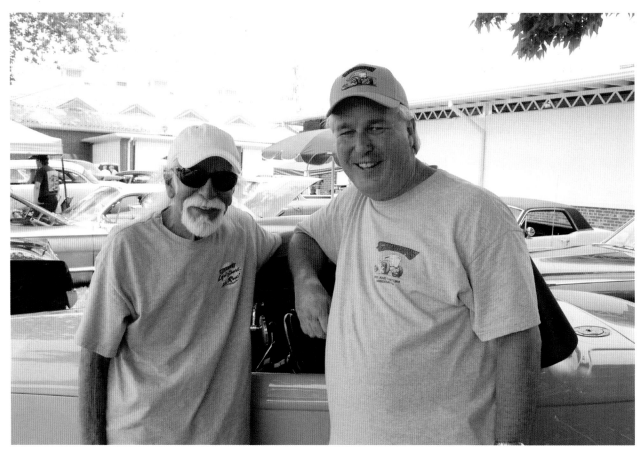

Automotive painting guru Roger Ward (left) and the author in front of Roger's taupe-colored 1932 Ford roadster at the 2012 Goodguy's Heartland Nationals.

Acknowledgments

They say that the only thing that remains constant is change, and that is certainly true when it comes to automotive paint products and practice. Other than getting good advice beforehand, painting an automobile simply takes practice. Contemporary paint products are designed to make the task as easy as possible. Whether you start on a complete vehicular repaint or just a fender, practice is the key. No matter what you paint, the first shot at it won't be perfect, which will allow you to learn with each new attempt. Evaluate your results after each job and then consult this book again to find out what you may have done wrong, and then get ready to do it again.

After discussing the steps required in painting a vehicle in the various chapters, I will walk you through a complete paint job on an older vehicle. The vehicle is not meant to be a show car by any means, but it does serve as a good example of the type of vehicle that you might be painting for your first project.

I must thank my longtime friend, Roger Ward, who has taught me most of what I know about auto painting. Roger painted his first car when he was fourteen years old, and has been refining his skills for almost sixty years now. Roger has seen a new development or two in the painting industry, has earned a fair amount of magazine coverage, and most of all has been a truly great friend over the years.

Thanks also go to Keith Moritz at Morfab Customs, Kevin and Wendy Brinkley at Harding's Auto Works, Jim Miller and Duane Wissman at Jerry's Auto Body, along with Steve "Bones" Bauer and Todd Pflanz at High Ridge NAPA for providing a wealth of information.

Wishing you the best in your painting projects,

Dennis W. Parks

Introduction

Even though automotive paint products and techniques have changed over the years, it is still possible to paint your own car or truck. With the products now available, you have perhaps the best opportunity ever to achieve a perfect paint job. What you must realize before you start, however, is that there is much more to painting a car than squeezing the trigger on a paint spray gun.

How To Paint Your Car tells readers virtually everything they need to know before painting their car, from disassembly and prepping the surface for primer, to buffing, polishing, and waxing the same finished surface. From that first coat of primer-surfacer to the last coat of paint (and beyond with polish and wax), this book explains everything you need to achieve that "I did it myself, and I'm proud of it" attitude. Whether you are planning to straighten some minor dents and repaint just the affected area, or repaint the entire car or truck, this book will tell you how to do the job correctly.

You must get the body as straight and as smooth as possible; painting over imperfections is only going to highlight them, rather than cover them. You must also mix primers, hardeners, top coats, and their respective catalysts as directed. The directions are included with each product—you just have to read them. If you can read and follow directions, you can paint your car. The chemistry of automotive paint has already been determined for you—there is no reason to try to "improve" the characteristics of any paint product. Mix the components as directed, apply them as directed, and allow them to dry as directed before applying successive coats, and you can apply a professional paint job to your car. The guidelines in this book will help make your car as ready for paint as it can be.

You must also have the right tools. As with most jobs, that requires the correct safety equipment. Today's paint products are safe to use, but only when they are used properly. Correct safety equipment, such as respirators, rubber gloves, and painter's coveralls, is essential. Learn what safety equipment is required for each type of paint product. This book will also tell the differences between conventional, HVLP, touch-up, siphon feed, and gravity feed spray guns, and which type is best for your particular needs.

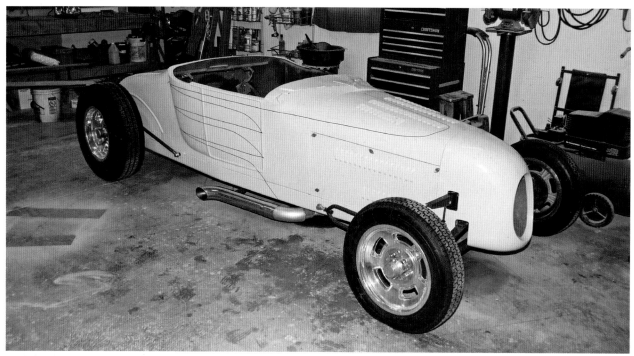

The author's former 1927 Ford roadster was painted VW Harvest Moon. At this point, scallops had been laid out with Fine Line tape, and the car was ready to be masked and painted.

Chapter 1
Automotive Painting Defined

Depending on the job at hand, paint can be applied to automobile bodies in more than one way. Initially, our automobiles roll off the assembly line with a fresh coat of paint. Eventually, our cars or trucks will need slight touch-ups to keep small nicks or scratches from blemishing their fresh appearance. Touch-up work is usually accomplished with a small brush attached to the cap of a bottle of touch-up paint. If wear and tear necessitates the painting of small body items or trim, you might use a spray can to bring that finish up to snuff. If your automobile has sustained collision damage, repair will usually involve repainting the affected panel(s) or sections with conventional paint spray guns.

The techniques used to apply automotive paint are determined by the type (and amount) of coverage needed and the condition of the existing surface material. You would not use a full-size spray gun to touch up a small scratch, or expect to use a touch-up brush to refinish an entire panel. Likewise, paint from a spray can may be "close enough" in color match and texture to refinish or modify a trim panel, such as a grille or body molding. If the entire vehicle is going to be repainted, however, use paint specifically manufactured for automotive refinishing.

To achieve a visually acceptable, compatible, and durable paint job, you must use products designed to suit the existing paint finishes or undercoat preparations. The finest paint job in the world will not last if the various layers of body filler, primer, sealers, and final top coat are not compatible. Simply put, do not try to be a chemist when it comes to repainting your car.

DETERMINING THE TYPE OF PAINT ON YOUR CAR

Before the advent of high-tech polyurethane paint products, cars were painted with either enamel or lacquer. Each had its own distinct characteristics. Enamels were quick and easy, generally covering in one or two coats and not requiring any clear coats or rubbing out. Lacquer, on the other hand, required multiple coats, but imperfections were easily rubbed

out and quickly repainted. Lacquer's fast drying time afforded painters the opportunity to fix blemishes almost immediately.

Although both paint products (enamel and lacquer) offer specific benefits, they cannot be used together on car bodies because they are not compatible. It would be all right, under proper conditions, to spray enamel over lacquer when surfaces are properly prepared, but lacquer applied over enamel almost always results in wrinkling or other severe finish damage. This is because the solvent base for lacquer paint (lacquer thinner) is much too potent for the softer materials used in enamel products.

Product compatibility factors are also extremely important today. Compatible materials are not confined to just enamel, lacquer, or urethane bases—every product in an entire paint system must be compatible with the surface material to which it will be applied, as well as with every other product in the system. For example, using a PPG reducer with a BASF hardener in a DuPont paint product is asking for trouble. The individual products were not designed as parts of a single compatible paint system, and as a result, the color, adhesion, and surface flow of that combination could be adversely affected. More information on paint chemistry and compatibility is found in Chapter 2.

Before arbitrarily purchasing paint for your car, you need to determine what type of material currently exists on the vehicle's surface: enamel, lacquer, or urethane. On newer vehicles, factory paint jobs are all going to be urethane-based, as enamels and lacquers are quickly becoming history. For your specific vehicle, it will be worth asking your local automotive paint supplier for information on which kind of paint the factory applied. For those cars still clad in factory paint jobs, their identification tags should list the specific paint codes. In addition, auto body paint and supply store professionals can determine the exact type of paint and color from the vehicle identification number (VIN) on older vehicles, or from a separate paint and options tag

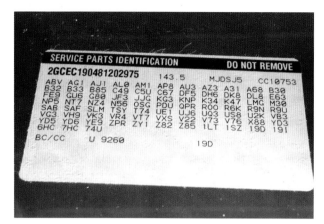

Not that Joe Public can make any sense out of a paint and options tag, but to a service technician, this tag provides tons of information. One of these codes—maybe "BC/CC U 9260" on the bottom—tells us that the paint is base coat/clear coat Victory Red. This particular tag is in the glove box, but can be found in other places on other makes and models. Consult a repair manual if you can't find the tag on your vehicle.

on newer vehicles. This makes material identification easy when you plan to match existing paint.

If your car or truck has been repainted with a type of paint or a color different from its original factory job, you will have to obtain paint code numbers from a paint can used during the repaint or from some other source, like the painter who completed the job. Hopefully, that person kept track of this information and will make it available to you.

If you are unable to determine specific paint codes or information relating to the type of paint used on your car, you will have to test an inconspicuous spot on the vehicle body with lacquer thinner; you could also test a spot on an area already slated for repaint. Dab a clean, white cloth with lacquer thinner and rub a spot of paint. If color comes off immediately, or the spot begins to wrinkle, the paint type is enamel. Should color wipe off onto the cloth after vigorous rubbing, lacquer paint is present. If nothing wipes off, the paint is probably a type of urethane.

To determine if finishes include coats of clear paint over their base color, sand an inconspicuous spot with 600-grit-or-finer sandpaper. White sanding residue indicates the existence of a clear coat finish, whereas a color residue demonstrates that the body was painted with a color material only.

Enough emphasis cannot be placed on the importance of determining the type of paint covering the surface of your car before you apply new coats of fresh paint. The only exceptions are vehicle bodies that have been stripped to bare metal in preparation

for complete new paint system applications. If you are still unsure about the type of paint on your car after this test, or if you have any other related questions or problems, consult an auto body paint and supply store professional. Be earnest and attentive in order to receive definitive answers and patient assistance. Remember, applying mismatched coatings to an existing finish can ruin the whole paint job.

NICK AND SCRATCH REPAIR

Minor nicks and scratches can sometimes be polished or buffed out. They must be shallow and expose only paint at their deepest point. If primer or bare metal is visible, you must apply new paint.

An easy and inexpensive way to repair nicks involves the use of touch-up paint. Small bottles of stock factory colors are commonly available at auto body paint and supply stores and a number of auto parts houses. Mostly supplied for newer cars, these touch-up paints match the paint code on your vehicle's ID tag. Apply them with a small brush attached to the bottle's cap or with an artist's fine paintbrush. For years, auto enthusiasts have successfully used the clean ends of paper matchsticks to apply touch-up paint. The choice is yours.

It is imperative to cover nicks as soon as possible, especially when bare metal is exposed. Oxidation quickly attacks bare metal, beginning a costly rust and corrosion process. Like a cancer, oxidation spreads

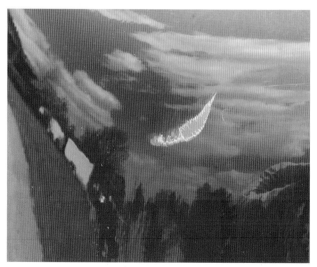

This blemish scars the driver's side bedside of the author's daily driver pickup and is a common type of damage that could happen to most any vehicle. This isn't a dent or a gouge—it simply has a few layers of "skin" peeled off. Since the factory primer is still intact, it hasn't developed any rust yet. In later chapters, you will see how to repair this common damage.

undetected beneath paint until damage is so extensive that flakes of paint peel off at random. Prior to the advent of convenient touch-up paint bottles, auto enthusiasts applied dabs of clear fingernail polish to nicks in an effort to protect bare metal and deter the progress of oxidation, rust, and corrosion.

Long, deep scratches may pose more serious problems than tiny nicks. Although you may treat minor scratches in almost the same fashion as nicks, long strokes with a touch-up paintbrush may be too rough or noticeable. Depending on the color and type of paint finish, you may be better off carefully sanding scratches smooth and then feathering in new layers of fresh paint with an aerosol touch-up can (available at some auto parts stores and auto body paint and supply outlets) or a regular spray paint device.

PANEL PAINTING

Except for a few special automobiles, most vehicles are composed of a number of separate sections welded or bolted together to make single motorized units. Auto body professionals generally refer to these sections as panels—for example, quarter panels or rear body panels. In addition to panels, cars and trucks have roofs, hoods, fenders, and doors.

In many body collision or simple repaint situations, painters have to spray complete panels in lieu of spraying specific spots. The determination of whether to spot-paint or cover entire panels depends upon the type and style of the existing paint finish, size of the repair area, and the ability to blend new paint into the surrounding body paint.

Spot-painting a number of minor ding repairs scattered over an entire hood panel would probably turn out looking like a spotted leopard. It is much easier to prepare and paint the hood all at once, and the results look more professional and uniform throughout. The same holds true for other panels in need of more than just a spot or two of new paint.

Some situations allow for painting just parts of panels, as opposed to entire units. These might include lower panel sections or featured grooves, ridges, or trim lines on doors, fenders, or quarter panels. Special graphics or vinyl stripes might also serve as perimeters to cordon off particular areas, allowing for partial panel repaints. A ridge or trim line draws the eye away from the paint itself, making minor color variations unnoticeable.

With the advent of base coat/clear coat paint systems, blending has all but eliminated panel painting.

Even though you may know the correct paint code, prep the surface properly, and apply the paint flawlessly, any panels painted separately from others will most likely not match the rest of the vehicle. Single-stage paint products can also blend well; however, base coat/clear coat is recommended for the novice. The blend creates the illusion that the affected area was never damaged, even though the actual color of the repaired area may not exactly match the adjacent panels. On the other hand, two adjacent panels painted separately are quite noticeable when reinstalled on the vehicle.

Color blending and uniform paint feathering are of utmost importance when you paint panels. Your ultimate goal is to apply paint in such a way that no definitive edges are visible, making those areas appear as if they had never been repaired or repainted. To help a primary painted panel's new finish blend in with surrounding panels, sometimes single-panel repaint jobs require that adjacent panels on either side be lightly sprayed with feather coats of paint.

COMPLETE PAINT JOB

On a partial repaint job, approximately 70 percent of the work involved is surface preparation, and only 30 percent is related to actual paint application. For a complete paint job, however, approximately 95 percent of the work is surface preparation, while only 5 percent is spent applying paint.

Many people do not understand that the condition of body surfaces prior to paint application directly affects the outcome of a paint job. Every speck of dirt, sanding scratch, pinhole, or other tiny blemish is magnified tenfold after paint has been applied over it. The flawless, even quality of the surrounding paint draws the viewer's eye directly to the imperfection. Automotive paint, even in multiple layers, constitutes a very thin coating, and it simply will not cover up even minor flaws the same way, for example, house paint might. If the surface isn't smooth, don't spray it!

All exterior body trim must be removed for complete paint jobs. You should take off door handles, trim pieces, mirrors, emblems, badges, key locks, radio antennae, and anything else attached to your car's body. This alleviates the need for intricate masking and prevents accidental overspray onto these pieces because of inadequate masking. Removing body trim also allows the paint to cover all vehicle body parts evenly and greatly reduces the chance of paint build-up or thin coat coverage on areas obstructed with handles, adornments, and add-ons.

Removing body trim and accessories requires the use of hand tools to loosen nuts, bolts, and screws. Other pieces held in place by adhesives or double-backed tape may require the use of an adhesive remover product. You must take your time and remove items in a controlled manner so that none of them are broken or damaged during disassembly.

Once you start taking parts off your car, you'll be surprised at the amount collected. In addition to door handles, key locks and trim, you'll remove light assemblies, reflectors, grille pieces, bumpers, license plates, mudguards, and a lot more. Therefore, develop a systematic storage plan so nothing gets lost or broken.

Keep plenty of sturdy boxes on hand to store related parts as you take them off specific body areas. Keep fender parts together in one box, door items in another, and so forth. This way, when you start replacing them after paint work is completed, you will be able to quickly and easily locate all necessary body and trim pieces, as well as their fastening nuts, bolts, screws, clips, and so on. In addition to boxes, resealable freezer bags work well for temporary storage of small pieces and parts. Use a permanent marker to note the contents on the storage label.

Expect to spend plenty of time sanding every square inch of your car or truck's body surface before picking up a spray paint gun. All imperfections must be smoothed

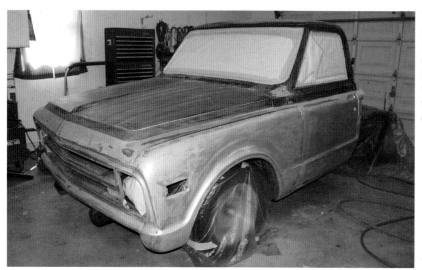

This '68 Chevy pickup was in the early stages of being completely repainted. Notice that the bumpers, bed, outside mirrors, grille trim, and side marker lights have been removed. Headlights have been masked off with masking paper, as well as the glass. Plastic sheeting covers the wheels and tires, along with the exposed portion of the chassis.

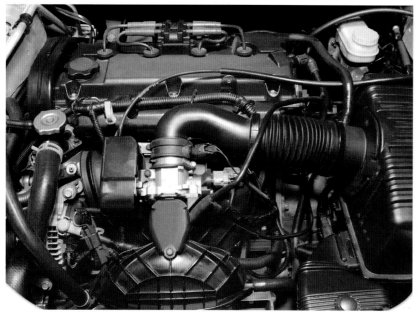

With today's crowded engine compartments, it is no longer as easy as it once was to repaint under the hood. To do the job correctly involves much more than just removing the engine.

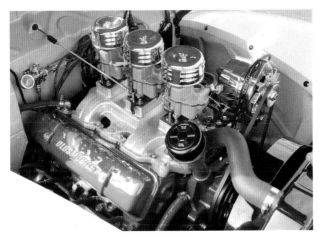

While older vehicles such as this 1940 Ford coupe may have more room in the engine compartment, to do a complete color change on a vehicle, the engine (or the front clip sheet metal) should be pulled to gain adequate access.

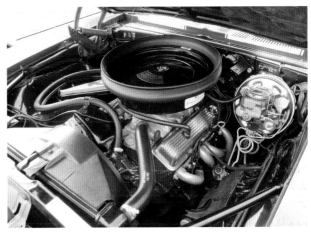

Even early muscle cars with or without smog equipment get cramped in the engine compartment when you add power brakes, air conditioning, and other accessories. Therefore, you should take this into consideration if you are anticipating performing a complete color change on a vehicle.

or repaired to give paint a blemish-free bonding base. By itself, paint is not thick enough to hide sand scratch swelling or pinholes. For those problems, products like primer-surfacers are used, which also have to be sanded and smoothed to perfection if paint is expected to lay down evenly and be visually attractive.

COLOR CHANGE PAINT JOB

Changing the color of a vehicle involves additional considerations, more difficult on some vehicles than on others. For a complete color change, it is necessary to paint the engine compartment, the doorjambs, and the interior. Unless you are extremely experienced with a detail gun and

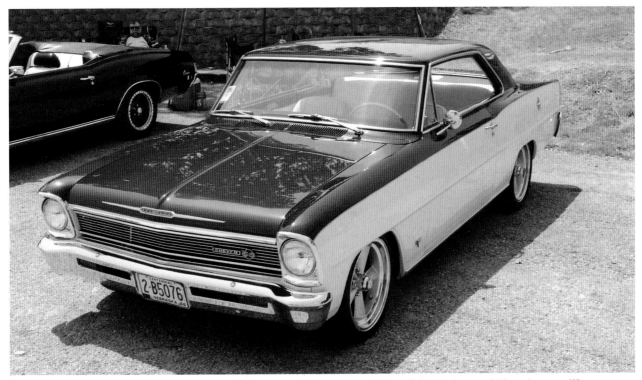

Even if the car of your dreams was not painted two-tone from the factory does not mean that it can't be when you repaint it, or vice-versa. Whenever you are painting your car (or truck), paint it as close to stock or as wild as you desire.

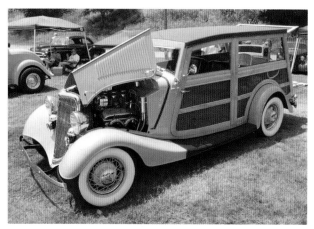

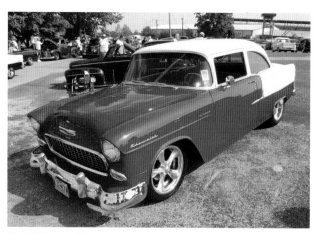

The gray paint, maple and mahogany wood, and wire wheels may allow this 1934 Ford to pass as a restoration in some circles, but the small-block Chevy engine under the hood makes it a hot rod. Still, it is classy no matter what you call it.

The 1950s proved that vehicles could be painted more than one color. It was common to see General Motors and Ford cars wearing two different colors, while many from Chrysler included three different colors. For this era vehicle, white complements most any color.

masking procedures, it is necessary to remove the engine to repaint the engine compartment. If the engine has already been removed from the vehicle you are painting, this is of little consequence, other than the additional sanding and surface preparation. This also holds true for the interior, although upholstery already covers much of it.

Color Selection

A crucial part of any paint job is picking the right color. If you are simply repairing and refinishing a dented fender on a late-model vehicle, this is not a big deal. However, if you are building that long-awaited hot rod or custom, color choice may be more difficult than you think. No matter what you are painting, or how you go about choosing the color, look at your anticipated color under as many different lighting conditions as possible to make sure it is right for your vehicle.

Because there are so many different automotive paint colors to choose from, it may become confusing or downright frustrating trying to pick just one dynamic

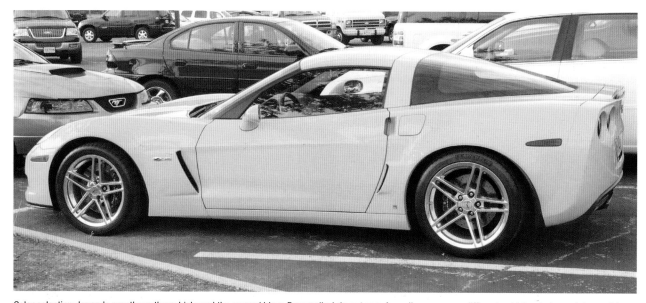

Color selection depends greatly on the vehicle and the owner/driver. Personally, I do not care for yellow on many different vehicles, but on a late-model Corvette, this particular hue looks great. I will admit, however, that some older yellow Corvettes were too soft for my taste. Within any color, there are certain shades that look better than others.

color for your car. Have patience. Look at car and truck magazines for ideas of the colors other enthusiasts are using. Attend car shows and talk to fellow car buffs about how they arrived at certain paint schemes. These conversations may lead you to good suppliers and products, and may help you avoid the mistakes your fellow enthusiasts have already made.

Many times, especially for older classic and vintage automobiles, certain color schemes prove more appealing than others do. While a pink 1957 Thunderbird may be a head turner, an equally pink

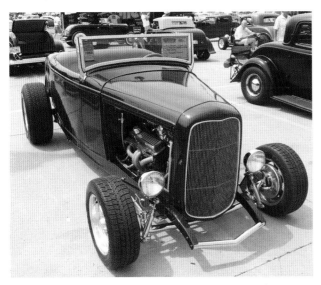

A selection of several 1932 Ford roadsters provides some comparisons in colors and may suggest different attitudes about the vehicle or its owner. Most any shade of red is popular, but is easily overdone.

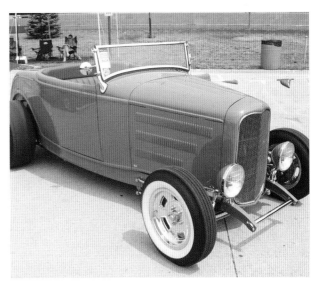

I find this aqua/turquoise color to be somewhat refreshing on this clean roadster; it makes me think of the Bahamas or Key West. While the car is well built, the color could be considered as trendy by some, making it easy to get tired of or difficult to sell. I do like the car though.

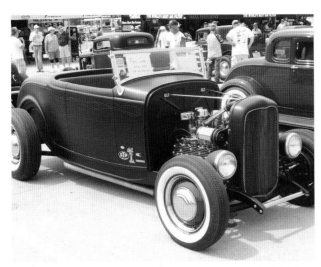

While the intent is to look like primer from the 1950s, this satin finish is most likely a modern urethane single-stage paint that has flattener added. This finish protects like paint (as it is paint), but it provides the nostalgic look of primer, and will not withstand weather unless it is top coated. The contrasting painted wheels, whitewalls, sponsor decals, and outline flames all work together to give street cred to the flathead engine.

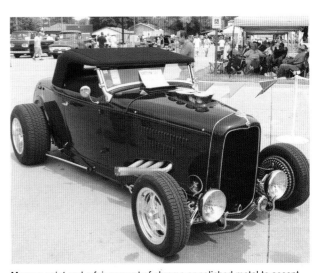

Maroon paint and a fair amount of chrome or polished metal to accent it usually always looks tasteful and sophisticated. The fact that this beauty flashes some cleavage in all the right places simply makes it more appealing.

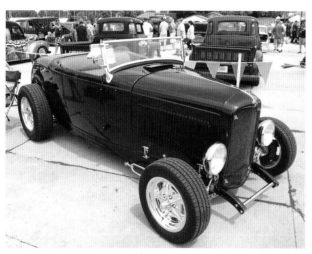

This Washington Blue (or similar) roadster is built much like the aqua roadster in previous photos, but seems more traditional in its appearance. That may not be a big deal to some enthusiasts, but it might be to others.

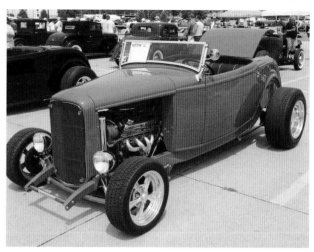

I like orange and I like it on this roadster. Solid colors such as red, orange, yellow, and black are typically safe colors to use on a hot rod. They are easy to keep clean, they photograph well, and they make the vehicle look like more fun. They also serve as a great canvas for graphics, should a new owner choose to make it "their" vehicle.

1956 Oldsmobile may look out of place. Experienced car painters have a knack for envisioning the outcome of cars painted specific colors. From their experience around body shops and car shows, and through reading thousands of auto magazines, they know which colors look best and are in style for most types of vehicles, from sports cars to pickups, and late-model sedans to classic coupes.

True auto enthusiasts are not hard to find. One of the best places is car clubs. Members have a keen interest in automobiles—why else would they belong to such an organization? Many clubs specialize in certain types of vehicles, like 1955 through 1957 Chevrolets, 1960s vintage Corvettes, all Mustangs, particular Ford F-100 trucks, MGs, and so on. If yours is an older project car that is finally ready for paint and you find yourself in a quandary as to what color to paint it, find a local club whose members share an interest in the same make, model, or general vintage. A few casual conversations with them should help you narrow your color choices to a select few. If there's any chance you may someday sell the vehicle, picking a color that's somehow in keeping with its style and vintage may make it a hotter prospect at that time. However, you should be wary of any trendy colors that may quickly lose their appeal.

Matching the Old

Choosing the right color for blending in repaint areas on newer cars is easy. You simply adhere to the vehicle's ID tag color code, or let an auto body paint and supply store professional decipher that information from its VIN or color and options tag.

A word of caution about color codes printed on VIN or color and options tags is in order. Occasionally the codes do not actually match the color that was really sprayed on the vehicle at the factory. With the vast number of automobiles manufactured each year, the percentage with incorrect codes is very small, yet it is a somewhat alarming number of vehicles. When you take the color code from your vehicle to the local automotive paint retailer to purchase paint, you should tell them that the basic color of the vehicle is blue, red, green, or whatever it happens to be. If the color code that you supply yields yellow paint, but your car is black, the paint employee will want to know before mixing a gallon or two of paint that you won't actually be able to use.

If this happens, you can choose a color from a large selection of paint selection charts. Automotive paint professionals have volumes of original equipment manufacturer (OEM) paint chips categorized by year and vehicle manufacturer. If you are looking for paint to match a 2008 Chevrolet Malibu, for example, you could go to the 2008 General Motors portion of the paint selection chart and probably find what you are looking for. Realize that similar colors from different years or manufacturers may be close, yet somewhat different. When you find a color that looks close, ask the paint store employee if the color you selected is actually for a Malibu. The color

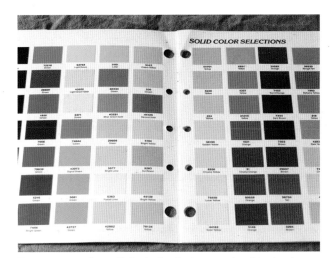

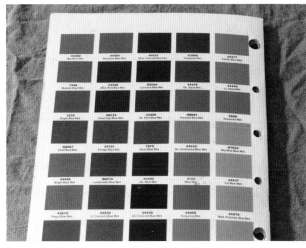

These two pages from a DuPont color chart are merely solid colors from a fleet colors catalog, yet there are still several shades to choose from. This does not include all of the factory colors available, nor does it include the many custom blends of metallics, candies, and pearls.

Oh, you know you want some shade of blue. This is simply a one-page selection out of that same fleet colors catalog. More colors than you can imagine are out there, making color selection one of the toughest choices when it comes to painting a vehicle.

you selected may be for a Camaro or a Corvette, but not the correct color for your Malibu. When there were fewer colors for cars, finding an exact match was much easier.

For each color code of paint, there are multiple formulas to provide an acceptable match by the vehicle manufacturer for any specific color. This is due to the robotic paint process used by the vehicle manufacturers. For example, the first ten vehicles going down the paint line are supposed to be black, followed by ten that are supposed to be white, followed by ten that are supposed to be red, then yellow, then blue. Controlled by computers, the paint spraying system is purged at each color change. In our example, nine of the first ten vehicles will be black, yet the tenth vehicle will be slightly lighter than the nine before it. The first two or three white vehicles will be slightly grayer than the middle "white" vehicles, while those at the end of the white session will be slightly pink, due to the red in the system. Of the red vehicles, the first few won't be as vibrant as the heart of the run, while the end of the run will have more of a yellow cast, or orange appearance to them. Of course, the yellow vehicles are also affected; the first few may yield a "dirty" yellow when compared to the middle of the batch or the slightly green appearing vehicles that would result from the end of the yellow run.

This characteristic is not limited to any one manufacturer or color, although certain colors of certain vehicles are more commonplace. Any paint supply

professional can determine the prime paint formula for your vehicle by entering the color code into the paint formula database. He or she can also discover the prime formulas for all the variants of the color code, and each variant has a code that indicates such properties as "less red, more yellow" or "less white, more red." Some color codes may not have variant codes, while some may have as many as ten or twelve. When a color code has variant color codes listed, the person mixing the paint will always supply the paint from the prime formula if the intended paint is for a complete paint job. If the paint is for a repair, color chips from each of the variant colors must be compared to the vehicle to obtain the correct color.

A second method of determining the paint formula for virtually any color involves the use of a color spectrometer. The average auto paint retailer usually doesn't stock this expensive tool, but they may be able to get one through their paint distributor. If you are trying to match a specific color that available paint codes can't identify, the extra effort of finding a color spectrometer may be the answer.

The color spectrometer scans a portion of the vehicle with the desired color, and then a computer downloads the data and deciphers the color, displaying the appropriate paint formula. Although paint matching cannot be 100 percent accurate all of the time, this process is extremely accurate on single-stage or two-stage paints. However, it is not designed for, nor capable of, determining the formula of tri-stage paints,

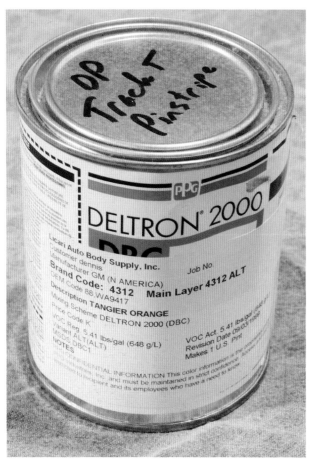

Paint labels tell you just about everything you need regarding the contents of the can, stopping just short of providing the actual formula. Most paint companies would consider that formula intellectual property or proprietary information. The label does tell where the paint was purchased, by whom, the OEM, the OEM's number code and name, and what type of paint it is. It also provides the VOC info, the quantity of paint, and the appropriate MSDS for the product.

or finishes which include special-effect additives, such as pearl or metallic.

SELECTING A NEW COLOR

Selecting a new color for the complete repaint of a vehicle might not be quite as easy. Valspar Refinish already has 100,000 different automotive paint colors on file, and developing new hues keeps its engineers busy. The days of walking into a paint store and simply asking for a quart of red paint are gone. Today, there are easily more than 600 different shades of red, so customers must be much more specific. They need to pick out a certain color chip from any number of color catalogs or have a particular paint code number available. Most other colors have as many variations.

One way to decide on a new paint color is to visit local automobile dealerships. When you find a car or truck with a paint scheme that you like, copy the vehicle's numeric paint code and take it to your local auto body paint and supply store. In lieu of actual paint codes, proper paint-mixing formulas may be located on computer files with just the year, make, and model of most any newer vehicle. Customers can confirm particular colors by comparing that information with corresponding color chips from paint color catalogs.

Custom Finishes

Along with color selection, you may want to investigate special custom paint additives. Metallics have improved since their heyday in the 1960s. Now, instead of large, bold flakes dazzling a car body, you can add specific doses of tiny micro-flakes to make an otherwise bland color light blaze to a magnificent and brilliant finish. A good number of newer car paint finishes include subtle metallic; you can see them firsthand on automobiles at almost any new car dealership or on color chips at your local auto body paint and supply store.

Pearl additives are another means by which you can make a solid color look custom. Years ago, auto body shops used fish scales to give stock colors a pearlescent sheen and to appear as different shades when viewed from various angles. In essence, a vehicle that appears white when viewed from the front may appear bright pink or even blue from a lower angle, or when viewed from the front or back.

Today's pearl additives are made by applying oxide pigments to milaceous iron oxide (mica) or aluminum. These tiny chips may be painted on one side, while remaining clear on the other. Depending on the pearl color selected and the angle of light reflected from one's viewpoint, these paint jobs can offer truly unique perspectives. With improvements in pearl products and stricter standards, they are now easier to blend for spot repairs than just a few years ago. Manufacturers used to advise painters to repaint the entire affected side of the vehicle from headlight to taillight, so each part of the full side displayed identical tints from all directions to avoid causing subtle "paint clouds" of varying paint degrees from appearing between panels or parts of panels. Today, the only real drawback to a pearl finish is that it absolutely must be clear coated for long-term color stability.

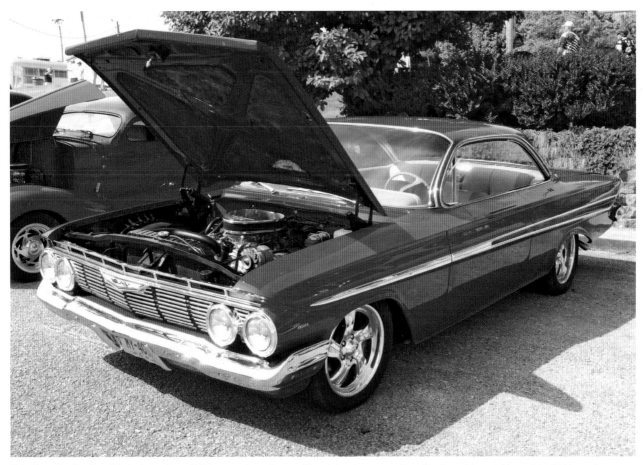

This Chevy hardtop is red, but what color red? Unless you have the specific paint code you are attempting to match, matching paint might be a chore. However, you can go to a paint dealer to browse their paint chip books and select a color that you like. You can also go to a new car lot, find a color you like, and ask for that specific color at the paint dealer.

CONSULTANTS

To paint it yourself, or not to paint it yourself? That is the question, and it's the second most important decision to make besides choosing the color itself. Before you simply jump in (and possibly get in way over your head before you know it), you should first find out what your choices are and what they will cost. If you want to get your daily driver painted, but lack the proper equipment or the necessary time, you may be better to have the work done by a reputable shop.

If, however, you are willing to purchase, rent, or borrow the proper equipment (for both paint application and safety), and have the time and workplace to make your investment worthwhile, go for it! Whether your repaint job consists of straightening or replacing a fender, painting a new set of steel wheels, or a complete color change, having done it yourself with pleasing

results will increase your self-esteem. Before jumping in, talk with those in the business to get a better feel for what your specific project will entail.

Professional Auto Painter

Automobile owners with little or no knowledge of the auto body repair and paint business are frequently surprised at the cost of a quality paint job. They have no idea of the amount of work involved during the preparation stages before painting, nor of the cost of materials such as primers, sealers, reducers, hardeners, and paint. Uninformed car owners have a difficult time understanding why some companies can paint cars for as little as $99.95, while other shops charge $5,000 or more for a top-notch, complete paint job. Of course, there is no real ceiling for the price of a paint job, as the labor involved will vary greatly depending on what you need to have done.

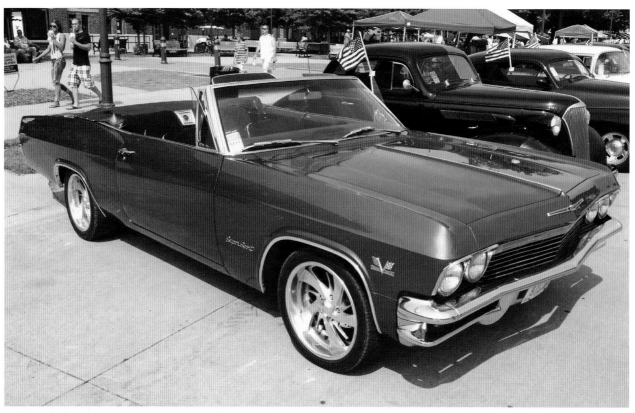

While these cars were common when I was in grade school, none of them looked this good. A nice, clean base color accented with some pearl comes to life in the sunshine.

Should you decide to have a professional paint your car, remember that you get what you pay for. Outfits that specialize in cheap paint jobs cannot afford to spend a lot of time preparing or masking cars. Their business relies on volume. The more cars they paint, the more money they make. Therefore, sanding and masking work is normally minimal, if done at all.

Due to minimal masking, close inspection of repainted vehicles by inexpensive paint shops generally reveals overspray on fender wells, leaf springs, emblems, badges, window trim, spare tires under pickup truck beds, and more. Rough surface spots may receive a quick pass or two with sandpaper, but extra time cannot be allotted for definitive sanding and feathering needs. These shops are not going to remove the bed from your pickup truck to paint the back of the cab, either.

Now, should you want a much more thorough paint job than the one just described (and most people do), these shops can provide better quality service. This will, of course, cost you more, with the price of "extras" quickly approaching that of a more thorough, lower

volume shop. Inexpensive paint shops are forced to use bulk supplies. Color choices are usually limited to the colors on hand in 55-gallon barrels. Frequently, shops like these will buy out paint manufacturers' supplies of discontinued colors at huge discounts and they pass these savings on to you. In many cases, paint shops use enamel-based products because they cover in one or two coats and do not require rubbing out or polishing work afterward.

Auto paint shops that specialize in overall quality and customer satisfaction are vastly different from high-volume shops. You will have to pay more for their services, but your car or truck will be meticulously prepared and then painted with a high-quality, durable, and long-lasting paint product. All exterior accessories will be removed, including the bumpers and grille. Masking will be complete and the work required after spray-painting will be accomplished professionally.

Skeptics may still not completely understand the enormous differences between paint jobs that cost only a few hundred dollars and those that command thousands. Simply put, professional paint technicians spend hours and hours sanding surfaces to perfection. Then they apply required coats of primer-surfacer to fill in tiny sand scratches and other minute blemishes. Those surfaces are also sanded to perfection.

The amount of prep work performed is what raises the price of an automotive paint job. This prep work is what distinguishes the final quality and longevity of the paint job as well. It is important to remember this, whether you are doing the work yourself or farming it out.

Once the surface has been meticulously smoothed, coats of sealer are sprayed on to protect undercoats from absorbing potent solvents included in paint. Be sure to allot sufficient drying time; professionals often use high-intensity heat lamps to speed this process. These lamps use a tremendous amount of electricity, which is figured into estimates as part of the overhead costs.

Once dry, color coats are applied and cured with assistance from heat lamps. Depending upon the type of paint system used, clear coats then might be sprayed over the entire vehicle. Normally, three coats are enough. When the clear has dried, painters carefully inspect car bodies for imperfections. Then, 1,200–2,000-grit sandpaper is used to smooth blemishes as needed, and additional coats of clear may be applied.

Satisfied that their job has turned out correctly, painters buff entire vehicle bodies with fine polish and a soft buffing pad. Afterward, vehicle parts may still have to be replaced, and this takes time—gaskets and seals must be perfectly positioned to function as intended. Care is taken so that parts are not bumped against newly painted finishes to cause nicks or scratches.

As if that were not enough, each vehicle is then detailed to perfection. I doubt many customers would pay their paint bill if glass, wheels, tires, weather stripping, and other parts of the car were dirty and covered with sanding dust when they arrived to pick it up from the shop. Most quality body shop owners insist that their customers' cars to be detailed before delivery; this way, the customer enjoys a freshly painted car and can relish the fact that it has been cleaned to perfection. The car stands out, looks crisp, and is a pleasure to drive.

When shopping for a professional auto painter, be sure to ask if your car will be detailed before delivery. Ask if all exterior accessories will be removed for painting, and whether or not any overspray will be removed or painted over. Be certain that maximum attention is paid to the masking process, and that quality paint products will be used throughout the job.

Finding a professional auto paint shop with a reputable track record should not be too difficult. Word-of-mouth recommendations are generally reliable. If a friend or neighbor has recently painted a car, ask how he or she feels about the quality of service. You can also talk to your auto insurance agent, fellow car enthusiasts, a local detailer, or your mechanic.

You might even ask the owner of a local specialty auto sales business. These folks are true auto enthusiasts—they have to be, in order to stay up-to-date on the latest classic car trends and make the best deals when it comes to the sale of classic and vintage automobiles. To them, a less than professional auto body shop is a nightmare. They expect to pay higher prices for quality work, but in return, demand that work be of the highest caliber. Dealers in this business get a lot of money for the cars they sell. They know that quality $5,000 paint jobs can easily raise values of special automobiles by $6,000 or more.

Your telephone book's yellow pages are loaded with auto body repair and paint shop advertisements. Call a few of the shops to get a feel for their professionalism over the phone. As you cut your list to three or four, take time to visit selected facilities to see firsthand what kind of operations they conduct. You should expect courteous and knowledgeable estimators and organized, well-lighted, tidy work areas. Talk to estimators and ask direct questions. Get estimates from each shop before committing to one. At the end of the day, compare prices and select the shop that offers the best service for the most equitable price.

AUTO BODY PAINT AND SUPPLY STORE

Auto body paint and supply stores are in business to keep body shops adequately supplied in paint products, body repair materials, and tools for both types of work. Paint and body repair suppliers constantly update auto body professionals with product information from manufacturers. Supply store professionals' knowledge about their paint products is second to none, even if they've never actually painted a car.

Novice auto painters can learn a great deal from professionals when both parties fully comprehend the paint project at hand. Be up front and honest with the professional. If possible, bring your car to the store's location so the professional can see your project firsthand. This way, he or she can best recommend a proper paint system to use and supplies you will need to complete the job.

Don't expect professionals to drop everything just to give you lessons in painting cars. Their primary job is to serve professional body shops, not teach auto painting. For the most part, Mondays and Fridays are their busiest days. Shop owners generally call in orders on Monday for supplies they will need for the week's work. On Friday, shops may need special deliveries of materials to complete jobs that customers expect to pick up that afternoon. Plan to visit auto body supply stores during the middle of the week when professionals may have more time to converse with you.

In addition to stocking everything from paint guns to sandpaper, auto body paint and supply stores carry information sheets and application guides on almost all of the paint-related products they sell. Paint manufacturers provide this material. You can get sheets on the use and application of primer-surfacers, sealers, and tri-stage paint systems, as well as just about every other product that you might ever put on your car's body. They are free, so take one for every product you intend to use. These information sheets are also available on the Internet from the manufacturers' websites. This is convenient if you have lost a particular info sheet (or spilled paint on it) and your paint/primer supplier is closed when you need the info.

Auto body paint and supply stores can match almost any color of automotive paint. However, if you want a specific color that is not displayed in any color chart or paint chip catalog, realize that it will have to be made by hand using trial and error methods. Expect to pay a lot more for this service than for stock colors, because of the added labor involved.

This situation arises when customers request a color match with a repainted car and they have no idea which color was used or who did the work. In those cases, professionals simply ask customers to find the closest match by searching through volumes of color chips. Then, he or she finds a suitable color by working with various tints and hues. To find a match, professionals mix paint by hand unless the customer provides a paint chip to match the car. This process takes hours, and is one reason why special,

hand-matched colors cost a lot more than standard quantities of those colors whose formulas are stored in company computers.

Ask your auto body paint and supply professional how much sandpaper of which grit you need to properly prepare your car's finish for new paint. Sanding chores are different with each job, and fine-grit paper does not last as long as one might expect. Along with sandpaper, purchase plenty of automotive paint masking tape and paper. Two-inch tape works great for some chores, while more detailed tasks require ¾-inch and ⅛-inch tape.

By and large, your auto body paint and supply store professional can be a fountain of information. Take advantage of this person's knowledge by being polite and courteous, and by asking intelligent questions. Be aware of the store's busiest hours and plan to visit during slack times.

Special Considerations

Automotive painting has surely become a high-tech business. Not only do painters have to be concerned about the finished product, but they must also be keenly aware of personal safety hazards involved with potent chemicals used in paint bases and hardeners. Professionals considered filter masks as health-conscious aids just a few years ago, but state-of-the-art positive-pressure respirators are more common now. Be aware of fire hazards, especially pilot lights on hot water heaters and home heating systems. Thinners and reducers are highly flammable, so keep cigarettes and other sources of ignition far away from your project.

Novice painters can apply special paint systems utilizing metallic and pearl finishes by following all label instructions and tips from application guides. Take advantage of this wealth of information at your fingertips to make your paint job progress as expected.

Be sure to spend an adequate amount of time preparing your car or truck's surface for paint. Too many times, enthusiastic novice painters get ahead of themselves. They believe that a thick coat of paint will hide blemishes or flaws. Don't settle for that. Plan to spend a day or two just to prepare your car's body surface for paint. Be sure that the paint system you employ is compatible with surrounding paint. And decide early on that you will practice on an old hood or trunk lid before starting work on your favorite automobile.

Chapter 2
Automotive Paint Chemistry

Automotive paint manufacturing is a highly technical and scientific business. Along with satisfying customers' needs with quality products, paint manufacturers must conform to increasing health, safety, and environmental standards and regulations. When manufacturers develop new products for the auto paint industry, they must meet all of the strict regulations related to personal user safety and overall environmental pollution criteria.

Just because a fantastic new product might be able to cover car bodies in one easy step, shine forever without wax or polish, and resist oxidation and other

VOC-COMPLIANT PRODUCTS FOR THE NATIONAL RULE UNDERCOATS

Product	Mixing Ratio	Hardener	Reducer	VOC
Pretreatment VOC Limit 6.5 lbs/gal				
Priomat® 1:1 Primer 3688	1:1	3689	NA	6.4
Priomat® 1 K Primer Surfacer 4080	NA	NA	+50% 3363 or 3365	6.1
Priomat® Primer 3255	NA	NA	+50% 3363	6.3
Primer/Primer Surfacer VOC Limit 4.8 lbs/gal				
Permahyd® Primer Surfacer 4100	NA	NA	0–10% 6000	1.5
Permasolid® H.S. Surfacer Plus 5110	4:1	3100, 3050, 3040, 3030, 3368, 3324	NA	4.4
Permacron® Vario Surfacer 8590	2:1	3100, 3050, 3040, 3030, 3368, 3324	+5–10% 8580 3363, 3365, 3366	4.7
Permacron® Tinting Surfacer 5100 (mixed 2:1 with color)	4:1	3100, 3050, 3040, 3030, 3368	+10% 8580 3363, 3365	4.8
Primer Sealer VOC Limit 4.6 lbs/gal				
Permacron® Non Sanding Surfacer 5030	2:1	3050, 3040, 3030, 3368	+15% 8580 3363, 3365, 3366	4.6
Permacron® Vario Surfacer 8590	2:1	3050, 3040, 3030, 3368	+15% 8580	4.6
Permacron® Transparent Surfacer 8550	2:1	3050, 3040, 3030, 3368	+15% 8580, 3365	4.6
Specialty Coating VOC Limit 7.0 lbs/gal				
Priomat® Elastic Primer 3304	NA	NA	NA	7.0
Priomat® Elastic Primer Filler 3306	NA	NA	+50% 8581	6.5
Permacron® 1.1 Elastic Primer Surfacer 3300	1:1	3301	NA	5.6

In 1998, the National Rule that regulates the VOC content of coatings used to refinish automobiles in the United States was issued. The regulation establishes maximum VOC limits and is broken down into eight different categories: pretreatment wash primers; primers/primer surfacers; primer sealers; single-stage top coats; two-stage top coats; three- and four-stage top coats; multi-colored top coats; and specialty coatings. Each category is limited to a certain weight of VOCs per ready-to-spray gallon of product. The manufacturers are the parties who are regulated by this and must manufacturer compliant products.

VOC-COMPLIANT PRODUCTS FOR THE NATIONAL RULE TOP COATS

Product	Mixing Ratio	Hardener	Reducer	VOC
Single-Stage Top coat VOC Limit 5.0 lbs/gal				
Permacron® Acrylic Urethane Series 257	2:1	3050, 3040, 3030, 3368, 3324	+5–10% 8580, 3363, 3365, 3366	4.9
2-Stage Multistage System VOC Limit 5.0 lbs/gal				
Permacron® Base Coal Series 293/295	NA	NA	+50% 33055, 3056 or +65% 3054	5.9–6.6 (depending on formula)
Followed by:				
Permasolid® H.S. Clear Coat 8030	2:1	3309, 3310, 3315, 3320	NA	3.7
Permasolid® H.S. Clear Coat 8030	2:1	3310, 3315, 3320	+0–5% 3363, 3365, 3366, 8550	3.9
Permasolid® H.S. Clear Coat 8030 (use with base coat equal to or less than 6.1 lbs/gal before reduction)	2:1	3309, 3310, 3315, 3320	+10–30% 9030 Accelerator	4.3
Permacron® Vario Clear Coat 8000 (use with base coat equal to or less than 5.8 lbs/gallon before reduction)	3:1	3309, 3310, 3315, 3320	+2% 8580, 3363, 3365, 3366	4.4
3-Stage Multistage System VOC Limit 5.2 lbs/gal				
Permacron® Base Coat Series 293/295	NA	NA	+50% 3055, 3056 or +65% 3054	5.9–6.6 (depending on formula)
Followed by:				
Permasolid® H.S. Clear Coat 8030	2:1	3309, 3310, 3315, 3320	NA	3.7

Additional Information

- No record keeping required for additional usage
- No HVLP spray equipment necessary
- No limits for surface preparation materials

debilitating factors does not guarantee it would be safe to use. It may require a different kind of application procedure or special high-tech filtering system to prevent deadly fumes from injuring users or poisoning the atmosphere. Therefore, every paint product needs to find an even balance to not only serve its intended function, but also be safe for users and the environment.

The research required to develop quality paint products includes continuing studies by paint manufacturers through their teams of scientists and engineers. In addition to the development of new and vibrant colors, researchers in this field conduct tests to determine the amount of hazardous materials created by various paint products and their application techniques. These scientists and engineers, along with those from related fields, have invented some water-based automotive paint products, although they are mostly undercoat materials.

Developers have also created a relatively new system of paint application that incorporates a high-volume spray with very low pressure. This system, referred to as HVLP (High Volume Low Pressure), allows more paint to adhere to vehicle bodies with far less overspray than encountered with conventional spray paint systems. In essence, since more material sticks to properly prepared sheetmetal surfaces, much less is lost to the atmosphere through clouds of overspray that ricochets off body panels into the air.

Through increased safety awareness and continued research, manufacturers are determined to develop environmentally safe paint materials that can be applied

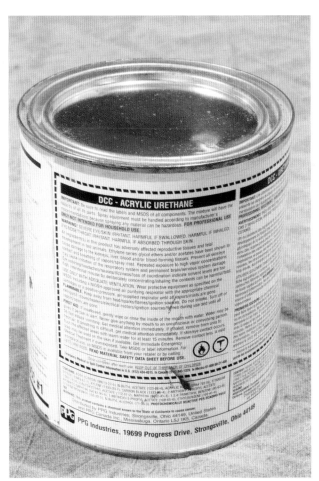

This label provides the pertinent safety info for the product. Should first aid be required when using this product, the info is as close as the product's container.

satisfactorily with minimal or no overspray, reducing pollution to practically nothing. This effort has taken time to design, develop, and implement, yet it should be on retailers' shelves in the very near future. Meanwhile, automotive painters must be especially aware of potential user hazards and take advantage of all recommended safety procedures and equipment. This includes the use of positive-pressure full-face respirators, protective hoods, quality rubber gloves, and painters' coveralls.

The chemistry surrounding automotive paint materials is quite complex. Although that information may be of interest to certain scientific folks, it really won't be much help to those who simply want to learn how to paint their car or truck. It's helpful, however, to understand some automotive paint properties in order to choose the proper products and achieve a professional-looking and long-lasting paint finish on your vehicle.

BASIC INGREDIENTS

Auto paint is made up of pigments, binders, and solvents. Pigments give paint material its color. Binders are used to hold pigment materials together and keep them in a state that remains solidly attached to vehicle bodies. Solvents are those liquid media (thinners and reducers) that transform solid pigment and binder materials into sprayable liquids. Solvents are, for the most part, the materials that evaporate into the atmosphere and cause pollution concerns.

Various pigment, binder, and solvent combinations produce different types of paint. Their differences are reflected in coverage techniques, drying times, repairability, and durability. In general, all paint materials are solid substances that have been mixed with a solvent and changed into liquid forms for spraying. Once solvents have evaporated, pigments and binders harden into colorful sheets that strongly adhere to auto body surfaces to offer pleasant appearances and oxidation protection for underlying metal.

In years past, auto painters were limited to either straight enamel- or lacquer-based paints. Enamels were relatively easy to apply and covered in just one or two coats. They did not have to be rubbed out, and they lasted a long time. Nitrocellulose lacquer paint required many thin coats and numerous clear coats over color bases, which had to be rubbed out in order to gain a deep, lustrous shine. It dried fast and allowed minor flaws to be gently wet-sanded and then painted over just minutes after the paint was applied.

Advances in paint chemistry brought new kinds of enamel and lacquer paint, referred to as acrylic. Acrylic simply means plastic. Although acrylic enamel and acrylic lacquer retain their same basic application and benefit characteristics, their durability and ultraviolet (UV) resistance has been greatly improved.

A new type of paint was introduced as acrylic enamels and lacquers improved. Urethane paint products, and more recently polyurethane, combined advantages of both enamels and lacquers to offer quick-drying ingredients that covered in one to three coats, and allowed blemish repair soon after a coat was sprayed on. One of the biggest advantages urethanes offer is durability. In a sense, urethane and polyurethane products were developed to resist the hazards of today's harsh airborne pollutants, acid rain, and other oxidizing elements.

More recently, waterborne paint has become commonplace in the automotive OEM and is making its way into the refinish and custom markets.

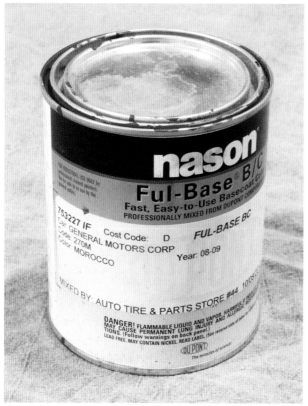

This label on the front of the paint can provides the necessary info for ordering more of this paint in the future. It doesn't provide the exact formula, but since it is not a custom mix this info will be adequate. In this case, Morocco from a 2008–09 GM product.

Waterborne paint products are mandated in much of Europe, Canada, and both coasts of the United States. Rather than solvents to make the pigment and binders into sprayable liquid, water is used. This does bring about a new learning curve to spraying paint, yet it is not difficult. The big difference in traditional solvent-based and waterborne paint products is that the latter requires different equipment to dry the paint.

Once again, although basic ingredients remain the same—pigment, binder, and solvent—their chemical compositions give paint its own individual characteristics. The addition of chemical hardeners plays a significant role by improving the way pigments and binders bond together and adhere to painted surfaces.

Paint and solvent mixtures use liquid hardeners (catalysts) in established proportions as recommended by label instructions and informational guidelines. You must use fresh air respirators (as well as their labels and information sheets) when using hardeners because hardeners contain isocyanate chemicals, which have been deemed health hazards when inhaled or absorbed through the skin.

There are four basic types of automotive paint produced today: acrylic enamel, acrylic lacquer, urethane, and waterborne. Any sales of acrylic enamel or acrylic lacquer are usually for restoration projects. Most professional painters strongly suggest that anyone painting his or her own car use urethane products, with base coat/clear coat being the first choice over single-stage. Except where waterborne paint is mandated, well over 90 percent of automotive paint sales are for urethane-based products.

Acrylic Enamel

No automobile painting book would be complete without some mention of lacquers and enamels, if only for historical perspective. For all intents and purposes, their use in automobile painting is obsolete.

According to PPG's Refinish Manual, "Alkyd (natural-based) and acrylic (plastic-based) enamels dry first by evaporation of the reducers, then by oxidation of the resin (binder)." This means that although the paint finish may appear to dry quickly through evaporation of its solvent base, the material continues to harden as resins combine with oxygen in the air. Heat from infrared lamps helps to speed this process.

As the curing process continues, a dry synthetic film solidifies over the top of the finish to offer a tough, shiny color coat. Wet sanding this coat to remove bits of dirt or debris destroys that film and requires touch-up painting to repair blemishes.

When compared to the durability of urethane products, alkyd and acrylic enamels fall short. Although they can cover in just one or two coats and do not require the use of isocyanate-based hardeners, they cannot hold up to the same kind of harsh environments or impact hazards. In addition, the application of any lacquer-based product over enamel will result in surface wrinkling or crazing. This is because the materials in enamel cannot hold up to the strong chemicals in lacquer.

For enamel paint to accept a top coat of lacquer material, custom flames or other artwork requires an application of special sealer to prevent lacquer solvents from penetrating and ruining enamel bases. For situations such as this, consult an auto body paint and supply professional for advice and recommendations that apply to your specific job.

Acrylic Lacquer

Acrylic lacquer resists ultraviolet sunrays, cracking, dulling, and yellowing much better than nitrocellulose lacquer. It has been a favorite paint among auto enthusiasts for years because it is easy to mix, can be applied at relatively low pressures, dries quickly, and can generally be repaired and recoated within 10 to 20 minutes after the last coat has been sprayed.

By its nature, lacquer requires that a number of coats be applied to achieve color and coverage expectations. After that, coats of clear lacquer are sprayed over color bases for protection and for required buffing. If painters were to buff lacquer color coats, tints would be adversely affected. Therefore, painters apply clear coats so that buffing shines them to a deep gloss without disturbing any underlying color characteristics. The process requires more time than enamel applications, but the extra shine and lustrous finish are worth the effort.

Many custom painters use lacquer because of its quick-drying nature. Frequently, custom designs require multiple masking in order to achieve unique paint schemes. Because lacquer dries in 10 to 20 minutes during warm weather, painters can apply masking tape over new paint and continue with their custom project without much interruption. To do the same thing in enamel, painters might have to wait for days until paint is dry enough to accept strips of masking tape without subsequent damage to its top film layer.

Years ago, most professional auto body painters recommended novices begin their auto painting careers using lacquer-based paint. This allowed them to repair defects almost immediately and continue with their work—lacquer is forgiving in that regard. Repaint efforts to repair scratches and cover areas exposed by bodywork are also easy to match on lacquer paint jobs. After mixing and spraying the matching original-finish paint color, painters can revive gloss and texture by polishing and buffing the finish.

Because of the amount of volatile organic compounds (VOCs) emitted by lacquer solvents, regulatory agencies have minimized the use of lacquer paint or required that it only be sprayed in down-draft paint booths equipped with special filters and air-purifying systems. This is a factor to consider when contemplating a complete paint job for your car. Be sure to talk it over with your auto body paint and supply professional, as he or she should be one of the first auto paint professionals to learn of any new restrictions.

Urethane

Perhaps one of the more familiar brands of urethane paint today is PPG's Deltron. Urethane enamels differ from alkyd and acrylic enamels in that their resins react chemically with isocyanates in the hardener. PPG's Refinish Manual states, "Urethane enamels dry by evaporation of the reducers and by a chemical reaction between the two principal base components (hydroxyls and polyisocyanates), which harden the paint film." In addition to maximum coverage and immediate high gloss without buffing, urethane enamels offer a much harder and more durable finish.

Acrylic urethanes are very versatile. They cover in just a few coats, dry quickly, can be wet sanded to repair minor defects or blemishes, and offer a durable finish with maximum scratch, impact, and ultraviolet light resistance.

Urethane paint products dry much better when subjected to heat. Professional auto painters frequently use paint booths equipped with heaters or infrared lamps to help urethanes cure to their maximum strength in a short time.

At the factory, urethane paint jobs are baked at temperatures around 450 degrees Fahrenheit. Factories use high temperatures because car bodies are bare and lack any plastic pieces that would melt under those conditions. This baking process further hardens paint pigments and additives, and then helps them adhere to body surfaces better than ever before. Baked-on factory finishes provide a solid base for repainting as long as the finish is properly prepared and scuffed.

For repaint jobs, auto painters generally use heaters or lamps at temperatures below 140 degrees Fahrenheit for about 30 minutes. Higher temperatures can damage sensitive engine computers or melt plastic assemblies. Product information sheets list specific heat application times for particular temperature ranges.

Along with DuPont and PPG, other paint manufacturers (including Glasurit, House of Kolor, and Metalflake) offer their own brands of urethane products. All of these companies believe they have the best products. Likewise, auto painters all have their own personal preferences. Two auto enthusiasts seldom agree that one kind is better than all the rest—these conclusions are based on all kinds of experiences.

One painter may have applied a certain product over an incompatible base to cause a less than satisfactory result; another may have used the same product differently to arrive at a perfect finish with plenty of gloss and adhesion.

As much as users may disagree as to which brand is best, manufacturers are adamant about two things.

First, painters must always use only those products included together as one paint system. In other words, if you decide to apply PPG paint on your car, be sure to use PPG reducer, hardener, primer, sealer, primer-surfacer, cleaner, and paint throughout the project. Never mix those products with any different brand. All products listed as part of a manufacturer's paint system are designed to be used together. Chemical bases and other important chemical combinations have been thoroughly tested and researched to give users the best results for their money. Inadvertently mixing brands is asking for trouble. Should you mix brands, you are taking the risk that the new paint finish on your car or truck will wrinkle, craze, mottle, orange-peel, or otherwise suffer irreparable damage.

Painters' second area of emphatic agreement pertains to the use of all recommended personal safety equipment. In addition to spraying paint in well-ventilated areas away from all sources of heat and flame, they insist that you wear respirators and augment that protection with a hood, rubber gloves, and painter's coveralls. These recommendations are clearly printed on paint product labels, which even go so far as to mention the kind of NIOSH (National Institute for Occupational Safety and Health)-approved respirator to use when applying that particular material.

Because paint manufacturers must meet strict regulations and exacting product standards, it is quite safe to say that all of their products should perform as expected when properly mixed and applied. To further ensure that your vehicle exhibits the deep shine and excellent adhesion of the paint finish as expected, be absolutely certain you follow all recommended surface preparation instructions. If you don't follow the instructions, the new paint you carefully spray onto your car's surface could dry to a separate film that would be easily peeled off in long sheets.

Remember, baked-on urethanes offer durable, hard paint finishes. Because of this, new paint solvents might not penetrate their surface to guarantee quality adhesion. You will be required to scuff the paint with 180–220-grit sandpaper before applying new paint so that the new paint can bond to the old. As all paint products differ among manufacturers, information of this nature must be confirmed with your auto body paint and supply professional for the specific job you are contemplating.

Waterborne

While all of the information provided for the three types of paint products just listed is still correct for those types of paint, there is a major development in paint products that must be mentioned . . . this is waterborne paint. This waterborne paint is a relatively new formulation of paint that uses water, rather than solvent to make it fluid, as does enamel, lacquer, and urethane products. Since most water sources throughout the world include a wide variety of minerals and chemicals, the paint manufacturers sell water-based reducers to mix with their waterborne paint. Although the content of this "water" will most likely vary from one manufacturer to another, you can bet that it is highly filtered, although should probably not be considered potable. This uniformity of water, just like the uniformity of reducer for solvent-based products, is what provides uniformity of the overall product.

Just as with all new products, you will hear good and bad about it, and to use it will require some changes in application and equipment. Additionally, waterborne products will vary from one manufacturer to another. One brand's claim may be that they have the best color matching ability, while another company may claim the best coverage or the widest variety of colors. Like any other new technology, choosing a product that serves your purposes best and then fully learning everything you can about it and how to make it work for you is the best advice I can give you.

The purpose behind the development of waterborne paint is to reduce the amount of VOCs being put into the air every time someone paints a car. Traditional solvent-based paint products typically contain a high level of these VOCs. While the regulations enacted apply mainly to the West and East Coast areas of the United States, and to all of Canada, clean air is something we can all live with. Since collision repair and custom body shops are responsible for the majority or paint work, you may not be affected if you are simply repainting a fender or just painting one vehicle. However, I must suggest that you check with your local auto body and paint supplier to verify what you must do to be in compliance. Regulations regarding waterborne paint do not specify water as the only material to be used, so it is possible that some paint manufacturers may develop paint that is neither solvent-based or waterborne. For now however, water is the most convenient material to use with paint.

Currently, and I say currently because the paint manufacturing business is currently buzzing with activity as it continues to refine existing waterborne products and develop others, waterborne paint is available as a base coat/clear coat system. Traditional solvent-based primers, sealers, and other undercoats are still used as described elsewhere to prep the sheet metal for paint. Likewise, traditional solvent-based clear is used as a top coat over the waterborne color coats. Most of these "under and over" products are already low enough in VOCs that they can still be used. Again, check with your local supplier of whatever brand products that you are using to see what is and what is not compatible. What this means for the hobbyist who may spray one or two cars a year, solvent-based paint systems are going to continue to be around for several more years, so if that is what you are familiar with, you can continue to use it.

Besides being lower in VOCs, waterborne paint has other benefits to both amateur and professional painters. Although waterborne paint drying times vary somewhat with the temperature and humidity just like traditional solvent-based products, the overall drying time is significantly shorter for waterborne paint. This requires less time between coats and masking for multiple color changes. Solvent-based paints often require 20–30 minutes or more before being dry enough for masking, while most waterborne paint takes only a tenth of that time. Yes, just two or three minutes are required before you are able to begin masking for another color. This time-saving aspect will be welcomed greatly by the collision repair industry and its patrons. Additionally and perhaps more important to the readers of this book is the fact that application errors can be corrected much more quickly. While you should still practice proper techniques to avoid runs, drips, and other errors, small defects can be repaired quite easily. If, say a bug flies into your wet paint or you are sweating and a drop of perspiration lands right in the middle of a horizontal panel such as the hood or the roof, it is no longer a big deal like it once was. With waterborne paint, you can allow the paint to dry naturally or with the aid of a blow gun, then sand the localized area of the defect with 600-grit sandpaper (dry, not wet) to remove the defect. Then apply a couple of new paint coats to the repaired area, along with the overall clear to the entire painted surface, and no one will ever know about the bug or perspiration problem.

Another good thing about waterborne paint is that when the complete paint job is finished, the paint film thickness of the paint on the sheet metal is thinner than that of solvent-based paint. This is due mainly to the fact that there are no hardeners used with waterborne paint and the water that is used to act as a reducer or thinner evaporates away.

A downside of waterborne paint is that it requires spray guns designed for waterborne paint (more about that in Chapter 4) and extremely dry air from the air compressor. The latter is important to all paint types, but become critical to the success of waterborne paint. Therefore it becomes critical to remember to drain the air compressor before and after painting sessions, along with installing a desiccant drier between the air compressor and the spray gun. This is not difficult to do, but is not something that the hobbyist or amateur remembers to do on a regular basis. After the paint is applied, it requires heat and air movement to dry. If the ambient air is humid, the air temperature must be even warmer to dry the paint properly. Depending on your location for painting, you may not be able to control air movement or ambient temperature. However, assistance is as close as your local automotive paint supply store. Whether you are painting your first vehicle or plan to go into the business, they can provide you with the exact information required for your local area. For a one-time paint job, you may simply need four box fans (one placed near each corner of the car) to get the job done. For a budding custom paint shop, your local paint rep can help to get your shop equipped along with give you additional training on paint application.

SPECIAL EFFECT ADDITIVES

Although there are more than enough colors to choose from for making your vehicle stand out from the crowd, there are also additives that can be mixed with the paint to provide special effects. The most common additives are metallic and pearl. Their use is not necessarily difficult, yet it does add another variable to the equation. If this is the first vehicle you have ever painted, you may choose to stick with a solid color. Yet, if you are repairing a fender-bender, including metallic or pearl to match the existing paint might be necessary.

Metallic

Many newer cars sport brilliant metallic paint finishes. Unlike custom paint jobs of the 1960s, these newer paint products suspend tiny metallic flakes so small that you have to look at the surface from just a few inches away to distinguish their presence. Along with a pleasant color base, metallic particles offer extra shine and gloss to many paint schemes, adding a flair of custom character to vehicles.

Painters can add recommended doses of metallic flakes to almost any paint base. They do this by scooping out small amounts of flake material with a spoon. Then, according to mixture instructions, they add ounces or fractions of ounces to the paint blend. A test panel is sprayed to check the outcome. If flakes are spaced too far apart, a little more may be added. Painters always start out with minimal metallic doses. This is because more flakes can always be added, but none can be taken out.

Often, the type of flakes may require a special spray gun for application, such as one with a large orifice. Otherwise, the spray gun may become clogged by the flakes. Keep this in mind if you are purchasing a new spray gun and plan to spray metallic.

If you order a specific metallic paint from an auto body paint and supply store, flakes will be added in during the mixing process. Paint codes used by auto body paint suppliers account for all additives required to make new paint mixes match original standards, including metallic flakes.

When applying metallic paints, vigorously shake paint containers before filling spray gun cups to ensure that all metallic particles are equally suspended in the solution. If necessary, visit the auto body paint and supply store just before painting and ask them to shake your paint container on their heavy-duty paint-shaking machine. While doing spray paint work, most professional painters shake their paint gun after each pass to ensure all particles remain thoroughly suspended and dispersed. This ensures uniform metallic coverage over all parts of the vehicle being painted.

For do-it-yourself painters who want to mix their own metallics, flakes are sold separately at most auto body paint and supply stores. They are displayed in small jars as a dry material; they do not come mixed with a paste or a liquid. You can purchase metallic flakes in different sizes and colors. You can also order metallic materials through custom auto paint outlets, like the Metalflake Corporation and Jon Kosmoski's House of Kolor.

Pearl

Have you ever glanced at a custom car and perceived it as white, and then during a subsequent glance realized it was light blue or pink? Chances are, your eyes are not failing you. Instead, the automobile in question has probably been painted with a pearl additive mixed with the paint.

Pearl additive consists of tiny chips of synthetic inorganic crystalline substances painted on one side and clear on the other. Auto body paint and supply stores sell concentrates of pearl, and the chips come mixed in a paste. Both materials are added to gallons of paint in amounts of from two to four ounces. Small measuring spoons are used to remove material from jars and then transfer it to the paint mixture.

When viewed from different angles, light reflection off pearl finishes causes painted surfaces to reflect different colors. The pearl additive determines the paint color. For the color you desire, check paint chips at the paint and supply store to select which combination of color paint base and pearl additive is going to work best. Now, if the factory originally painted your car with a pearl-type color, a paint and supply store should automatically include the prescribed pearl dose to your paint mixture. To be sure, ask the professional at the time you place your paint order.

If you are trying to jazz up a stock paint color by adding pearl yourself, you must verify that pearl is compatible with the paint product you intend to use. In most cases, pearl works well with just about any paint base. But why take a chance on ruining an otherwise clean paint job when all you have to do is ask an auto body paint professional? Other than that, it is recommended you add just a bit less pearl than the prescribed amount listed on the information sheet or container label. Then, shoot a test panel and visually inspect the results. Add a little more pearl if necessary. This way, you won't have to worry about putting in too much pearl, which could ruin your paint job by making it look washed out or milky.

For the ultimate in special effects, paint manufacturers have designed paints that change colors, depending on the angle from which they are viewed. This is similar to the effect that pearl additives give, yet is much more pronounced. A common application changes from green to purple, while another application changes from blue to pink. This paint is a premixed product, rather than the result from the end user adding a special effect additive. PPG markets its two color-changing paints as Radiance and Harlequin, while DuPont markets its as ChromaLusion. Like pearl and metallic additives, these products are best left to professional or advanced amateur painters.

Clear

Clear paint is just that—clear. Spray clear paint over the top of certain color coats to serve as a protective film, and then polish it to perfection without disrupting an underlying base of color, pearl, or metallic. Clear paint was preferred almost exclusively over lacquer paint jobs, because polishing lacquer color coats could disrupt their color uniformity. It also added resistance to sun rays and potential paint finish hazards.

Today, clear coats are commonly found on stock factory paint jobs. According to PPG's Refinish Manual, there were two reasons for introducing base coat/clear coat finishes: first, the application of clear paint over light-colored metallic paint finishes greatly increased their durability; second, this process reduced the solvent needs for paint color applications to help manufacturers meet the government's emission standards. In essence, base coat/clear coat paint systems allowed painters to apply only a 1-mil thickness of color when it was covered with 2 mils of clear. Conventional paint color applications normally call for 2 to 3 mils of coverage.

Custom paint jobs almost always call for protective coats of clear paint. This is so polishing and waxing will not directly touch or adversely affect exotic color blends, metallic flakes, pearl additives, or custom graphics. Along with that, certain clear coat products contain chemical ingredients that are designed to ward off the harmful effects of ultraviolet sun rays and help color coats resist premature fading.

To determine if your car has been painted with a base coat/clear coat system, take the color code numbers from your factory-painted car to the auto body paint and supply store. You'll learn which system was used from the store's paint books or computer. If yours is a repaint, sand an inconspicuous spot with 600-grit or finer sandpaper. White residue is an indication of clear paint in most cases, providing, of course, that the vehicle is not painted white.

MULTI STAGE SYSTEMS

Years ago, vehicles were primed and then painted with single-stage paints. There were no clear coats to protect the color, or metallic or pearl additives to enhance it. Plain, solid colors, with little protection (other than owner-applied wax) were commonplace. For the most part, the automobile factories have gotten away from single-stage paint. By using multistage paint systems, they can provide a wider variety of color effects, while providing a more durable paint finish.

Base coat/Clear coat

A base coat/clear coat paint system could also be referred to as a two-step paint system. One step involves color application, while the second refers to the application of clear paint. In theory, base coat/clear coat paint systems are the modern-day equivalent of the old practice of spraying lacquer color coats, and then coating them with additional coats of clear. Apply base coats of color to achieve coverage (the number of coats necessary differs with each color). Apply two to three coats of clear once coverage is achieved, then sand and buff the vehicle for superior shine.

Tri-Stage

Some new colors may require three steps—a fact that can be determined by color code deciphering or paint chip selection at an auto body paint and supply store.

Before spraying toners or another color, candy paint jobs require an application of a base coat of gold or silver. Basically, that base coat will always show through somewhat, as toners are a light mixture of color blended in with clear paint. The first toner coat may not seem to cover a gold base at all, but additional light coats of candy toners will eventually cover to an exciting degree, but still allow shades of the base to be observed. "Translucent" is the best way to describe the final semitransparent effect. You can get an idea of this by holding a lollipop up to a well-lighted surface—although the lollipop color dominates, the surface color behind it will add some degree of color.

The same basic premise holds true for tri-stage paint systems. A base coat of white will make a color coat of purple, for example, a different shade than a base coat of gold or silver. The desired final finish color, along with the paint system brand selected, will determine what base color must be applied to achieve the intended results. Application guides available at the auto body paint and supply store list recommended flash times between coats and any other pertinent information regarding use of that particular paint system.

The third step of a tri-stage paint system is the application of clear paint. With this type of system, wet sanding, rubbing out, or polishing a color coat that has been applied over a base coat could remove enough color pigment to cause parts of the base coat to show through, creating a break in an otherwise uniform paint application. Therefore, coats of clear paint not only protect underlying color coats, but also

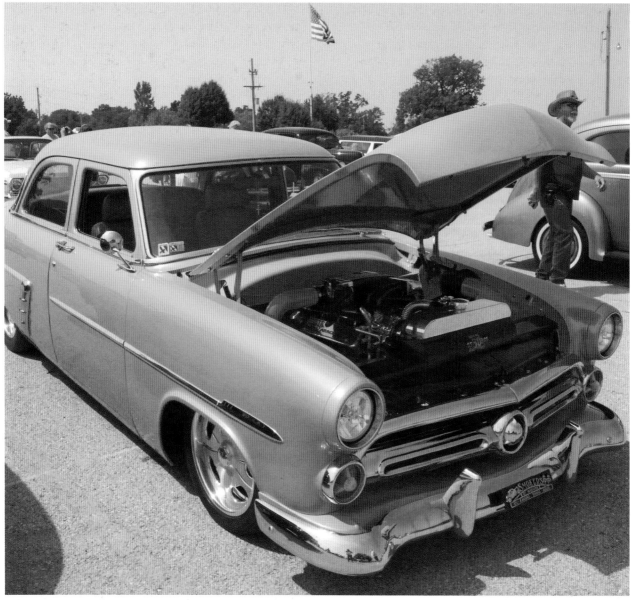

I originally saw this car from several hundred yards away at a major hot rod event, but was drawn to it simply because of the color. From a distance, it appeared as though it was school bus yellow, but closer inspection revealed that its paint included pearl. While you may not want this type of finish on your daily driver or work truck, it sure makes a special interest vehicle come alive when parked in the sunlight.

allow painters to buff and polish surfaces to a deep, lustrous shine without ever touching color.

Although base coat/clear coat paint systems are highly recommended for novice painters, the use of a tri-stage paint system is not recommended. With the number of variables associated with painting, such as mixing paint, application procedure, and correct time between coats, the addition of a third stage variable increases the chances for error exponentially.

VOLATILE ORGANIC COMPOUNDS (VOCS)

Many parts of our planet have become so polluted that government agencies and research institutes have taken bold steps to curtail the creation of any new pollution sources, as well as to drastically cut back on sources that have been in existence for years. The automotive paint industry is not immune to these emission standards and has, in fact, worked a great deal to curb pollution caused by paint overspray and solvent evaporation.

Volatile organic compounds (VOCs) are chemical substances that rise into the atmosphere from paint overspray and solvent evaporation to unite with nitrous oxides and produce ozone. Some forms of vegetation also emit VOCs, but we should know not to mess with Mother Nature. Ozone is a major component of smog. In layman terms, VOCs are those elements in cans of paint that evaporate. Chemical solvents are responsible for VOCs, since pigments and binders (resins) are the solids that form films on auto body surfaces. Solvent is a generic term used to describe the material in paint that keeps the mixture in a liquid state; lacquer paints have lacquer thinner, while enamels and urethanes have reducers. Any gallon of paint could include up to 90 percent solvent. Thinners and reducers are 100-percent solvent.

States like California, New York, Texas, and New Jersey have passed laws relating to the emission of VOCs by local companies, including automotive paint shops. In addition to mandating that shops install high-tech paint booths with downdraft ventilation systems, they insist that these booths come equipped with special filtering systems designed to burn off or otherwise filter out VOCs. Many of these areas have now further mandated the use of waterborne paint exclusively.

To aid in stemming the amount of VOCs escaping into the air by way of paint overspray, some companies, such as Accuspray, have developed High Volume Low Pressure (HVLP) spray paint systems. These units are capable of producing 64 cfm (cubic feet per minute) of air at 5 psi (pounds per square inch). They also warm air to approximately 90 degrees Fahrenheit. More of the paint actually lands on the vehicle (instead of bouncing off it) since the spray is low pressure. This results in less overspray, thereby reducing the amount of product required by approximately 25 percent.

Paint manufacturers are striving to develop new paint products that will dramatically reduce the amount of VOCs escaping into the air. Waterborne paint products have yielded mixed results; however, research and development continues. Existing research suggests that base coats will eventually be waterborne, and that single-stage, solid-shade base coats, and all clears will eventually be high solids. As far as lacquers are concerned, it's just not conceivable to get their VOC content down to the levels imposed by the new laws. Manufacturers have accepted that lacquers are going to be phased out completely. Shops have to accept that as well.

As confusing as this issue can be, the best way to stay on top of it is to maintain contact with your local auto body paint and supply store. Professionals will be among the first to know of drastic changes in the auto paint industry. They will also be among the first to receive new and updated technical material on new paint products and compatible systems for use on previously painted automobiles in need of touch-up. In the long run, rest assured that any new paint technology will be well researched and made compatible with paint systems used on today's vehicles.

The development of waterborne paint has made great strides since the previous edition of this book was published. Although many vehicles have been painted with waterborne paints from the factory since the 1980s, the development has greatly improved since then. Auto manufacturing facilities and auto collision repair shops on both the East and West Coasts of the United States, all of Canada, and much of Europe have already been mandated to use waterborne paint. Your local automotive paint and body supplier will be your best source of information regarding local requirements and restrictions.

Hobbyists still use both solvent and waterborne paints. Paint reps say that if you have painted a car or two with solvent paint, and are going to paint no more

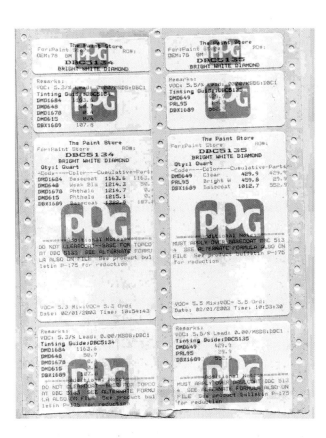

This is the formula for the base coat (left) and the midcoat (right) for a tri-stage paint system on a Cadillac. Note that the label for the base coat instructs "DO NOT CLEARCOAT." Likewise, the midcoat instructs "MUST APPLY OVER BASECOAT." These two products, basecoat and midcoat, must be used in conjunction, along with the application of clear, to obtain the factory color. *The Paint Store*

than one or two cars a year in your home garage, you can still use solvent paint with no problems. This is good news as you probably already have all the equipment you need and are familiar with the various paint products and their uses. However, if you are thinking about opening your own commercial shop, you need to consider using waterborne paint. If you have no experience with solvent paint, you should probably jump right into waterborne paint from the beginning, as it is here to stay.

OVERVIEW

You can use almost any paint system if your car or truck is scheduled to be stripped to bare metal and you are contemplating a complete paint job. It could be single-stage urethane for a relatively simple two- to three-coat coverage, with no rubbing out or buffing requirements, or a complete base coat/clear coat system that will mean more spraying and rubbing-out work, but a much more durable and bullet-proof finish. Preparations are about the same; you'll have to treat bare metal to coats

of epoxy primer and primer-surfacer, and then sand to perfection before applying either a single-stage or multistage system.

Concerns over personal safety while using hardeners with isocyanate ingredients may cause you to opt for a single-stage product. Since small specs of dirt or debris cannot be wet sanded smooth, you will have to apply paint in an extra-clean and dust-free environment.

By far, your best source for product information is your local auto body paint and supply store professional. This person can address concerns about your car's existing paint surface and any special mixing or application techniques unique to the new paint system you have chosen. He or she can also supply useful information concerning local climates and weather conditions. Professionals should also be aware of uncommon regional factors, which enable them to guide you through purchases of temperature-related thinners and reducers, and other specific techniques required for that area.

Chapter 3
Supporting Products

The process of painting cars would much easier and less technical if only one paint product were necessary for all automotive uses. Wouldn't it be nice if you only had to buy one gallon of product, and it would take care of all primer, sealer, and color concerns? Unfortunately, that is not the case. Along with the various paint bases that actually put color on vehicle bodies, numerous other products are necessary in specific situations to guarantee maximum color longevity, adhesion, and sheetmetal protection.

Spraying paint directly onto bare metal will not result in the smooth finish you expect. The color may wash out, the paint may peel or crack, and a host of other problems will quickly surface. Likewise, painting cars whose vinyl and rubber parts have been treated with lots of silicone will likely produce fish-eye problems, because the silicone has settled on the metal and made it resistant to paint adhesion. And what about flexible urethane plastic parts, such as bumpers and ground effects? Without a flex-additive, the paint on these components would randomly peel and crack.

As they do with paint products, manufacturers supply auto body paint and supply stores with information sheets and application guides for their sealers, primers, primer/surfacers, paint removers, and cleaners. Mixing instructions and flash times are explicit, just as they are for paint.

A complete paint system includes all the products needed to accomplish any paint job. Starting with wax and grease remover, paint manufacturers design all of their sealers, primers, thinners, retarders, reducers, and paints to be compatible with each other. Calibrate mixing sticks from each manufacturer so that as parts of one item are mixed with others, the outcome will be

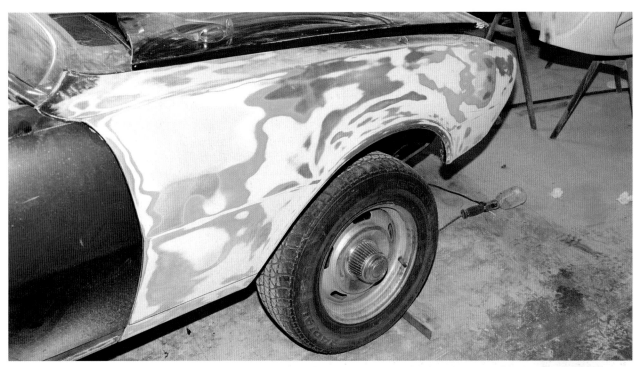

Not that you absolutely have to go down to bare metal prior to painting a vehicle, but you should definitely go down to a solid substrate prior to adding various fillers, primers, and paint products over it. If you are familiar with the vehicle in question, you may just need to scuff the existing surface prior to repainting it. However, nothing is more certain than starting with bare metal. Scuffing down to bare metal reveals that this fender has had multiple layers of paint and/or filler on it previously.

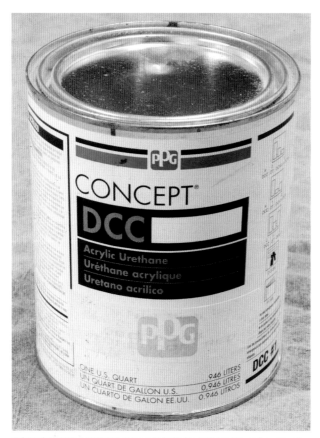

Although the label is faded, it does include the color name and number for the paint that is used on the author's former 1929 Ford Model A Tudor. For anyone that may be interested, it is Toreador Red.

a perfectly blended paint product that will serve the purposes of metal protection, paint adhesion, and color holdout as intended.

Paint support chemicals are all of the products you will need to prepare auto body surfaces for paint (undercoats), as well as those additives designed to be mixed with paint to overcome specific problems. Since it is impossible to depict every kind of paint-related problem for every vehicle and every circumstance, you may have to confer with a paint and supply professional or professional auto painter for unique problems. By being up-front with professionals about the kind of paint job you expect to apply and your lack of painting experience, you allow them an excellent opportunity to share their technical paint knowledge with you and possibly solve more problems than you knew you had.

PAINT REMOVERS

You can remove paint from car bodies in three ways: sanding, media blasting, and chemical stripping. Auto

body repairers remove paint from selected areas with coarse sanding discs on a high-speed sanding tool. More intense paint removal projects, like those for rusty and neglected hulks, require controlled media blasting. Both of these methods not only remove paint, but they also take off undercoats and anything else covering bare metal.

Another method of removing paint down to bare metal is to use chemical strippers, which loosen paint material and make it easy to gently scrape off with a firm plastic squeegee or putty knife. Careful—the process is messy! Scraped-off globs of paint fall to the floor. You must also be concerned about personal safety while using potent chemical strippers. Wear heavy-duty rubber gloves, eye protection, and a respirator as directed by the product label.

The use of chemical paint strippers is generally saved for complete new paint jobs, as opposed to auto body repair work to fix localized dents. For repair work, most auto body professionals quickly remove paint with a sander after the majority of dent repairs have been completed. This is because it is much easier to see surface imperfections, wrinkles, and low spots on painted body panels than on those with bare, shiny metal.

Sanding

For small projects or localized repair, an electric or pneumatic sander works quite well. You can easily remove paint from the immediate area that requires undercoat and paint application.

Using a 36- or 40-grit sanding disc, you can remove paint from a car body in no time. The extra-coarse discs also do a good job of removing all paint or body filler remnants from tiny dings and other hard-to-reach crevices. The heavy pattern of rather deep sanding scratches on sheet metal also serves as an excellent base for filler material adhesion.

Media Blasting

Media blasting will probably be quicker than using a hand-held sander if you are completing a body-off restoration, or working on a relatively small part that can be removed from the vehicle. This would be a more efficient way of removing paint and underlying primers from a complete body shell or chassis. With both media blasting and a hand-held sander, there is a down side. Either method, if concentrated on one area for too long, will cause excessive heat buildup from

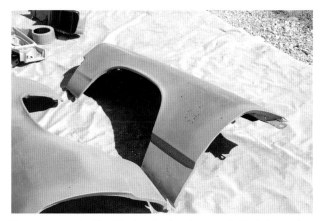

These are a couple of front fenders that have been media blasted, removing paint and body filler in the process. The process leaves a slight texture that makes for good adhesion of epoxy primer and body filler if necessary. Getting down to bare metal is usually the best way to begin a repaint job, unless you know exactly what lies beneath the surface before you start.

friction, which can warp the sheet metal. You must then repair the warped metal before you can get back to your paint preparation.

Another drawback of media blasting is that, on a car body or truck cab, it is virtually impossible to remove all of the blasting media that accumulates between panels and within crevices. Some media will never be removed from your vehicle because it will fall into your paint or interior upholstery.

On the other hand, a good thing about media blasting is that with the correct media (plastic, walnut shells, etc.), and under the correct air pressure, it can be used on fiberglass or other nonsheetmetal components. You must verify that the person who does your media blasting is competent in the various media available and the correct usage.

Chemical Stripping

When the vehicle body is in almost perfect condition, chemical paint removers work well on automobiles in need of a complete new paint job. In other words, use chemical paint removers when there is no compelling reason to roughen sheet metal with a sanding disc or take the chance that a mistake with sandblasting equipment could cause panels to warp damage by high-pressure media blasting away at its surface.

Although chemical strippers can easily damage nonmetallic items, such as rubber moldings or plastics, controlled applications and gentle material removal should result in a clean, shiny body surface with no ill effects. To reduce the possibility of scratches or other scraping damage, consider using a heavy-duty plastic squeegee to remove wrinkled paint from body surfaces, instead of a metal putty knife.

A number of different brands of paint removers are available, but you might want to seek an auto body paint and supply salesperson's advice as to which particular product might be best suited to your needs. Use a sheet of heavy-duty plastic or cardboard under the edges of your car while removing chemically impregnated paint residue. This way, once you strip the body, you can remove and discard the scrapings safely according to any local hazardous waste control regulations in effect in your area.

Chemical strippers are available in two basic forms for dipping or brushing. Dipping it is a practical way to remove all paint and primer when the body needs to be removed from the chassis. For best results, disassemble every component as well as possible before dipping. This allows the chemical stripper to get into all of the places where rust may be hiding. This process removes all rust, leaving only shiny metal. Of course, if a band of rust is all that is holding the lower portion of a door or fender onto the upper portion, the lower portion may no longer be attached when the parts are lifted out of the rust removal vat.

Brushed-on chemical strippers should be reserved for relatively small jobs, such as a door or fender. Doing an entire vehicle by hand would be more expensive than disassembling it and having the components dipped.

WAX AND GREASE REMOVERS

Every surface must be as clean as possible before it is ready for an undercoat or top coat. Remove all traces of dirt, grease, oil, silicone, and other contaminants. After a thorough and meticulous wash, wipe off the body with a wax and grease remover. Each paint system will have its own recommended product.

The best cleaning results can be obtained by using one cloth dampened with wax and grease remover to initially wipe surfaces with one hand, followed by a clean dry cloth in the other hand to remove lingering residue and moisture. Be absolutely certain that the cloths you use are clean and completely free from all traces of wax, polish, oil, or anything else. To be sure, buy a yard or two of soft flannel material at a fabric store, wash it in your washing machine, and then cut it into workable sizes about 2 feet square, and then fold it

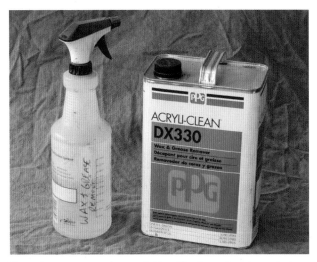

Wax and grease remover is essential to getting the surface clean prior to sanding or spraying undercoats or top coats. Rather than pour the cleaner onto a cloth or paper towel, invest in a cheap spray bottle to apply the wax and grease remover, and then wipe it off with a clean towel. Just be sure to label the bottle with its contents with a magic marker or pen, as this bottle is labeled.

into a handy size so fresh sides can be unfolded for use when one becomes soiled.

Clean every part of any surface to be painted with a wax and grease remover product. If this chore is not completed, you run the risk of contaminants on the surface ruining an otherwise professionally applied paint job. Be sure to follow label instructions, including the use of rubber gloves and any recommended protective respiratory device.

To ensure that auto body surfaces are as clean as can be, supplement wax and grease remover cleaning with an additional wipe down using a glass cleaner. Ammonia in these glass-cleaning products helps to remove tiny traces of residual contaminant material and assists in the removal of lingering moisture particles. Glass cleaner is simply sprayed onto surfaces and then wiped dry with a clean, soft, lint-free cloth.

UNDERCOATS

There are many misperceptions about what primer is and does. Many believe this term simply refers to one product that adequately prepares car bodies for paint. Others think that a thick primer will hide dents and scratches, even out body surfaces, and allow paint to cover evenly. Some people even believe that primer will eliminate rust problems—quite the opposite! Many

primers (except epoxy primers) are actually very porous, therefore soaking up moisture. This works to increase the buildup of rust beneath the primer.

Simply put, primers are materials that are applied directly over properly prepared bare metal. Their category in the overall package of any paint system includes different products designed separately to provide a variety of surface preparation functions. Together, they could be clumped under the term undercoats: those materials applied to auto body surfaces in preparation for paint applications. Generally, these include epoxy primers, primer-surfacers, and sealers.

Epoxy Primer (Etching Primer)

Use waterproof epoxy primers, like PPG's DP40LF, to protect bare metal from oxidation problems. Use a spray gun to apply catalyst-type epoxy primers mixed with a hardener according to label instructions. One to two coats is recommended. Painters usually apply these kinds of primers to bare metal before the application of any other product for two reasons: first, since they are waterproof, they protect the sheet metal; second, epoxy primers offer excellent adhesion to metal, and they serve as perfect bases for additional undercoat products and top coats (paint).

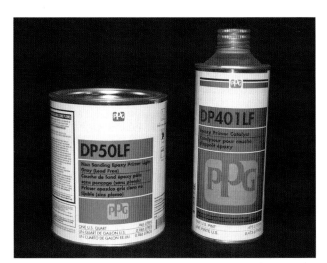

One of PPG's most popular products among painters is its DP line of epoxy primers. Available in a variety of colors and in a lead-free formula, it is an excellent choice of primer for providing corrosion protection to bare metal. It is also suitable for use on other materials as it greatly increases adhesion properties. It must be mixed with DP401LF or DP402LF hardener, each of which gives the mixture different characteristics. DP401LF makes the DP products suitable as a primer on flexible parts, while mixed with DP402LF serves as a sealer.

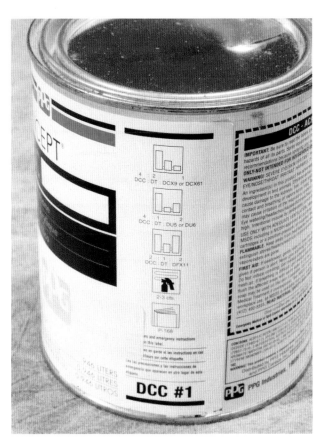

This label's instructions provide mixing instructions and the recommended number of coats, as well as the bulletin number (P-168) for additional info. Three different mixing ratios are provided since there are three different hardeners available for this product.

As with other paint products, each manufacturer offers its own epoxy primer, and you are advised to use only those designed for the paint system you have chosen. Catalyst-type primers in the same category are manufactured for different purposes, although the basic purpose of epoxy primers is to protect bare metal and offer quality adhesion bases. Some are designed to comply with strict military standards that require excellent corrosion resistance and exceptional adhesion capabilities. Others are made for aluminum surfaces or fiberglass materials.

In order to maximize oxidation, rust, and corrosion protection for sheetmetal car bodies in regions with exceptionally harsh corrosion environments, like ocean coasts and areas where winter roads are salted, auto body painters have applied catalyzed epoxy primers to bare metal and then again over subsequent primer-surfacer undercoats. If you live in such an area, you should confirm the need, usefulness, and application procedure for additional epoxy primer coats with your auto body paint and supply professional.

Primer-Surfacer (Filler Primer)

After an automobile body has had its sheet metal repaired and received its required coats of epoxy primer, minor flaws might linger, such as sanding scratches. To cover them, painters use primer-surfacer products manufactured by the same company that produced the rest of the paint system. Because of their high solids content, primer-surfacers cover tiny imperfections and allow painters to sand the coated surfaces to smooth perfection.

These products must not be confused with body fillers; the materials used in body fillers offer a great deal more strength and durability than primer-surfacers. Fillers are designed to cover sheetmetal imperfections up to ¼ inch in depth without cracking or chipping when applied well. Spray primer-surfacers only on surfaces to fill very slight sand scratches or other tiny blemishes. They are a final means by which to smooth body surfaces to perfection.

The final undercoat products designed to be sanded and smoothed are primer-surfacers. Undercoats applied after them are simply used to seal base materials against the absorption of paint solvents, or to increase overall paint adhesion. Therefore, it is imperative to apply their coats uniformly and all sanding be executed in a controlled and systematic manner.

Although some primer-surfacers may resist moisture to a point where wet sanding can be completed with no problems, other products can actually absorb water. Therefore, while your car sports only a primer-surfacer finish, resist temptations to wash it or drive during periods of wet weather.

Should moisture find its way into primer-surfacer finishes, it could become trapped inside this porous, talc-based material and remain there after paint has been sprayed and cured. At that point, moisture could find its way to bare metal and start a rusting process, or, if thwarted in that direction by epoxy primer, it may travel toward the surface to cause problems with the paint finish.

Different primer-surfacers are designed for specific applications. While one may be best suited for use over an epoxy primer and serve as a base for a urethane top coat, another may designed for use over aluminum or fiberglass surfaces in preparation for lacquer paint. Be sure to read information sheets and application guides for any primer-surfacer product you intend to use,

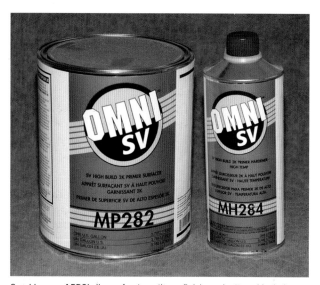

Omni is one of PPG's lines of automotive refinish products and includes the same types of products, just less expensive. Most paint companies have multiple lines, with each line having different qualities, such as faster working time for professional shops or less expensive for the budget conscious. I used this product on a budget repaint project and was happy with the results.

and remember that auto body paint and supply store employees can provide selection assistance.

Be sure to purchase enough sandpaper of the proper grit to smooth the primer-surfacer after application. Just about every job requires more than one sheet of sandpaper, especially for those that entail entire full-body paint jobs. One coat of primer-surfacer is usually applied, and the cured surface block sanded with 150-grit. Another coat is then sprayed on over the first, and finish sanded with 320-grit and then perfected with 500-grit.

Most professionals use a guide coat (usually a black spray can enamel) over primer-surfacers. After adding the guide coat, you sand with a sanding block until the entire guide coat has been removed.

SEALERS

Paint manufacturers produce a number of sealers for an assortment of specific applications. Sealers protect undercoats from the materials and solvents in subsequently applied paint top coats, and add maximum adhesion capability for those top coats. Sealers also ensure uniform color match.

You must consider the use of a sealer when applying new paint over an existing paint surface, especially when you are not exactly sure what type or brand of paint is currently on the vehicle's finish. Most sealers

do not require sanding after they have been applied and cured. They simply form a sort of barrier between the undercoat and top coat.

Along with protecting undercoats from the absorption of paint solvents, sealers help to keep sand scratch swelling to a minimum. For example, imagine that some minor sand scratches are still present after you meticulously sanded the last coat of primer-surfacer. Absorption of a paint solvent will cause primer-surfacer sand scratches to swell and become more visible. As solvents evaporate, paint solids will fill the voids left behind by sand scratches to result in dull, scratchy-looking finishes.

Sealers also offer paint top coats a uniform base to maximize color uniformity. A properly prepared surface sprayed with an appropriate sealer, as your paint system requirements designate, gives paint its best chance of forming an even film with uniform solvent evaporation to ensure all painted areas exhibit the identical color without blotches, clouds, or bleed-through. This is especially important when painting a light color over an existing dark hue.

Sealers are also advantageous for those jobs on which new paint will be sprayed over factory finishes that were baked on at temperatures around 450 degrees Fahrenheit. Because those stock paint jobs are so hard and durable, new paint may have a difficult time penetrating the surface to achieve maximum adhesion. Spraying new paint directly over existing finishes without scuffing or sealing base surfaces is a common mistake of inexperienced painters. The results of this can range from massive random paint flaking, to the extreme, in which fresh paint layers can be peeled off in sheets.

Sealers can make the difference between an adequate paint job and an excellent one. Confirm with the paint and supply salesperson the exact kind of sealer product to use with your paint system. Be sure to refer to application guides and information sheets for mixing instructions and other pertinent product user recommendations.

TACK CLOTHS

The very last thing most painters do before actually spraying paint is wipe off body surfaces with a tack cloth. The special material used to make tack cloths allows them to pick up very fine particles of lint, dust, and other debris. As mentioned earlier, coats of paint almost always magnify imperfections on a primered surface. The process of wiping off body surfaces with a

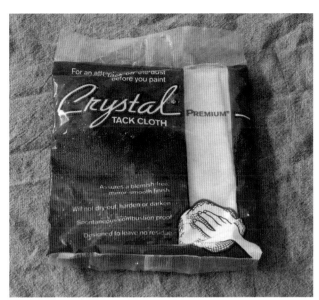

After cleaning the surface with wax and grease remover, but prior to spraying any color, go over the vehicle with a tack cloth and a light touch to remove any remaining dust or dirt.

tack cloth helps ensure that bits of debris are removed so imperfections are not created. Do not rub tack cloths hard against the surface to be painted, as the residue may cause fish eyes.

You can buy tack cloths at any auto body paint and supply store. Their cost is minimal, especially when compared to the kind of intricate dust and lint removal they provide. It works best to open and unfold tack cloths and then lightly fold them back again. This fluffs them up to make them more manageable. Be sure to take note of any package instructions or user recommendations to ensure adequate and complete cleaning.

THINNERS, REDUCERS, AND RETARDERS

In order for paint pigments and binders to cure and harden into a unified solid substance, the liquid parts of each paint mixture must evaporate. Solvents are the agents used to turn solid pigments and binders into liquids for sprayability. Thinners, reducers, and retardants all fall into the category of solvents.

The chemical makeup of various solvents, although similar in design and purpose, varies according to the type of pigments and binders used in particular paint products. Lacquer thinners are designed to work with lacquer-based products. Enamels require solvents containing different chemical blends known as enamel reducers. Lacquer thinner is not compatible with enamel products, and reducers are not generally compatible with lacquers. For all intents and purposes, the word thinner is associated with lacquer, and the term reducer applies to enamels and urethanes.

A retarder is either a thinner or a reducer with an extra-slow evaporation time. Retarders are used for paint jobs that are sprayed during exceptionally hot weather, typically above 95 degrees Fahrenheit. Their function is to evaporate much more slowly than other thinners or reducers so paint does not dry too fast—which may cause checking, crazing, cracking, or other problems.

All of these paint solvent materials are designed for use under certain climatic conditions. They possess slow, medium, and fast evaporation abilities. In addition to temperature factors, you may need to use a specific solvent to compensate for very heavy or very light humidity. In essence, fast-evaporating solvents are used during paint work in cool temperatures, and slow ones employed during hot weather.

But using a fast solvent on a cool and very humid day could cause blushing, a condition in which moisture is trapped in paint after the fast solvent has evaporated. In that case, use a medium thinner or reducer to allow moisture time to evaporate along with solvent so that the resulting paint film dries completely and evenly.

Paint products are designed to be sprayed under climatic conditions of 70 degrees Fahrenheit and 30 percent humidity. Conditions such as these are perfect for laboratory tests, but you would have to paint cars in a controlled spray booth equipped with a dehumidifier and heater to achieve these perfect conditions all the time. To help you compensate for the lack of such a facility (which easily costs $100,000 or more), paint chemists have designed various solvents that react differently under various atmospheric conditions. To help inexperienced auto painters choose the correct solvent, labels on thinners, reducers, and retarders include best-use temperature ranges.

To determine which rated solvent is best under the specific humidity conditions for the region you are working in, consult with an auto body paint and supply professional. Professionals are familiar with the atmospheric and climatic conditions in their areas. They want your paint job to result in a beautiful finish so you will be satisfied with their products and continue to buy merchandise from them in the future. Therefore, you should be able to rely on their advice about the use of various products and their application techniques.

Auto body paint and supply stores can provide definitive information sheets and application guides, as well as list specific paint-to-thinner and reducer mixing ratios. Since paint is a liquid in the can, and although it has already been mixed with certain amounts of solvent, even more solvent is needed to make the solution sprayable. Use mixing sticks for this function according to product label instructions. Some mixing sticks' calibrations are designed for use with certain bases and solvents. You must be sure to use a mixing stick designed specifically for the brand of paint product you use. Calibrated mixing sticks are readily available at auto body paint and supply stores—don't confuse them with wooden stir sticks!

SPECIAL ADDITIVES

A variety of additives are available to prevent or eliminate various problems that may present themselves as you paint your car or truck. Among these are fish-eye eliminators, chip-resistant coatings, and special additives for use on flexible components. For the most part, these additives should not be used unless your paint project involves the problems or circumstances these tools are designed to address.

Fish-eye Eliminators

Fish eyes may appear as tiny surface finish blemishes that resemble small circles of popped paint bubbles, which seem to occur almost as soon as paint hits an auto body surface. Silicon residue often causes these flaws. Small traces of silicone do not allow paint to settle evenly; rather, they cause material to encircle the speck of silicone and form a volcano-like shape.

Fish-eye problems result from extended use of silicone-based vinyl dressings on body side moldings and other trim. Excessive dressing applications create random overspray away from trim, and infiltrates surrounding paint surfaces to become embedded in finishes. Silicone particles commonly remain even if the painted surfaces were cleaned thoroughly before paint application.

Auto body paint protectants, like polyglycoats and other silicone-based materials, can also cause fish-eye problems. In severe cases, silicone materials are absorbed by paint finishes to the point that underlying metal becomes saturated with silicone, making quality repaint efforts an almost impossible task.

Although fish-eye preventers are available, their use is not widely recommended, as you are just fighting fire with fire, or actually silicone with silicone. The best way to eliminate fish-eye problems is to thoroughly wash the entire vehicle before doing any paint prep work. Use a bucket of warm water with some ordinary dishwashing soap, such as Dove or Ivory, to clean the entire painted surface of the vehicle. Use a wax and grease remover to help remove any other residue once it is clean and dry. If you are going to be repainting the entire vehicle, use a somewhat more aggressive cleanser such as Comet to wash the vehicle to help eliminate fish-eye problems.

For the extreme case in which thorough cleaning does not eliminate fish-eyes, paint manufacturers have developed paint additives, which overcome the dilemma of fish-eyes and allow paint to flow uniformly and cover evenly. Various paint manufacturing companies label their fish-eye eliminators under certain names, like PPG's Omni AU MX194 Fish Eye Eliminator, Glasurit's Antisilicone Additive, and DuPont's Fish Eye Eliminator 9259S. Be sure to use only homologous products; use PPG's Fish Eye Preventer with PPG paint products, etc.

Container labels provide the proper mixing instructions. In addition, it is recommended you use the fish-eye eliminator product throughout your entire paint job. Do not simply mix in a prescribed dose to paint one panel that seems to exhibit fish-eye problems; rather, use that same mixture for the entire repaint to guarantee that color tints and coverage smoothness is the same.

Use multipurpose vinyl dressings sparingly to reduce fish-eye problems during future paint touch-ups or repaints. Instead of spraying trim pieces directly, spray dressing on a soft cloth first and then wipe it on parts in a controlled fashion. Afterward, be sure to wash the entire car thoroughly with a high-quality car wash soap to remove traces of lingering silicone residue.

Flexible Additives

Newer cars frequently feature flexible urethane bumpers, spoilers, splash guards, and ground effects that are usually painted in body color. For the most part, paint products used to cover these pieces are the same as those used to paint bodies. However, since these types of parts are flexible, a special additive is mixed in with lacquer or enamel paint to allow its thin film to bend and conform along with the body part without cracking, peeling, or chipping. This kind of additive is critical if you want the painted finish on

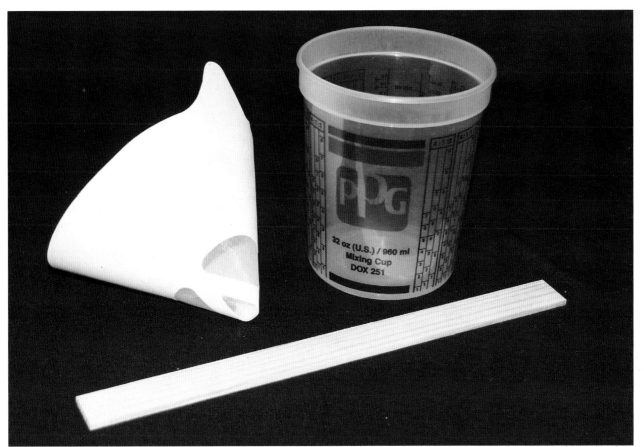

Even though you should ask your paint supplier to shake up your paint in their paint shaker, you still need to stir it by the time you get to your painting location, so make sure you have some paint stir sticks. You also need to stir undercoat products as well, as those products have more solids that settle to the bottom of the container. Stir sticks also come in handy for use as sanding blocks and as a means to check gaps between panels. Paint strainers are essential to use when pouring paint products into your spray gun cup; the slightest impurity can give you more headaches than you can imagine.

flexible parts to last. The use of flex additives is not as common as it was at one time. With lacquers and enamels, flex additives were a necessity; however, they are not required with urethane products.

According to PPG's Full Line Catalog, its Flexative Elastomeric Additive can be mixed directly with acrylic lacquers, acrylic enamels, urethane-modified acrylic enamels, and acrylic urethanes to repair flexible body parts. Specific instructions call for part surfaces to be clean and then sanded to promote paint adhesion. Once again, each paint manufacturer recommends using only its own brand of flexible additive with its brand of paint products.

In addition to flexible painted bumpers and bumper guards, be alert to using a flexible additive when painting any other similar material. This includes flexible spoilers, fender flares, entire front nose pieces, and mud flaps.

ADDITIONAL ITEMS

So you have your wax and grease remover, primer, sealer, paint (color), clear, sandpaper, masking tape, a new spray gun, and the appropriate safety equipment. What could you have possibly forgotten? A few more items will make your painting job easier. Except for the cleanup solvent, these items are usually free, so you might as well use them.

Spray Out Cards

An extremely handy tool that will help you ensure proper paint coverage is a spray out card. They are available from your paint and supply professional, and in most cases are free for the asking. If there is a charge, it is minimal, and well worth the price. The spray out card is black and white, with some text printed on it.

Before spraying any paint on your vehicle, apply paint to the spray out card, using the same procedure as on your vehicle. Use the same overlap pattern, spray gun settings, and time between coats. Apply enough coats to the spray out card so that the black and white and text is completely covered. The number of coats required to do this is the number of coats that will be required when painting your car as well. This spray out card also serves as a test for color match.

Stir Sticks and Paint Strainers

You will also need stir sticks and paint strainers. Even though your paint products (undercoats or top coats) have been mixed at the factory, they will still require stirring by the end user. Paint retailers usually provide stir sticks free upon request, or for minimal charge.

Paint strainers filter out impurities or grit. Some professional painters strain paint products as they pour them into the mixing cup, while others do not. However, they all strain the product as it goes into the spray gun cup. Whether you are spraying primer, sealer, or top coat, it must be strained to avoid getting dirt and debris in your spray gun.

Cleanup Thinner or Reducer

Ask your paint supplier what product to use for cleaning your spray gun. Instead of using the same expensive thinner or reducer that you are using with your paint products, most paint retailers have some less expensive products designed for that purpose. Some professionals may not carry a less expensive product, but it is worth asking. Other than the expense, there is nothing wrong with using the same reducer for cleanup as you mix with paint. Just be sure that you have something to clean your spray gun with before you fill it up with a product that has a short pot life.

OVERVIEW

Compared to a decade ago, decisions regarding automobile painting have increased dramatically.

Not only do you have tens of thousands of colors to choose from, but you also have to determine which kind of solvent, primer, primer-surfacer, and sealer to use—and, for that matter, which products you do not need to use. The technology surrounding the auto paint industry has really become high-tech. Even professional painters sometimes have to suffer through difficult decisions relating to paint procedures on cars that have been repainted one or two times with an unknown type of paint, or worse yet, more than one type sprayed onto different body panels.

Before starting your paint job, research thoroughly what has to be done to prepare the vehicle's surface, and which paint products you'll need to complete the job safely, effectively, and with excellent results. Haphazardly starting a project with little concern over a systematic and organized approach does nothing but delay the overall process, causing frustration over missed completion dates and the extra work needed to go over areas that were not properly serviced the first time.

Remember that all automotive paint products are potentially dangerous. Just about every product is flammable and you have to be keenly aware of all heat and flame sources whenever working with them. Flash fires involving clouds of flammable gases will quickly engulf your shop, garage, carport, and most importantly, you. Have a fire extinguisher available at all times just in case.

Personal safety has become an intense issue with the use of automotive painting chemicals. Every label of every product will clearly recommend the use of certain personal safety equipment. Heed those recommendations to protect your health. Should you have any questions about the intended use or function of any auto paint product or piece of related equipment, do not hesitate to consult an auto body paint and supply salesperson, manufacturer information sheet or application guide, professional auto painter, or paint manufacturer.

Chapter 4
Tools, Materials, and Safety

It is almost impossible to complete any job without the right tools, materials, and equipment. Automotive painting is no different from any other chore, and you must expect to buy, borrow, or rent some rather specialized equipment if you expect to prepare an auto body surface properly and then paint it with results comparable to that of a professional.

Auto body paint and supply stores carry a wide selection of repair and painting tools and equipment. In most cases, this merchandise is designed for commercial use and is made of heavy-duty materials and quality. The cost may be high, but you can expect each item to last a long time with proper maintenance. You might opt instead to purchase required equipment from tool outlets or other stores that sell the items. These other places might carry less heavy-duty items, which may cost less.

The Eastwood Company sells tools and equipment especially designed for both part-time and serious auto restorers, auto body repair technicians, and painters. Eastwood tests all of its tools and equipment in its field laboratory, a quality shop where auto restoration and repair projects are ongoing. Eastwood advertises that each item listed in its catalog has been used in their shop with satisfactory results. Talk to other auto enthusiasts to see what equipment and suppliers they've had good luck with on their paint projects.

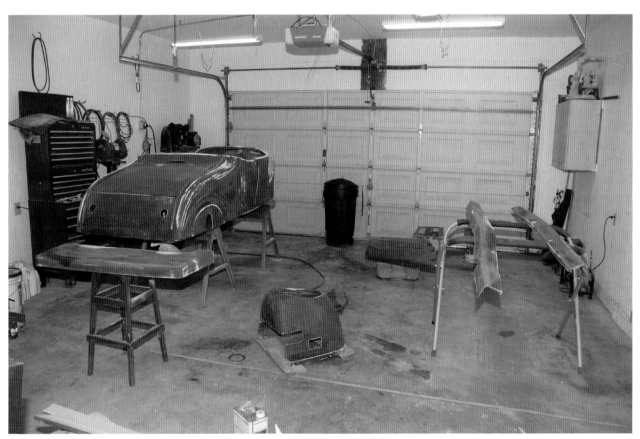

While I am admittedly not a professional painter, I have accomplished much in the way of automotive painting in this two-car garage. It is approximately 20 feet wide and 28 feet deep, and has white painted walls to help reflect all available light. To vent, I raise the garage door a foot or two and place a box fan (blowing outward) in the doorway behind the camera position. It is not the ideal situation, but I have been satisfied with the results. Lighting along the walls would be a great improvement, as well as racks to hang small items for painting.

In lieu of purchasing or borrowing tools or equipment, you could rent items at a local rental shop. Although most rental shops make valiant attempts to keep their inventories in top condition, you may have some trouble finding paint guns that spray as expected; dry paint easily clogs tiny air and material ports if they are not immediately cleaned after each use. Therefore, you might seriously consider spending a few dollars to buy your own paint spray gun so that you can guarantee it will be taken care of properly and will operate as expected every time.

WORK AREA

If you wanted to apply a nonskid paint job to your car that was rough enough to prevent a sheet of ice from falling off of it, you could apply almost any paint in a desert sandstorm and call it good. A little smoother texture, you say? Then try painting your car in a carport with a dirt and gravel floor. But, if what you really want is a smooth, blemish-free, lustrous, deep-shine paint job, consider renting a regular auto spray booth or spending a little time to devise a makeshift paint booth in your garage or workshop.

The auto paint industry constantly faces new and updated limitations on where and how to spray due to the increasing regulation of waste compounds. The advent of High Volume/Low Pressure (HVLP) systems is a great help, but along with them, painters in certain regions are required to use high-tech spray booths equipped with downdraft ventilation systems and overspray-capturing mechanisms.

To offset the staggering price of their booths, some paint shops make them available for rent—under supervised conditions, of course. You may be able to find rental booths through advertisements in your telephone book yellow pages or online under the heading "Auto Body Repair and Painting." You can also check with your auto body paint and supply professional, auto parts store salesperson, and even make a few calls to local body shops to determine if they rent their booths, or know of any other body shops that offer theirs for rent.

A definite problem exists when renting paint booths, however, in that you have to transport your car to that location. Whether it is driven or towed, you have to mask the car at that booth's location, along with possible part dismantling, such as lights, and required cleaning. Be sure to transport your car and yourself on a dry day with dry roads.

Should you decide to paint your vehicle at home, you must provide a suitable work area. A garage or shop should be fine. Be sure to provide plenty of air ventilation to account for overspray. You will need an air compressor, lots of light, and an electrical source to operate a fresh air respirator compressor, if called for.

Rather than spray cars in an open garage and cover everything in the place with speckles of overspray, consider enclosing an area with sheets of clear plastic. Long, wide sheets of clear plastic sheeting are available at lumberyards and hardware stores. Roll an edge of plastic around strips of lath and nail them to the ceiling or rafters. Use heavy-duty duct tape to secure bottom edges to the floor. Consider placing plastic across open rafters as a makeshift ceiling to prevent dust from the attic space from falling onto your paint surface. Be sure not to put plastic too close to light fixtures, as hot bulbs could melt or ignite it.

Put a large fan near the front of your workspace to aid ventilation. Cut a hole in the plastic for a fan to bring in fresh air from outside of the enclosure. Tape a thin, lint-free cloth over the fan's cage to trap dust or debris. Leave the garage door open to assist in ventilation, but be certain that local breezes will not flow directly from the outside in through the open door. If that is a problem, determine when breezes are minimal, maybe early in the morning, and plan to paint at that time.

Minimize dust by wetting down the gravel or dirt driveway near your garage or workshop. You might even have to leave a light sprinkler spray in place during paint work to keep dust particles from being kicked up and blown all over your painting surface. Wetting down the floor in your workspace is often suggested to keep down dust; under certain circumstances, this may be necessary. However, this practice should be avoided if possible. Wetting down the floor introduces humidity to your painting environment, which may cause more problems than what you are trying to eliminate. Be careful and avoid using electrical devices when working on a wet surface—doing so could get you electrocuted.

SAFETY REGULATIONS

Fortunately, for users of most paint products, the paint manufacturers have been saddled with the responsibility of making their products environmentally safe and user-friendly. The manufacturers are continually striving to lower the amount of VOCs in their products. There is nothing that the user can do to lower the amount of VOCs in the paint itself; however, end users must obey local laws that govern the use and disposal of these products.

Protecting the Environment

Most federal and local laws governing the use of paint products are aimed at protecting the environment. In the United States, California has the most restrictive laws. Check with your local paint supply professional for the latest laws in your area.

Painters in California are restricted to using waterborne products for most of their painting, along with downdraft spray booths for certain spraying operations. In the parts of the country that do not require the use of waterborne products, these products are typically not available in paint supply stores. The good thing about this is that you can use whatever product your favorite paint supply store has to offer. If the product is on the shelf, it has been deemed compliant with whatever local laws are in effect.

Most regulations depend upon the amount of painting to be done. A shop that advertises and operates as an auto body repair and refinish business is obviously going to be under the watchful eye of the local authorities that govern that type of activity in your area. However, if you are purchasing only enough of those same products to repaint one car or truck, other than perhaps a pesky neighbor, no one is going to notice or care for the most part. To make your life easier, though, exercise common sense, and don't advertise the fact that you are using volatile chemicals to any of your neighbors who are not fond of your interest in automobiles. Remember that these chemicals are regulated because of the dangers they pose to human health and the environment, and the health and safety of you and your neighbors is paramount to painting at home.

What do you do with the leftover paint products when the job is over? That will vary in your particular area; however, pouring it on the ground is a definite no-no. Some paint professionals dispose of your leftover paint products for a nominal fee, as they have to pay to have it disposed of (at least it will be disposed of properly). Information sheets for all paint products provide disposal recommendations. If you have any questions as to the correct procedure for product disposal, you can verify what is appropriate in your area by checking with your local paint professional.

Protecting Yourself

Although the government may not care that you are spraying paint in your own garage, your body will. Decades ago, painters could get by with tying a bandana over their mouth and nose and be all right, as the prime concern was avoiding multicolored nose hair. Those days are now long gone.

You may not be breaking any laws if you do not wear the proper safety equipment, but violating this law will kill you in time. If you don't take proper precautions, you may not die tomorrow or next week, but paint products are among the most dangerous available. Don't take unnecessary risks.

The paint manufacturers list the necessary safety equipment (breathing masks, skin protection, etc.) and include precautions on the labels and information sheets for all of their products. It is imperative that you follow their recommendations.

Charcoal filter masks are suitable for most (but not all) undercoat products. These are relatively inexpensive for masks with replaceable cartridges, and disposable units are even less expensive. Replace charcoal filters after 24 hours of use in a painting environment. When not in use, store the entire mask in a resealable freezer bag.

Any paint product that contains isocyanates (epoxy primer, or any product that requires mixing with a hardener) requires the most complete protection. Isocyanates are not only inhaled, but they are also absorbed through tear ducts in the eyes or through skin pores. It is necessary to cover your entire body when using these products—equip yourself with painter's coveralls, rubber gloves, goggles, and a hat.

I recommend a fresh-air-supplied hood if you're considering a profession out of painting automobiles. This hood covers the entire head and face, and connects to its own air compressor to supply fresh air to the user.

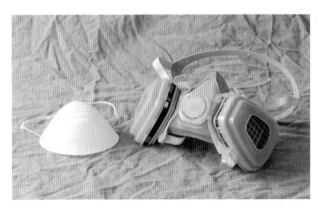

These two masks are essential for responsible respiratory health when doing automotive body and paint work. The simple paper filter mask on the left should be used anytime that you are sanding or otherwise in a dusty environment. The filter mask on the right should be your minimum requirement when spraying primer or paint.

Even though I've usually enjoyed access to a garage when automotive painting or priming, I know that is not the case for everyone. Whether you have a huge garage, a small garage, a carport, or simply a driveway in which to do your automotive painting, you need to keep the paint in and the dust and dirt out for the best results. I will say, however, that my best friend (who has been painting cars for close to 60 years now) has been turning out fantastic paintwork without a spray booth for his entire career. Still, you want to prevent paint (and especially clear) from getting on everything in the vicinity, keeping dust and dirt to a minimum will help you obtain professional results. To do this, you may choose to build a temporary spray booth.

For your temporary spray booth, you may choose to use plastic piping, or electrical conduit and the associated fittings, or you may choose to weld up a framework out of metal. Any of those work if you go about it properly. After building the framework out of the material of your choice, drape 3-mil-thick clear plastic sheeting over it, and you have a temporary spray booth. However, I have included some rough sketches of a temporary spray booth built out of 2x4 lumber, a bunch of nails, some bolts, and the aforementioned plastic sheeting. This method is freestanding, uses common carpentry practice to construct, and can be disassembled for storage or could be used to create a permanent spray booth. Just to keep everyone legal, I must warn you to check with your local building codes and enforcement officials before constructing anything like this, especially if the curious public can see it.

Regardless of what materials you use, you must first decide what size to make it. The sketches that follow build a booth that is 28 feet long, 16 feet wide, and 8 feet high. This gives you plenty of room on all sides for most vehicles. I would suggest allowing at least 3 feet on all sides if you can. You will need additional height if you are painting a monster truck, but 8 feet should be the minimum for most anything as you will need to walk around, even if you are painting a go-kart. You will need two sidewalls, and you may decide to build them in multiple sections depending on their length. As shown on the sketches, each sidewall is made of two 14-foot-long sections that are bolted together. If this is something that you think you may need to assemble, disassemble, and store multiple times, you can utilize more, but shorter sections to make them easier to manage.

If you decide to go with the carpentry route for your temporary spray booth, begin with two pieces of 2x4 lumber that are each as long as the sidewall (or the modular portion thereof). One of these will be the lower (or sill) plate, while the other will be the upper plate. Place each of these on an edge, side by side, and mark for the 2x4 studs that will give the wall its height. In my sketches, I placed the studs on 16-inch centers, just as in home construction. However, if this is a temporary construction, you could probably get away with placing the studs on 24-inch centers. If you are going to add in light fixtures in the walls, you will need to determine what size to frame them in and modify your studs and wall framing accordingly. You can now use 16d nails to nails each stud perpendicular to the sill plate and then nail the upper plate onto the opposite ends of the studs. If this is temporary, you can probably get by with two nails in each end of each stud, but if it is permanent, you should go with three nails.

Build the first end wall in mostly the same way, just not

SIDEWALL (TWO REQUIRED)

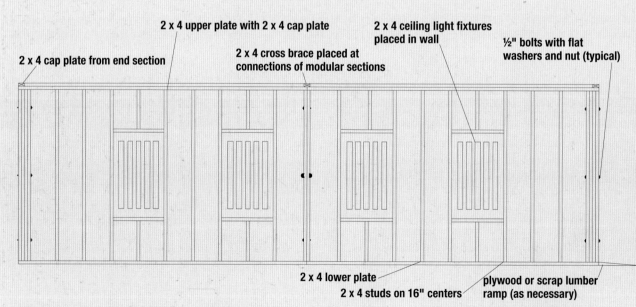

2 x 4 upper plate with 2 x 4 cap plate

2 x 4 ceiling light fixtures placed in wall

½" bolts with flat washers and nut (typical)

2 x 4 cap plate from end section

2 x 4 cross brace placed at connections of modular sections

2 x 4 lower plate

2 x 4 studs on 16" centers

plywood or scrap lumber ramp (as necessary)

This sketch shows a full sidewall made up of two smaller sections that are bolted together. A number of fluorescent light fixtures built into the walls would certainly increase visibility while painting. In a commercial spray booth, these lights need to be explosion-proof, but you may be able to work around that in a temporary booth. Still, you should work safely.

FRONT WALL (ONE REQUIRED)

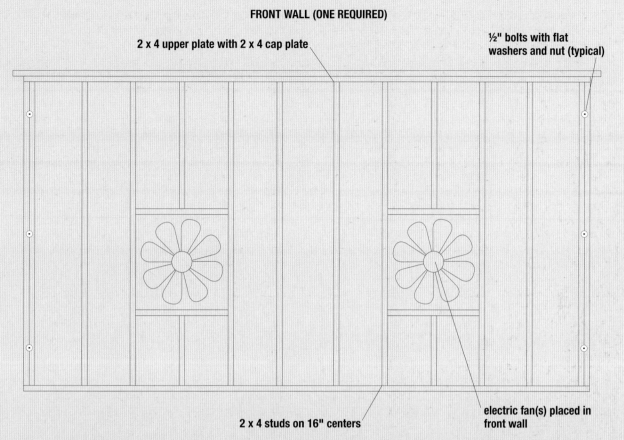

2 x 4 upper plate with 2 x 4 cap plate

½" bolts with flat washers and nut (typical)

2 x 4 studs on 16" centers

electric fan(s) placed in front wall

The front wall and back wall should be the same width as each other and constructed in similar fashion to the two sidewalls. Notice how the cap plate extends beyond the upper plate by the width of the sidewall. This allows you to nail the cap plate of one to the top plate of the other, tying them together in the process. Several intermediate cross braces should be used to both tie the sidewalls together and to secure the plastic sheeting.

as wide. In the sketches, I show framing for two fans. One is better than none and will probably be sufficient if you are using an HVLP spray gun, as overspray will be minimal with that. Regardless of the number of fans, place them low in the wall. Install the fan(s) to blow air out of the spray booth, and place a disposable air filter on the inside of the booth. The last wall is the one that will allow your car to move in or out of the temporary spray booth, so you will need to frame it with a more than adequate size opening in it. You sure do not want to scrape new paint off your car as you are moving it out of the spray booth.

With all four walls framed, you can now erect them. This requires a minimum of two people, and a third doesn't hurt. Place one of the sidewalls in its intended position with the first wall located at the appropriate end and perpendicular to the sidewall. Brace the two walls together, and then add a cap plate atop the end wall's upper plate that also overlaps the end of the upper plate of the sidewall. The cap plate of each end wall should be as long as the end wall plus the width of each sidewall. Depending

on how much help you have available, you can install one cap plate on the end wall and secure both sidewalls at the same time. Then repeat the process for the entry wall, securing it with a cap plate that spans both sidewalls. You should then add several cross braces spanning both sidewalls to tie them together and to attach plastic sheeting later. Since these walls are unsecured to a subfloor, you should probably bolt the walls together at the corners. As shown in the sketches, three bolts, two flat washers, and a nut are required at each corner. You can drill holes for these most anywhere, but I would suggest one at approximately a foot up from the bottom, another one foot down from the top, and another somewhere in the middle.

If my instructions make any sense, you should now have a wooden structure in your driveway or somewhere. The next step is to install the plastic sheeting walls and roof. Depending on the size of your new spray booth, you may be able to work with one piece of material, or it may take multiple pieces. Ideally, you have one piece of 3-mil clear plastic sheeting to unroll or unfold on the top and to cover the walls as well. After positioning the plastic sheeting as necessary, use a staple gun to secure it to wooden framework. Leave the plastic sheeting loose on the door portion of the entry end. Tie the "garage door" up as you move your vehicle into the spray booth, and then untie it to let it hang down. Be sure you have access for an air hose to enter the booth, as well as for you to enter and exit. The temporary spray booth should not be sealed 100 percent, or you might suck the walls in when you turn on the exhaust fan or possibly develop condensation depending on your weather conditions. Neither of those are good things while painting your car.

BACK (DRIVE-THROUGH) WALL (ONE REQUIRED)

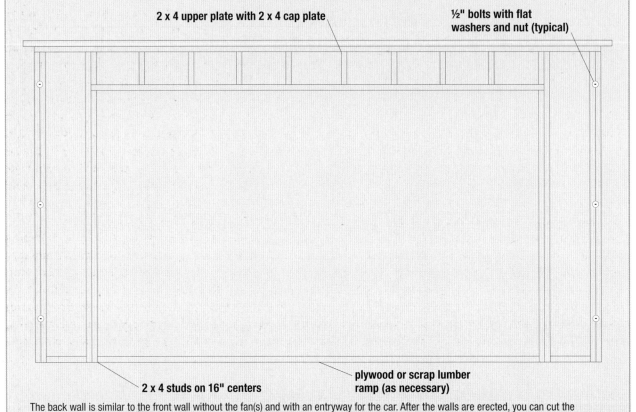

2 x 4 upper plate with 2 x 4 cap plate

½" bolts with flat washers and nut (typical)

2 x 4 studs on 16" centers

plywood or scrap lumber ramp (as necessary)

The back wall is similar to the front wall without the fan(s) and with an entryway for the car. After the walls are erected, you can cut the doorway out of the sill plate if you choose, put a piece of plywood over it, or just push a little harder to move the vehicle in or out.

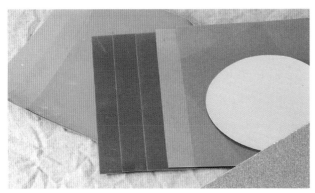

Various types of sandpaper are required when completely refinishing an automotive paint job. At the left are 2000,-, 1,500-,and 1,000-grit wet or dry for wet sanding the finished clear. Next are 400-, 320-, 240-, and 180-grit wet or dry used during block sanding. The round pad is 80-grit for scuffing an existing paint surface or to smooth body filler. The long strip at the bottom is 36-grit for roughing in plastic body filler.

When used in conjunction with painter's coverall's and rubber gloves, it offers the ultimate in protection from isocyanates. However, the cost for such a unit may be prohibitive for people who are painting their first vehicle.

As long as you are using a charcoal-filtered mask (with fresh cartridges), and you are wearing goggles, a hat, rubber gloves, and a pair of painter's coveralls, you will be safe. These materials can be purchased for around $50—an extremely small price to pay for health.

Paint products are most dangerous when they are being atomized, as when sprayed from a paint spray gun; however, they can be nearly as bad when the dried paint is being sanded. Wear a filtered mask during this time as well.

Lighting

Except for extreme conditions, you cannot have too much light to paint. Light reveals imperfections more clearly, allowing you to correct or remove them before they are painted over. Proper lighting exposes all areas of the parts or pieces that you are painting, providing you the opportunity for complete coverage with paint, and eliminating touch-up later.

You must be wary that your homebrewed lighting setup doesn't cause excessive localized heat that may cause blemishes in the paint. Most paint spray booths feature fluorescent light fixtures that are cooler than most other types of light.

Room to Work

Your work area must not be cluttered despite the fact that bodywork is dusty and dirty. You must have room

to walk around the vehicle or parts thereof that you are painting. Can you imagine the agony of straightening a fender or door to perfection, only to trip and fall into it just after applying a fresh coat of paint?

Your painting area should have adequate lighting, proper ventilation, a flat surface for mixing paint, and the means by which to hang small parts or subassemblies. Remove any unnecessary obstacles from your temporary spray booth to maximize safety and efficiency.

SANDING

Quality paint jobs cannot be accomplished when paint is applied to improperly prepared surfaces. Paint products are not designed to fill cracks, crevices, or other surface irregularities. Rather, they sink into these imperfections to magnify their depth and roughness. Therefore, spend as much time as necessary to sand all coats of primer-surfacer or existing paint surfaces to absolutely smooth perfection. All professional painters agree that most of their time is by far spent preparing cars for paint, rather than actually spraying them. A variety of sandpaper grits and useful hand tools are available for smoothing chores.

Sandpaper

Sandpaper is rated according to its relative coarseness; low numbers are the coarsest, and higher numbers are finer. For example, 36-grit sandpaper is extremely coarse and 1,200-grit is superfine, almost smooth. Auto body paint and supply stores carry the widest selection of sandpaper grits, both in the type used for dry sanding only, and those that can be used dry or with water. Save wet sanding for those operations required to smooth

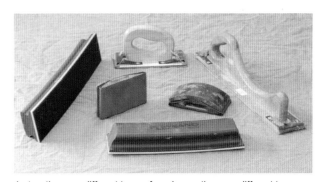

Just as there are different types of sandpaper, there are different types of sanding boards and sanding blocks. The Flexsand block in the front and at the left use a hook-and-loop method to attach the sandpaper, and are used for sanding slightly curved surfaces. The two wooden-handled sanding boards are for sanding flat areas and clamp the sandpaper in place. The two smaller rubber sanding blocks in the middle are slotted on both ends and conceal tacks that secure the sandpaper.

blemishes on lacquer or urethane paints after they have been sprayed and cured.

To complement their assortment of sandpaper grits, paint and supply stores carry these products in various sizes and shapes. You can buy sheets of sandpaper measuring about a foot square that can be cut or folded to suit user needs. You can also take advantage of sandpaper strips with or without adhesive backing for use on long sanding boards, or adhesive-backed discs for use with circular pads on dual-action (DA) sanders. Be sure to purchase enough sandpaper to complete your job, as one sheet is rarely enough for more than one small repair operation.

Sanding Blocks and Boards

For flat and even sanding, you must use a sanding block or board. Using your hand alone will result in minute low spots or grooves, caused by the hand's irregular shape and nonrigid nature. Knuckle protrusions featured on the palm side of your hand cause the sandpaper under them to dig in, while the rest of the sanding area receives only slight pressure and minimal smoothing. Sanding blocks and boards, on the other hand, provide flat, rigid bases that easily receive and disperse identical pressure over entire sanding surfaces.

Sanding blocks and boards are available at auto body paint and supply stores and some auto parts houses. There are three common sizes: the smallest, a little larger than the palm of your hand, is handy for reaching into tight areas confined by body designs or other obstructions; a medium size works great for sanding touch-up areas that encompass small panel areas; long blocks and boards work best for sanding chores on full panels, deck lids, and hoods. As a general rule of thumb, use the largest sanding board or block that works within the area that you are sanding for the best results.

ONE-OFF TOOLS

Custom sanding blocks and boards are designed for special applications. Rounded bases provide an excellent means for sanding curved body features, like grooves and arched fender flares. Small hand pads work best for smoothing imperfections near ridges, acute corners, and other unique spots too small for normal blocks or boards. Most of these items are also on display at your local auto body and paint supply store, and are available through auto-related equipment and tool outlets. Of course, when it comes to sanding, many oddball items found in the shop work well within body seams or crevices. Craft impromptu sanding blocks

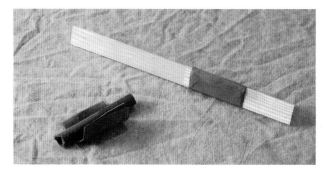

Even with all of the commercially available sanding devices, some body contours call for improvisation. Short sections of radiator, fuel line hose, or paint stick can be wrapped with the sandpaper of choice to get into those otherwise difficult areas. Just remember that a sanding block must provide a uniform backing surface to properly do the job.

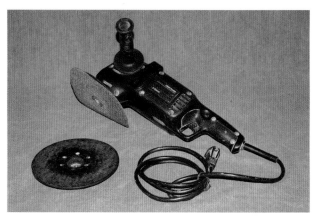

Unless you are a professional autobody refinisher, a sander such as this might be a more versatile tool than a DA. A variety of sanding discs are available for removing existing paint off your car or grinding down welds on your metal working projects. You can also use this type of sander as a buffer with the correct attachments (not shown).

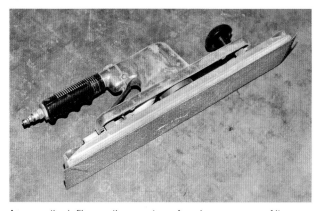

A pneumatic air file uses the same type of sandpaper as some of its handheld cousins, but saves excessive elbow strain. Saving effort and therefore time makes it a must-have in a collision repair shop, but the hobbyist can do the same work with a manual long board sander for much less money. These work best on large flat surfaces.

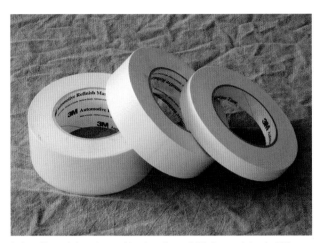

Automotive paint grade masking tape is available in a variety of widths, with the most common being 2 inch, 1½ inch, and ¾ inch wide as shown from left to right. Three-quarter inch is the most common and will serve most of your masking needs. Wider sizes are especially good for masking off trim and window moldings. Only automotive paint grade tape should be used when doing this type of work on your vehicle as common household tape will not endure the chemicals in automotive paint.

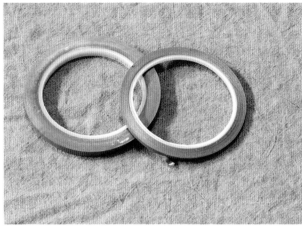

For laying out flames or scallops, or masking around intricate details, narrow Fine Line tape is the stuff to use. It is narrow, thin, and flexible, which allows it to be easily applied in curvaceous areas without bunching or pulling off the surface. It is available in different widths, most under ½ inch.

from just about anything, radiator hoses to paint stir sticks. Whichever tool helps you achieve a smooth panel is precisely the tool you need at the time. As long as the sanding "block" and the body panel shape are compatible, you're in good shape.

SANDING MACHINES

Sanding machines usually consist of pneumatic or electric hand sanders. Their use is not always required, especially for small jobs. However, on complete repaints or vehicles that have undergone body repair, these tools can help to cut the amount of time spent sanding. Beware, however, as a powerful sanding machine in the hands of an inexperienced operator can quickly do more harm than good.

High-speed rotary sanders are most commonly used to remove old paint, old body filler, and rust deposits on sheetmetal panels. They can also be used to remove or smooth grossly jagged fingers of fiberglass that stick out from cracks and other collision damage to panels on fiberglass body vehicles. For the most part, these tools are employed by auto body repair technicians, although painters do use them to remove years of accumulated paint and rust deposits from vehicles scheduled for full paint jobs.

With bases shaped like long sanding boards, air files make quick work of smoothing layers of plastic filler on wide panels, like door skins. Their internal mechanisms operate bases in a rapid back-and-forth direction. Users must constantly keep these tools moving because if allowed to rest on one spot, their forceful action will cause definite grooves, waves, or other imperfections. Like rotary sanders, air files can cut the amount of work required if used properly, or quickly cause more work if you are not careful.

DA (dual-action) sanders are a mainstay in professional auto paint shops. Their unique design causes a circular pad to move in orbital directions instead of just spinning in a high-speed circle. An offset counterweight working in conjunction with an oval-shaped mounting mechanism allows DA pads to be forced back and forth and side to side in a very fast movement. Speed controls allow for intricate sanding, and assortments of sandpaper grit discs can be used for anything from initial sanding to fine finishing.

DA sanders are available in different sizes and power ranges. Large tools work best for body repair jobs, and small ones are handiest for paint preparation work. You will find DAs at auto body paint and supply stores as well as some tool houses.

MASKING

No matter how skilled you are with a spray gun, any unpainted areas must be covered with masking paper or tape. The time and effort to clean up overspray will quickly exceed that needed to mask off the area.

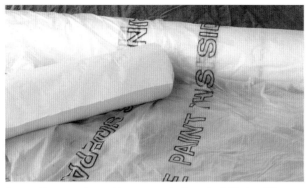

Use masking paper for masking areas wider than about 3 inches. It is commonly available in 12- and 18-inch widths at auto parts stores, but is available in several different widths at your auto paint and body supplier. Masking paper can be cut easily with scissors and can be folded to fit within the desired area. If you are covering a large area to prevent it from being covered with overspray, rolls of very thin film are available. These come in long rolls about 32 inches wide, but fold out to about 10 feet wide.

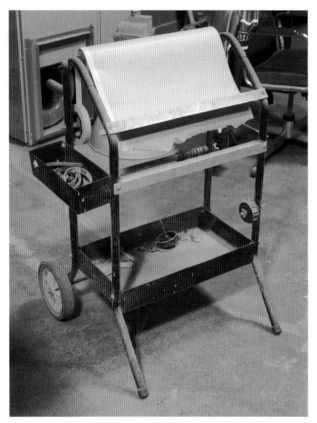

Common in every professional auto body shop is a rolling masking paper dispenser. This one has an 18-inch single roller, but others have multiple rollers with various widths of paper. The benefit of this device is that it attaches masking tape to one edge of the paper as you pull the masking paper from the roll and then the paper and tape is torn against the cutting bar. This is much easier than attempting to hold paper in place and then affix tape to the edge.

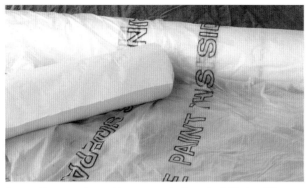

Tape

Almost everyone is familiar with masking tape. But did you know there is a drastic difference between the rolls of masking tape found at ordinary hardware stores and those specifically designed for automotive painting jobs? There is, and the difference in their designs makes a definite difference in the outcome of your paint job.

Ordinary household masking tape is not treated to withstand potent auto paint solvents. Paint can penetrate weak tape to ruin the finishes underneath. In addition, adhesives used in ordinary masking tape are not designed to easily break loose from surfaces and can remain on painted bodies after the bulk of material has been pulled off. Lingering traces of tape and adhesive residue might require use of a mild solvent for complete removal, a chore that could threaten the finish or new paint applied next to it.

Whether your job consists of a very small paint touch-up or complete paint job, you have to realize that automotive paint masking tape is the only product designed for such use. Using any other type of inexpensive alternative is just asking for problems and aggravation.

Auto body paint and supply stores sell masking tape in various widths. Sizes range from ⅛ inch up to a full 2 inches. Each masking job presents different needs, and having more than one size of masking tape on hand will help you accomplish those chores more quickly and easily. For example, it is much simpler to place a few strips of 2-inch-wide masking tape over a headlight than having to maneuver a sheet of masking paper over that same relatively small area.

For masking designs, or to ensure perfect masking tape edges along trim and molding, many painters initially lay down a thin ⅛-inch wide strip of Fine Line plastic tape. Made by 3M, Fine Line is very maneuverable and adheres well around curves without bending or folding. It is easy to use as a primary masking edge along trim and molding edges. After you have the Fine Line in place, you can add ¾-inch or wider tape anywhere along it, sparing you the task of getting each piece right at the edge of the masked part.

Painters use more rolls of ¾-inch masking tape than any other type. Its versatile size works great for securing paper and covering small items such as key locks. For a complete vehicle paint job, expect to use at least two rolls of 2-inch-wide tape and three rolls of ¾-inch. If you anticipate masking along trim or molding pieces, have a couple rolls of ⅛-inch Fine Line handy. Expect to pay anywhere from $2.50 to $5 per roll for

TOOLS, MATERIALS, AND SAFETY

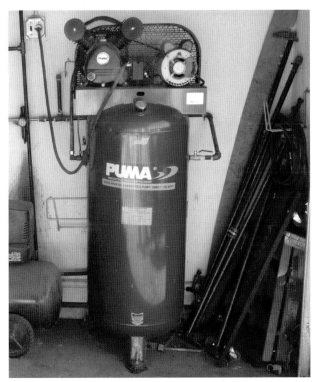

When I got serious about automotive painting and began using HVLP spray guns, the 25-gallon portable unit just couldn't keep up. To solve that issue, I purchased this Puma, six horsepower, 220-volt, single-phase air compressor. It develops 12 cfm and has a 60-gallon tank. Note that I have installed rubber insulators between it and the concrete floor.

quality automotive masking tape. Each roll is generally 60 yards long, the same as rolls of masking paper.

PAPER

Seldom will you find professional auto painters using anything but treated masking paper for any masking job. Inexperienced painters use newspaper with mixed results at best. Although newspaper material may seem inexpensive and appropriate for paint masking chores, it is porous and lets paint seep through to mar surface finishes underneath.

Rolls of quality automotive paint masking paper are available at auto body paint and supply stores. Their widths range from 4 inches up to 3 feet, with 12-inch widths being the most frequently used size. This paper is chemically treated to prevent paint or solvent penetration, a most important asset. Two rolls of 12-inch paper should be enough for most jobs. You'll need a roll of wider paper to cover roofs, hoods, and trunk lids in situations where they will not be painted at all, or will be sprayed a different color than body sides. A roll of 4-

or 6-inch paper could be handy for intricate masking, as is necessary around doorjambs, trunk, and hood edges.

To make their masking jobs easier, professional painters use masking paper and tape racks designed to distribute paper with tape already attached to the edge. To help you easily retrieve strips of masking paper, consider mounting a heavy dowel on the side of your workbench with long brackets, so rolls can rotate freely as you pull off needed lengths.

AIR COMPRESSOR

You could buy the most expensive auto paint products made, spend weeks and weeks preparing your car or truck's surface to perfection, use the most highly advanced spray paint gun available, and then ruin your paint job by relying upon an inadequate air compressor or a holding tank loaded with moisture and oil residue.

One cannot overemphasize the importance of a clean, dry, and controlled source of air pressure for any spray paint job. Miniscule particles of water, oil, or rust will find their way from holding tanks to spray gun nozzles unless they are captured and retained somewhere between the compressor and spray gun. If allowed to accumulate, and eventually exit a spray gun's nozzle, these contaminants will blemish the paint finish with fish eyes, dirt nibs, and possibly blushing problems all over the surface.

Most professional paint shops use a minimum 10-horsepower rated air compressor. These units simultaneously supply plenty of air for the operation of pneumatic tools and some painting equipment. For the hobbyist, a smaller compressor may be satisfactory, as long as the compressor is rated at 5-horsepower or greater. This is not to say that smaller compressors cannot be expected to work fine for small jobs, but 5-horsepower compressors offer plenty of compressed air without having to run constantly to supply it.

The more a compressor works to maintain proper pressure, the hotter the air supply becomes. As heat generation continues, the compressor introduces moisture into the air system through condensation inside piping. This is not good. You want your air compressor to build up a reserve of compressed air in its holding tank, and then shut off for a while to cool down.

Volume

About the best way to determine what size air compressor will work best for your needs is to compare the required cubic feet per minute (cfm) of air needed

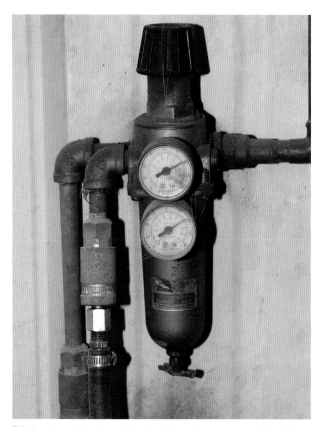

This is a heavy-duty air regulator that also splits one-source air line into two service lines. In this case, the air supply line comes in from the right, passing through the regulator, and exiting one of the lines to the left. The knob on the top is turned to regulate (or set) the exiting air pressure and is shown on the respective gauge. The knob at the bottom is a petcock for draining condensation.

be more appropriate when using HVLP, or other high demand pneumatic tools.

Pressure

To ensure that you have the recommended air pressure at the tip of your spray gun, hold the trigger on your gun wide open while adjusting the air pressure regulator controls. Although a control gauge setting might show 40 psi while in a static condition, operating your paint gun may cause it to drop down to 20 or 25 psi. It is important to apply auto paint at the psi rating indicated on the container label or in the product's application guide literature.

Another factor that causes false pressure gauge readings is the size of the air hose used to supply your paint gun. Small-diameter hoses experience friction loss and cause pressures to dwindle once they arrive at the paint gun 25 feet away. PPG's Refinish Manual suggests ¼-inch hose is too small for standard production paint guns. It suggests a preferred hose size of ⁵⁄₁₆-inch inside diameter in maximum lengths of 25 feet. For HVLP spray guns, ⅜-inch inside diameter air hose is recommended.

Regulators

Air pressure is adjusted by tightening or loosening the knob on the air compressor's regulator. Smaller, homeowner-type compressors typically have a built-in regulator, while larger compressors usually have a separate regulator plumbed into the air line that exits the compressor air storage tank. Some shops may have

with your spray gun and the application of particular paint products, to the cfm rating on the compressor you plan to use. If the compressor can easily supply the required cfm at the prescribed application pressure, you should have no problem. But if you need 12 cfm for your spray gun and your 2-horsepower compressor can supply only a maximum of 9 cfm, you will need to rent or borrow a higher rated unit to meet the minimum 12-cfm requirement.

Your compressor must also have an adequate capacity. As an example, a 5-horsepower compressor with a 20-gallon tank that supplies enough air for a conventional spray gun may not be able to keep up with the demands of an HVLP spray gun. Instead of being able to spray a complete coat of paint at one time, you may have to stop in the middle (or several times) to allow the air supply to catch up. The same 5-horsepower compressor with a 35-gallon tank may

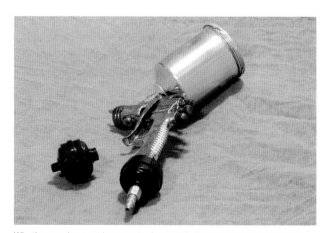

Whether you have moisture traps in your air line or not, sooner or later you are going to experience moisture finding its way to your spray gun. To prevent that moisture from causing problems with your primer or paint, install a filter/drier between your air hose and your spray gun. This should eliminate any oil or moisture from entering your spray gun.

MINIMUM PIPE SIZE RECOMMENDATIONS

Compressor Size	Capacity	Main Air Line Length	Size
Up to 2 hp	6 to 9 cfm	Over 50 ft	3/4 inch
3 to 5 hp	12 to 20 cfm	Up to 200 ft	3/4 inch
		Over 200 ft	1 inch
5 to 10 hp	20 to 40 cfm	Up to 100 ft	3/4 inch
		Over 100 ft to 200 ft	1 inch
		Over 200 ft	1 1/4 inch
10 to 15 hp	40 to 60 cfm	Up to 100 ft	1 inch
		Over 100 ft to 200 ft	1 1/4 inch
		Over 200 ft	1 1/4 inch

The size and capacity of your air compressor along with the distance the compressed air must travel from the compressor to the air tools that it operates is a determining factor on what size pipe should be used. Copper or galvanized pipe should be used to plumb your air supply to where it will actually be used.

multiple regulators in the air line. In a general purpose shop, one regulator adjusted to provide sufficient pressure for the particular tool that requires the most air would be adequate. In a larger shop that may include mechanic work, priming, and painting, each area would need a regulator to control the air pressure.

In addition to regulators that control the flow of air to the entire air line downstream of their installation, many spray guns utilize their own regulators. These work in much the same way, but provide the user more accurate control when spraying.

Regulators are often designed to include driers and filters as an all in one air management unit. These can be pricey however, so if you are just starting to equip your shop, you may choose to add driers and filters separately.

DRY AIR

After you have figured out which air compressor to use, consider installing a piping system with a water trap or air dryer at the end. Even for home use, a small air supply system with 3/4-inch to 1-inch pipe could be advantageous. A copper or galvanized pipe running downhill away from a compressor toward a water trap

or dryer allows moisture accumulations in heated air to flow away from the compressor and toward the trap or dryer. Since the hot air has time to cool inside pipes, moisture suspended in the air condenses into droplets that can be captured and retained as a liquid in the trap.

Driers

Remember that condensation that I mentioned a few paragraphs ago? You have to get rid of it somewhere. Of course, the best way is to drain the air storage tank on a regular basis. However, even if you have drained the tank at the beginning of the workday, a full day of compressor use will create some amount of moisture, depending on ambient temperature and humidity. Since moisture is an enemy of air tools and can absolutely ruin a paint job, installing a drier in the air line somewhere between the air compressor and the outlet will increase the life of your air tools and potentially save a paint job.

Most driers contain a desiccant material that soaks up moisture. This eliminates the need to drain moisture from the drier, but the desiccant will sometimes need to be replaced or reactivated.

To minimize the necessary length of air hose, consider installing an air supply system made of 3/4 or 1 inch (or larger for commercial applications) copper pipe or galvanized pipe. This can be surface mounted to the inside walls and ceiling of the shop, so it is never too late to install, regardless the age of the building. This size piping will not experience the friction loss that is common with smaller diameter hose. Multiple quick disconnect plugs can be plumbed into the system at convenient locations so that air hoses are not running all the way across the shop floor.

To keep portable air compressors mobile and to prevent their operational vibration from causing damage to solid piping mounted to walls, it is recommended that you connect your compressor to your piping system with a short, flexible air hose. By doing this, you can easily disconnect the air compressor from the piping system to move it to wherever it is needed for other kinds of jobs.

Hoses and Couplings

Air hoses are the flexible link between your air compressor and the air tools that you are using. Besides having the proper fittings on both ends so that there is no air leakage, air hoses must be of the proper size to work efficiently. Many homeowner's and upholstery shops use 1/4-inch self-coiling hose, as it keeps itself coiled up nicely when not in use. However, that kind of hose simply isn't going to pass enough air to operate the types of pneumatic tools that will be used in a body shop. Although you may be able to skimp by with a 5/16-inch inside diameter hose, one with a 3/8-inch diameter would be a better choice. Simply put, even if your air compressor can provide enough pressure and volume, using an air hose that is too small hampers your capabilities. You should also limit the length of air hoses to 25 feet; otherwise you will experience significant pressure loss due to friction through the hose.

Filters

In addition to eliminating moisture, it is good to filter out anything else that might be floating around in your air supply. This includes the rust that forms on the bottom of the tank since you forgot to drain the tank on a regular basis. Filter housings are installed inline much like regulators and driers. In addition to the air line connections, the filter housing includes a cup that can be removed from the filter housing. The cup is where the actual filter is located. The filter can be removed, the cup wiped clean, and the filter cleaned or replaced.

One cannot overemphasize the importance of a clean, dry, and controlled source of air pressure for any spray paint job (yes, this applies to primer as well). If you allow too much air pressure to accumulate inside the hose, your vehicle may be blemished with fish eyes, dirt nibs, and blushing problems by the time you're done spraying. However, miniscule particles of water, oil, or rust will find their way from holding tanks to other air-powered tools as well, unless they are captured and retained somewhere between the compressor and equipment being used.

PAINT GUNS

There are many brands of automotive spray paint guns to choose from besides the three most popular—Sata, Sharpe, and DeVilbiss. You should be able to use equipment from any one of these name-brand manufacturers with good results. Two basic types of spray guns are available; the standard production model is biggest and generally features a one-quart capacity cup. A smaller gun, referred to as a detail gun or jamb gun, features a 6- or 8-ounce capacity cup, and its trigger assembly is mounted on top, as opposed to standard guns with handle grip triggers.

A full range of various spray paint guns and their accessories are available at auto body paint and supply stores. Prices start at about $60 and go upward, depending upon the brand and precision quality. Paint cups are generally extra, costing around $25 for detail gun cups, or around $35 for production models. Along with paint guns, you can purchase air valves that attach to spray guns in-line with their air supply. These valves help to fine-tune air pressure at the gun to perfect spray patterns.

Professional automobile painters rely on their paint guns to provide uniform spray patterns with each use. To achieve this, they clean their guns thoroughly after each use. Spray gun quality is the number one factor when considering such a purchase. Better to save up extra money to buy a top-of-the-line model than settle for second best on an unfamiliar import. The problems with cheap paint guns relate to inadequate spray patterns and difficulty in finding replacement parts. Take your paint gun purchase seriously and opt for long-lasting quality instead of make-do availability.

Just as professional photographers suggest buying a camera from a camera shop, professional painters will suggest buying your paint spray gun from an automotive paint and supply professional. Cameras and paint spray guns are available at other outlets; however, a knowledgeable salesperson may not be. Having a knowledgeable person who has actually used a spray gun like the one they are selling you has some advantages. Product literature may suggest a particular setting for inlet air pressure, while real-world experience can assure you that a higher inlet pressure is necessary. If you do not have access to this firsthand knowledge, your brand-new spray gun may never operate as well as desired. Inlet air pressure settings are critical with HVLP spray guns, so it is worth your while to ask someone who knows for their recommendations, rather than relying solely on product literature. What works and what works best may not be the same.

Waterborne vs. Solvent

The big question that you must ask yourself now when purchasing a spray gun is what type of paint will you be using. If you favor waterborne paint, you must use a spray gun that utilizes noncorrosive, stainless-steel internal components. Yes, you are correct . . . the water in the paint makes the insides of the spray gun rust if you use a nonwaterborne-compliant spray gun. This is also the same reason waterborne paint sells in plastic containers, not metal. While researching this book, I found a few Internet posts that say you can

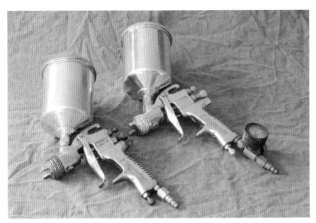

These are two of my HVLP spray guns from DeVilbiss, which have improved my results as well as minimized overspray in my garage. The gun with the blue anodized knobs uses a 1.3 (mm) spray tip and is used for spraying top coats (color and clear). The gun with the noncolored knobs uses a 1.8 (mm) spray tip and used for applying primer. Spray tips are also available in different sizes and can be interchanged for spraying different types of coatings, such as sprayable polyester body filler or truck bed liners. Shown on the primer gun is a regulator for adjusting the air pressure entering the gun.

use solvent-type spray guns for waterborne paint; you may be able to, but I do not suggest it. One reason is that waterborne paint products and solvent-based paint products tend to gel if/when combined. Gel in your spray gun cannot be conducive to future paint jobs. Next, water of any type (from a waterborne paint product, condensations, etc.) may cause the internal components of a spray gun to rust and corrode. There simply is no reason to intentionally inflict that kind of damage on your spray gun.

CONVENTIONAL SPRAY GUNS

Conventional spray guns typically require air pressure of 60 psi or more. This relatively high pressure blasts paint at the surface with such force that over 65 percent of the material actually goes up in overspray. In addition to this overspray, the additional air pressure is more likely to stir up existing dirt and debris, and allow it to fall into fresh paint.

HVLP (High Volume Low Pressure)

Concern over atmospheric pollution has caused government agencies, civic groups, auto paint manufacturers, auto painters, and paint equipment companies to acknowledge paint VOCs, overspray, and material waste as pollution problems, and they are striving for economical, common-sense solutions.

One viable means of reducing VOC and overspray pollution is by use of High Volume/Low Pressure (HVLP) spray paint systems.

When HVLP spray paint systems were introduced, they were composed of a spray paint gun and a turbine system that replaced the conventional air compressor. Although the HVLP concept made sense and was generally accepted as a good idea, the actual equipment met with less than widespread approval. The new turbine system caused the air pushing the paint onto the vehicle to overheat, causing the paint to dry too soon, sometimes even before it was actually landing on the vehicle. The turbine systems have been redesigned so that they do not get as hot. However, perhaps a more practical solution is the development of HVLP spray guns work with conventional air compressors; this allows experienced painters to use a system more familiar to them, and also makes the purchase of an air compressor easier to justify for the novice painter. The conventional air compressor is more versatile around the shop than an HVLP turbine paint system.

HVLP works by increasing the volume of paint that can uniformly pass through the spray gun's ports and nozzle, so that a relatively low pressure is all that is needed to propel the paint material. The end result is more adherence to auto surfaces and much less waste (up to 50 percent) through overspray from paint particles bouncing off surfaces at high pressure.

Much literature for HVLP spray guns recommends air pressure of 10 psi at the tip of the spray gun. This is not to be confused with the air pressure at the inlet of the spray gun where the hose connects. Depending on the design of the spray gun, the inlet pressure must sometimes be near 60 psi to obtain the suggested tip pressure.

Most painters who have used both conventional spray paint guns and HVLP systems agree that a vehicle that takes a complete gallon of paint when shot with a conventional gun can be completed with three quarts or less when an HVLP system is used. With the price of paint material alone being what it is, the purchase of an HVLP spray gun certainly pays for itself in a couple of repaint jobs, if not on the first one. Not only are you saving paint material with an HVLP spray gun, you'll experience a great reduction in the amount of overspray, which should be of major importance to the part-time auto painter who is working in his residential garage or workshop. The fewer red flags you send to your neighbors—who may not approve of your car hobby anyway—the better off you will be.

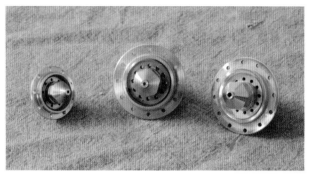

From left to right are the spray tips from a detail gun, a top coat gun, and a primer gun. They are 1.0 mm, 1.3 mm, and 1.8 mm, respectively. Although it may be difficult to see the difference in the size, the tip at the center of the nozzle is where the paint comes out. The detail gun is similar in design to the larger guns, just smaller.

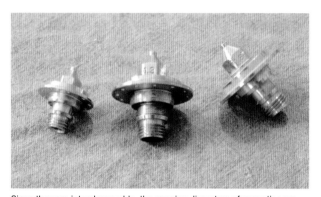

Since they are interchangeable, the opening diameters of spray tips are always marked. These are Devilbiss spray tips, and the diameters are plainly stamped on the outside of the nozzle, out of the line of fire so that paint does not obscure them. From left to right, we have 1.0 for the detail gun, 1.3 for the top coat gun, and 1.8 for the primer gun.

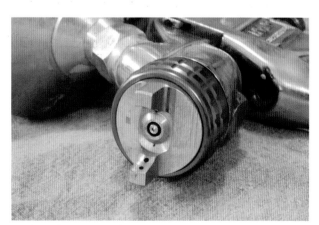

Several air passages in the flange portion of the spray nozzle funnel the air to far fewer passages in the cap, increasing the air pressure and distributing it more precisely around the tip of the nozzle. These tiny orifices must be kept clean for a spray gun to work properly.

Siphon Feed

Besides conventional or HVLP, spray guns can be further classified as siphon feed or gravity feed. Whether a production gun or a detail gun, the paint cup of a siphon feed gun is mounted below the air nozzle. This design requires more air pressure to siphon the paint material up, out of the cup. With a non-HVLP siphon feed spray gun, approximately 75 percent of the paint material ends up as overspray.

Gravity Feed

As you might expect, a gravity feed spray gun has the paint cup mounted above the air nozzle. This allows gravity to do the work of some of the air pressure, allowing for the use of a lower inlet air pressure. However, on a non-HVLP spray gun, this will still result in approximately 65 percent of the paint material ending up as overspray.

Production Gun

If your painting is going to be limited to large body panels, such as doors, fenders, and hoods, a full-size production gun will suit your needs. Commonly having a one-quart paint cup, this gun can spray a fair amount of material before you need to refill.

Detail Gun

The difference between the full-size production spray paint gun and the detail model is maneuverability. As

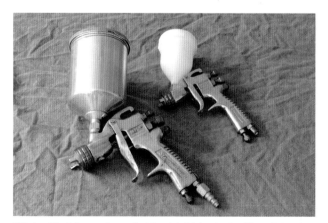

Side by side, it is easy to see that the detail (aka doorjamb) gun is much smaller than the full-size production gun. However, it is equally as important for a complete paint job. Although the HVLP guns are much better than suction feed guns overall, they are considerably taller with their gravity feed cups. This makes a detail gun so much handier in confined areas, such as when painting doorjambs or wheels.

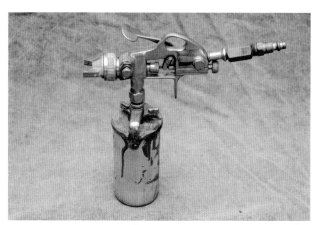

Working much more like an airbrush, a non-HVLP detail gun is operated by your forefinger on the lever at the top. Adjust the air pressure with the knob under the air inlet, and use the knob near the nozzle for fluid control.

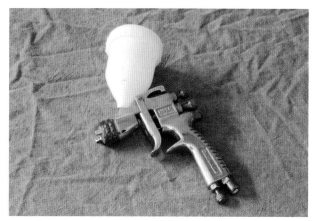

For all intents and purposes, the HVLP detail gun is designed and operates just like the larger production guns. Not that it is a big deal, but the design of this detail gun seems slightly more balanced in your hand than a non-HVLP detail gun.

the larger unit is perfect for complete paint jobs and panel repaints, the detail gun is perfect for intricate painting jobs, like small touch-ups requiring fine spray patterns and doorjamb painting. The top-mounted trigger on conventional detail guns is operated by the full length of a user's index finger. This comfortable position allows painters to operate these lightweight units in confined spaces with maximum control. HVLP detail guns, however, are simply smaller versions of production-style spray guns.

PAINT GUN MAINTENANCE

Spray paint guns need consistent and conscientious cleaning and maintenance. Bits of dry paint and debris easily clog small air and material passageways, and once they become plugged, it is difficult to clear them.

Clean your spray gun after each use. Each paint system (including waterborne) has certain wash solvents designated as part of the overall paint system. Be sure that your auto body paint and supply professional describes which cleaning product is best suited for the system that you are using. If you are spraying waterborne paint and run out of the designated cleanup material to clean your spray gun, you can use isopropyl (rubbing) alcohol, found most anywhere that first aid supplies are sold.

Professional body shops have special enclosed cabinets they use for gun cleaning. Solvent is forced through gun assemblies under pressure while trigger units are maintained in an open position. Without a cleaning cabinet, you have to fill your gun cup partly full with solvent, swish it around, and empty it to

remove the bulk of the remaining paint product. Then, refill it again with clean solvent and spray it through the unit. This should clear out the inner passageways.

Once you've done that, fill the cup about one-quarter full with clean solvent and spray it through the unit. Then, thoroughly clean the cup. Once that's done, spray clean thinner through the gun head again to be sure that nothing but clear solvent comes out. Use only those brushes designated for spray paint gun cleaning on housings, air caps, and other parts. Never use sharp objects to clear clogged air caps or other ports. The slightest scratch damage to finely machined spray gun parts can ruin otherwise perfect fan sprays.

Use a clean cloth, damp with the proper solvent, to clean bulk paint drips or splotches from exterior surfaces. When you're satisfied that interior ports and passageways are clean, run plenty of clean, dry air through the unit to remove lingering deposits of solvent. Hang or place guns in a vertical position for storing after completely drying them with clean cloths.

ADJUSTING YOUR SPRAY GUN AND TEST PATTERN

Paint companies recommend specific spray gun setups for applying their products. A sample recommendation for the DeVilbiss JGV-572 base coat spray gun is "Fluid Tip—FW (0.062 inch); Air Cap #86." This indicates a specific fluid tip and air cap to use with this particular paint product, available from the dealer of the spray gun. This is another reason why you should purchase your spray gun from a paint supply outlet, rather than a tool store that sells a variety of tools, without servicing

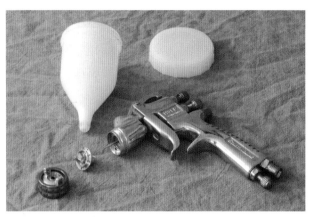

After emptying the paint cup and spraying clean thinner through the gun, disassemble it to clean each individual piece. You should also remove the air control knob from the back of the gun and pull out the needle so that it can be cleaned. Put small parts in a cup with thinner to soak while you are wiping down the larger parts. When it is all reassembled, reconnect an air hose and blow dry air through the gun to blow away any residual cleaning thinner from the internal passages.

any of them. A similar recommendation would apply to primer and clear coat spray guns by same manufacturer, Sata or Sharpe. These settings are available from information sheets and application guidelines, or from your auto body paint and supply professional.

Most full-size production spray paint guns have two control knobs. One controls the fan spray, while the other manages the volume of paint that exits the nozzle. They are located at the top rear section of most models. About the only way to achieve proper spray patterns and volume is to practice spraying paint on a test panel and see what works best for your spraying technique. If you move the spray gun slowly, adjust the gun to spray less paint. Conversely, if you move the spray gun faster, adjust the gun to spray more paint. If the equipment and operator are not balanced, runs, drips, or dry spots are the result. Various paint products and their reduction ratios will spray differently, especially with different recommended air pressures.

The fluid control knob will always be the knob inline with the spray nozzle. Begin by turning this knob almost all the way out, then squeeze the trigger all the way back. Begin turning the fluid control knob inward until you feel pressure on the knob. This allows the full amount of paint volume. When blending colors, you may need to adjust this fluid control knob inward to reduce the volume of paint being applied.

The fan control adjusts the pattern of the paint spray. Turning this all the way open creates an elliptical pattern,

while turning this knob all the way in results in a circular pattern. The larger elliptical pattern is desired in most situations. A third adjustment found on some spray guns is merely an air micrometer used to fine tune the amount of air entering the spray gun and is typically wide open.

Secure a piece of masking paper or cardboard to the wall with masking tape. Then with your spray gun adjusted, full of paint, and connected to an air supply, hold the nozzle of the gun about 8 inches from and perpendicular to the masking paper or cardboard. Now squeeze the trigger to completely open and close in one smooth motion. You can now adjust the knobs one at a time as described above to obtain the correct spray pattern. Spray more tests until you get it right, and then spray your car.

Many painters keep test panels in their spray paint booth. Usually, these are nothing more than sheets of wide masking paper taped to a wall. They can spray paint on the test panel and then adjust the gun's control knobs to get the right pattern and volume. At that point, they begin actual painting.

Periodically during paint jobs, painters may notice a flaw in their gun's fan pattern. To check it, turn to the test panel and shoot a clean section with a mist of paint. If it looks off, check the controls and the air pressure. If the pattern is still flawed, disconnect the paint gun from the supply hose and clean it. Chances are, a small port or passage has become clogged and must be cleaned before continuing the job.

As the surface to be painted becomes more confined or difficult, as on some front end sections, reduce pressure or change fan sprays to hit a smaller area. Make these adjustments with the help of the test panel.

OVERALL SAFETY

Many veteran auto painters realize they should have paid more attention to warning labels and other safety concerns during their apprentice years in the auto paint field. Comprehending too late the health hazards involved due to the amount of sanding dust, paint overspray, and solvents they have inhaled over the years is a sobering prospect indeed.

Inhalation

Painters must be aware of all the respiratory protection available to them, especially with the advent of paint hardeners that contain isocyanates (present in all two-part paint products). Although many painters still spray cars while wearing only heavy-duty filter masks

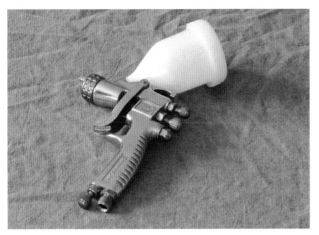

Whenever you purchase, rent, or borrow a spray gun, you should pay particular attention to the instructions to find out which knobs do what. You should then take the time to practice with them to find what actually happens when you adjust them. On this gun, the top knob is the fan control, which controls the spray pattern. The next knob (always in line with the fluid needle) is the fluid control, which controls the volume of air being dispensed. The third knob located at the bottom of the gun is merely a method to fine tune the air coming into the gun.

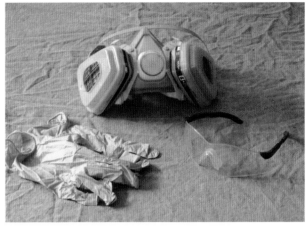

Making at least a small investment in these items makes your spraying experience more enjoyable. Disposable gloves help keep your hands and fingers paint free. Cleaning your hands with paint thinner quickly tells you where every nick and cut is located. At the very least, use a filtered spray mask. Finally, buy a pair of safety glasses just to make sure you don't splash paint products into your eyes.

for protection, smart painters opt instead for full-face, fresh-air respiratory systems. These units may be a bit cumbersome, but the amount of personal safety they afford easily overshadows their inconvenience.

Because of increased awareness to hazardous materials, government agencies have demanded that chemical manufacturers comply with more and more standards relating to user safety. Therefore, you commonly find recommendations of NIOSH-approved respiratory protection on almost all paint product containers. Be sure to read respirator package labels too—they list the types of materials the filter guards against, and those materials that are not filtered at all. Auto body paint and supply stores carry assortments of filter masks and fresh-air systems.

Osmosis

Manufacturers advise painters to wear goggles or full-face respirators since particles of paint overspray readily enter your body through your eyes by way of moist tear ducts. This is an important consideration during sanding as well. Most auto body paint and supply stores carry a selection of lightweight painter's goggles.

Skin Contact

Wear rubber gloves any time you handle thinners, reducers, hardeners, or any other paint product chemical.

Manufactures have developed special impermeable coveralls because paint chemicals can enter painter's bodies through pores in their skin. Designed to be used only once and then discarded, disposable coveralls serve two functions: first, they prevent paint chemicals from coming in contact with your skin; second, the material used to make the coveralls is lint-free, which means that concerns over lint falling off of your clothes and onto paint finishes is greatly reduced.

Professional painters who take full advantage of all personal safety equipment suit up in the following way for maximum protection while painting: first, don a pair of painter's coveralls, and then rubber gloves. Tape both pant legs closed around the ankles, and tape both arm sleeves around the wrist. Then pull on a painter's hood, which covers the neck and entire head, except for the face. Next, strap on a full-face, fresh-air respiratory mask, which, when connected to its air compressor supply hose, offers the user plenty of fresh, clean air.

This complete outfit gives painters full protection against harmful chemical liquids, paint overspray particles, and vapors. Seriously consider these protective items—none of them is very expensive (except for the fresh-air respiratory system), and rental businesses may even have these kinds of respiratory units available at more affordable rates.

Chapter 5
Surface Preparation

Automobile painting consists of a series of tasks that ultimately combine to produce a quality paint job that looks great, feels smooth, adheres securely, and lasts a long time. How good each step looks depends on the step that came before, and poor work anywhere along the line detracts from the end result. In other words, make sure you complete each stage of the painting process thoroughly and to the very highest level you can achieve. If you mess something up, take the time to fix it just right. Remember, the time you spend painting the car will be nothing compared to the amount of time you'll spend enjoying it once you're done. The car will be a rolling testament to your skills. Let the world know you're good!

Auto body surface preparation encompasses those jobs that actually get surfaces ready for paint. These tasks include dismantling some parts, removing old paint and rust, applying primer material, finish sanding, and cleaning surfaces with wax and grease remover and tack cloths. Of course, before you can take on surface preparation, any bodywork that that needs to be done must be addressed before doing any paint work. For good information on automotive bodywork, please refer to my book, *The Complete Guide to Auto Body Repair*, available from MBI.

PART REMOVAL

Experienced auto painters and auto enthusiasts can always seem to tell which cars have been repainted and which have not. Yet the goal of every auto painter—going for a stock look—is to finish the job so that no one can tell his or her work is not the very paint put on at the factory.

Telltale signs of repainted automobiles could be anything from tiny strips of paint overspray on window moldings, door handles, or light assemblies, to slight sanding scratches on the surface finish (also an indication of bodywork). To a prospective buyer or car show judge, these imperfections raise red flags. A buyer may suspect that the vehicle has been in an accident and perhaps suffered substantial, now-hidden, damage. The car show judge will deduct points because the work is sloppy.

Serious auto painters carefully remove all mirrors, door handles, key locks, trim, reflectors, and other removable body accessories to guarantee that no overspray accumulates on them. Removing the items alleviates overspray concerns, allows for controlled and thorough body preparation, and prevents paint build-up along their edges.

If you come across items for which you cannot determine a proper removal procedure, consult a service manager at a dealership, a professional auto body repair shop, or an auto paint facility. It makes no sense to take chances on breaking parts when help is just around the corner.

Another good source for this information is a factory repair manual for your vehicle. A dealership can probably help you obtain one for a late-model car or truck. For older vehicles, the Internet and eBay are good sources. Aftermarket publishers also make manuals for a wide range of vehicles. Auto parts stores typically carry these. Be sure to skim the book first to make sure it

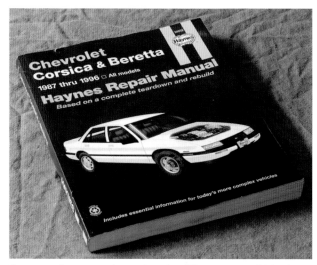

If you are not someone who repairs automobiles on an everyday basis, disassembly and reassembly necessary for a repaint of your car may have you befuddled at times. A repair manual like this one from Haynes or a Chilton's manual make for a good resource. These are commonly available from your local auto parts store or bookstore.

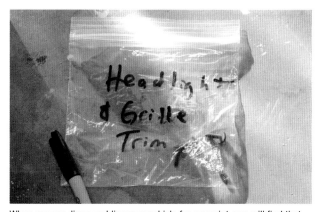

When you are disassembling your vehicle for a repaint, you will find that there are LOTS of nuts, bolts, screws, and other fasteners to keep track of. A box of resealable freezer bags and a permanent marker will help take care of that. Label the general area where the particular fasteners belong on the outside of the freezer bag. One step better might be to include a piece of paper that labels the specific parts, i.e. "3 Torx head screws each headlight bezel," or "8 bolts grille."

contains the information you need. A good manual will come in handy for other repairs too.

Removing parts is a phase of the project in which big gains appear to come quickly. Don't let your eagerness to tear into it rush you: before you start, create a good, sensible plan for removing and storing everything, so you can get it back together properly. Have plenty of large coffee cans and boxes on hand when you start the project. Use a heavy felt-tip marker to label boxes. Use one box for each general car section; for example, driver's side front fender and door, passenger side taillight, side light and reflector, and so on. Be certain to put small screws and nuts back onto the part after you remove it. That way you'll have ready access to them, and know their proper location when it's time to put everything back on.

Removing Bolt-on Components

Most auto body accessory parts such as door handles and mirrors are secured with screws, nuts, or bolts. Some emblems, badges, and trim on newer cars are attached with adhesive or double-backed tape. Before prying or yanking on something, carefully inspect it to determine just how it's mounted. You'll need to replace everything you break, and that costs money, and with rare parts, it may also take time.

If your screwdrivers and wrenches don't fit a screw or bolt head on your vehicle, don't force it—you could damage the tool or the fastener or both. GM, Ford, Chrysler, and AMC use bolts with multipoint Torx-

heads, shaped somewhat like an asterisk or star. You'll need Torx drivers or ratchet bits to remove them. Tool houses and auto parts stores should carry them.

Some door handles are removed by loosening a heavy-duty screw located on the door-edge horizontally in line with the handle. The handle is then pulled out from the door skin so the linkage arms can be dislodged. Most other door handles are secured by two screws or nuts accessed from inside the inner door space. Their removal requires that interior door panels be taken off first for access to the handle support.

Screws or clips secure most interior door panels. You will have to examine the door panels on your car to determine how they are attached. If no screws are visible anywhere around the perimeter of the panel, chances are good that it's secured with plastic clips pushed into retainer mounts. Pry them loose, but before you start prying, be sure to remove armrests, window cranks, and door handles.

Two large Phillips head screws secure most armrests. Window cranks on older cars are kept in place with a small C-shaped metal clip that snaps off the crank's operating shaft for removal. Newer cars may have pop-off plastic caps that run from the swivel knob to the shaft. Use a small-bladed screwdriver to gently pry off caps to access screws or nuts that hold cranks in place.

Remove door handles on older cars just like their matching window cranks, by removing their C-shaped metal clips. Newer car handles will have a screw or two holding them in place. After removing the screws, you might have to pry on the handle housing to pop it loose from the door panel opening in which it rests. Remove any linkage arms from the handle to the door latch mechanism as well.

Light assemblies are normally secured with screws located on the back of the housing assembly. Remove taillight units from inside the trunk or hatchback areas, or pull them straight out from the outside. Some lights may require you to remove lenses first by taking out two or four Phillips or Torx head screws. Reflectors should be easily removed by loosening screws located at either end of the lens or from inside the corresponding compartment.

Grilles may be a bit tricky to remove. Clever automotive engineers hide mounting screws and clips in such ways that it is sometimes almost impossible to figure out how they stay in place. Look for Torx, Phillips, or Allen head screws around the perimeter edge of grille sections. Although many grilles consist of

Fasteners for some parts are not going to jump out at you, so you may have to look for them. The two screws that secure the front turn signals into the bumper are easily seen in this photo, but you will need to get down on their level to find them on the actual vehicle.

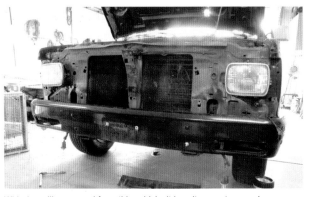

With the grille removed from this vehicle, it is quite easy to see why our vehicles have a grille . . . they are ugly without them. The grille, headlight bezels, and front valance (gravel pan) have all been removed simply by unscrewing no more than two dozen screws or bolts.

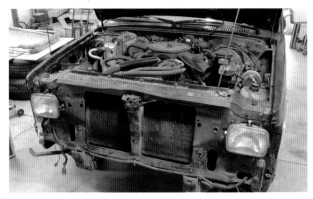

When removing bumpers and other heavier items, remember that it may be necessary to use some sort of penetrating oil to loosen rusty fasteners. You should also use some sort of lifting device or a helper to hold the part while you remove the last few bolts. While you may choose to not do this while disassembling the vehicle since you are going to repaint it anyway, please use some help during reassembly to avoid scratching or denting your freshly painted parts.

a combination of parts, entire assemblies can sometimes be removed as single units if all the right screws are loosened. Special clips hold separate pieces together.

Leave headlights in place if possible, especially if their current light beams are correctly adjusted. Should you decide that they have to be removed, do not touch the two screws that have springs beneath them. These are the directional adjustment screws used to move the headlight up or down, or right to left.

Bumpers on older cars are a snap to remove. Their support bolts are in plain view and there is generally no question as to how they are dismantled. Newer car bumpers are not always that easy to figure out. Since many of these units consist of a number of different parts, it may appear that they couldn't possibly be removed. Splash guards and other urethane accessories may cover them to the point that the only visible part of the assembly's support is located under the front or rear section of the car. Take your time removing bumpers, and enlist a helper if necessary. These units are heavy and you should take precautions so they do not fall on you while you're under the car loosening support bolts.

Adhesive

Once the interior door panels are removed, you will notice a piece of plastic or other material between the panel and door skin. This is a vapor barrier. Its function is to prevent water from entering the passenger compartment after it has seeped past window trim moldings. Be sure to keep those vapor barriers intact. You can simply roll them up to the top of the door and tape them out of the way.

Remove weather stripping if you need to paint door edges. Examine the stripping closely to see how it is secured—some stripping is attached with adhesive. Use an adhesive remover unless it is stout enough to withstand being pulled off. You may be able to use a heat gun or blow dryer to loosen the adhesive as you pull off the weather stripping.

Other kinds of weather stripping are secured with plastic pins with large heads inserted into prefabricated holes. The protruding parts of these pins are pressed into holes around the doors' perimeter edges.

Body side moldings and other trim pieces are secured to car bodies in several ways. Some feature protruding pins that snap into retainers; others have pins that are secured from the inside with flat metal retainers, and many are simply glued in place with adhesive or double-backed tape. To determine how these parts are

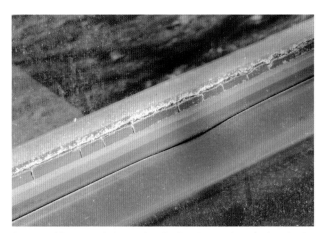

Rubber molding around window glass is often damaged, cracked, or simply missing. If it needs to be replaced, pull it out prior to priming and painting so you don't have to mask around it, then replace it to finish off the paint job.

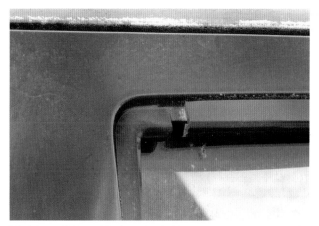

I don't know if this molding has shrunk this much over the years or what, but it looks pretty funky, if not outright bad. Again, this molding should be, can be, and will be replaced to complete the paint job.

secured to your car, you will have to gently pry up on an edge to inspect the back. Be very careful while doing this, because many plastic pieces are brittle and will crack if pried too far.

PAINT REMOVAL

The amount of old paint you need to remove depends upon the paint's condition, whether the vehicle requires bodywork, and how extensive the paint job will be. You can apply new paint over old paint if the existing finish is sanded with all oxidized paint material removed, and the surface is left flat, even, and smooth, and the original paint is not lacquer-based. If the original paint is lacquer based, the area to be painted needs to be stripped to bare metal and a compatible undercoat applied for the top coat being used. Otherwise the new paint will suffer adhesion problems. If the car needs bodywork, you'll have to take that area down to bare metal so that the filler material has its best opportunity to bond completely.

Painting decisions are easy when the vehicle needs bodywork or has deep paint blemishes. But if the old paint looks dull and oxidized, and you simply want to repaint it to look nice, here are some questions to ponder: is the existing paint too thick to support a new finish? Is there rust anywhere on the body? Does the entire car need a new paint job, or will repaint efforts to a couple of panels do the trick? Take some time to decide how much painting you need to do.

The best way to remove paint depends on the condition of the vehicle's existing paint surface. Cars with excellent bodies that require no sheetmetal repair should have paint removed using the mildest method.

This would probably be a chemical stripper or mild paint-stripping scouring-type pad.

Sanding

The Eastwood Company offers Strip Disc kits that include three 7-inch stripping discs and a cushioned backing pad that attaches to angled sanders (buffers) with 6,000-rpm maximum speeds. They strip paint quickly and completely without creating excessive heat, and their design will not harm valuable body panels. They are recommended after you've removed the bulk of old paint with a chemical stripper. An assortment of chemical strippers is available at auto body paint and supply stores. Be sure to read label instructions and plan to wear recommended protective equipment.

High-speed rotary sanders with coarse discs remove paint in a hurry. These work great for bodywork because the rough sanding scratches left behind make an excellent surface for filler to bond to. High-speed sanders and coarse discs also work well to remove rust.

Block sand with 80- or 100-grit sandpaper to remove surface rust from otherwise solid sheet metal. When *all* of the rust has disappeared, either bare metal or painted metal is present, the panel should be wiped down with wax and grease remover, then coated with epoxy primer. The coarse-grit sandpaper's sanding scratches provides excellent adhesion for the epoxy primer. Any existing dents or dings should be repaired or filled, and then coated with a high build primer-surfacer, prior to block sanding.

One caution with power sanding tools is that they generate a lot of heat. If you keep the tool in one area for too long, the sustained friction can generate enough heat to warp the panel. The risk of warping is greater on new cars, with their relatively thin panels.

Media Blasting

Another way to remove old paint is by sandblasting, or more common today, media blasting. This equipment works especially well for older cars with surface rust. Sandblasting media works fast to remove paint and traces of rust caught in tiny cracks, crevices, and pits. You have to contend with messy cleanup after your blasting is done, but the extra work is well worth the effort, as you'll discover that old paint and rust removal is accomplished quickly and thoroughly.

Sandblasters require controlled use with a compatible pressure and media combination. Too much pressure mixed with harsh media causes sheetmetal warping problems and other damage. Remove all accessories for the safest results, as sandblasting takes off chrome and paint, and it can quickly pit glass. Remove all vulnerable body parts or protect them with tarps or other suitably heavy material. Test the material first to be sure the sandblaster won't power through it.

Sandblaster manufacturers and suppliers offer charts that indicate which media to use at which pressures for different kinds of jobs. Media are rated according to their size—the lower the number, the smaller the particle size. For use on car parts and bodies, typical ranges are from number 40 (0.016 inch) to number 12 (0.004 inch). Media also come in work mixes that combine different amounts of various sized particles. Consult a salesperson at a sandblasting equipment store or professional at an auto body paint and supply store for help in selecting the proper media.

As important as media size is the pressure at which the material is blasted. Be sure that your pressure settings are correct—since you can shoot media from 200 to 400 miles per hour, take care to prevent unwanted body damage. In addition, you need to protect yourself from sandblasting media. Always wear heavy-duty leather gloves, long sleeves, and a quality sandblasting hood.

It is also recommended that you wear a NIOSH-approved respirator. Certain media materials (like silica) produce dust particles that could be harmful to your respiratory system. Along with respirators and gloves, purchase sandblasters and media at auto body paint and supply stores. Home-use sandblasting equipment ranges from $40 sandblasting guns that siphon media from a bucket to first-class units around $400.

Various sandblaster nozzle sizes require air compressors with specific horsepower. For example, a 3/32-inch nozzle requires a 2- to 3-horsepower air compressor to supply 7 cubic feet per minute at 80 psi. A 1/8-inch nozzle needs a 3- to 5-horsepower air compressor to supply it with 15 cubic feet per minute at 80 psi. Charts continue up to a 5/16-inch nozzle, which calls for a 40-horsepower air compressor to supply 125 cubic feet per minute at 80 psi. Again, check the charts at places that sell sandblast media to be sure the nozzle size, media, and air pressure that you plan to use will work in combination for your job.

Chemical Stripping or Dipping

Chemical stripping, also known as chemical dipping, is the best method if you want to start with fresh metal prior to repainting, as when resurrecting a vehicle that has been sitting outside in the elements, or even one that has been kept inside. Unlike media blasting, which may leave the sheet metal warped or pitted, chemical stripping removes all of the layers of primer, paint, wax, grease, dirt, and whatever else may be on it. Chemical stripping reveals shiny, bare metal once the process is complete. Yet there are some drawbacks to dipping a metal body or component. When submerged, the rust removal liquid gets into all surfaces, cracks, and crevices, exposing all to the environment. If you can access all of these surfaces and apply epoxy primer, you will be able to ward off rust quite successfully. However, unless you are dipping a single layer of sheet metal, chances are that you will not be able to apply epoxy primer to all of the bare surfaces. If you are in a dry climate, you may not have any problem; however, if you are in a humid climate, rust will eventually form on this bare metal.

If you are stripping a fender or other relatively small component, you can strip it yourself with a product known as aircraft stripper. It is best to remove the panel to be stripped from the vehicle if at all possible, as the stripper is much more difficult to mask than paint. When using paint stripper, be sure to use a proper respirator and rubber gloves. If the product is strong enough to remove paint, you can imagine what it will do to your skin and lungs.

For best results, use 100-grit sandpaper or a Scotch-Brite™ pad to scuff the panel prior to applying any of the stripper. This breaks open the seal of the existing paint, allowing the stripper to soak in to the paint it is supposed to remove. Apply the stripper as directed by the manufacturer. Allow the stripper plenty of time to work into the paint and begin loosening it. As the paint begins to loosen and bubble up from the surface, you can scrape it off with a putty knife. As top coats come off to yield undercoats, you may need to apply more stripper.

When you've stripped the entire surface, you must neutralize the effects of the stripper with lots of water. Unneutralized stripper attacks any primer or other paint coats that you may apply. Completely dry the surface after it has been neutralized and rinsed with water. It should then be wiped down with wax and grease remover, and then coated with an epoxy primer to prevent rust from forming on the bare, albeit clean, sheet metal.

If you desire to have an entire body hulk or more than one single panel stripped down to bare metal, you would be well advised to have it dipped by a professional service that specializes in this type of work. To find a company that does this, you may have to ask auto restorers in your area, or look in *Hemmings Motor News* for advertisements. When you find a company that does this work, call them ahead of time to see if you need to schedule an appointment to drop off your car body or parts. Sometimes there is a waiting list. The wait may be longer if you are bringing in a complete body hulk and several other pieces, while if you just have a few small pieces, they can usually fit them in with other jobs.

You can also ask for an estimate to have your pieces dipped. Most companies have a set price for doors, hoods, deck lids, etc. They are familiar enough with vehicles to know what it is going to take to strip a small Model A Ford roadster, compared to a large mid-1950s Cadillac. A recent estimate for a 1956 Ford pickup cab and doors was just under $500, to give a basic idea of the cost.

Prior to taking your parts to the stripper, you need to disassemble them as completely as possible. If you take off the doors, hood, and deck lid, you will get a more compete stripping job than if you leave these items in place. You also need to find out if there is any body filler in the vehicle already by using a magnet or a grinder. If the magnet doesn't stick to what should be a metal surface, there is at least some amount of body filler present. If you are contemplating taking the part in question to a stripper anyway, doing some grinding ahead of time won't hurt anything. If body filler is present and is thicker than about an $\frac{1}{8}$ inch, you should grind it out before going to the stripper. Anything less than an $\frac{1}{8}$ inch can usually be removed by the stripping process. Bear in mind that only metal pieces should go into the chemical dipping tank.

The stripping process consists of two different dipping operations. The first dip is into a "hot tank" filled with a caustic solution to remove wax, grease, and paint from the metal. Depending on the number of layers of paint or other chemicals on the metal, this process takes about four to eight hours. Remove the parts from the hot tank and rinse them with plain water for three to four hours to remove all traces of the caustic solution. Next, dip the pieces and parts into a second vat filled with a derusting solution. At this time, the material is connected to an electrical charge in just the opposite manner from chroming and powder coating. In those processes, the current draws the chrome and powder material onto the material, while here the electric charge pulls rust away from the metal. Depending on the condition of the metal and the amount of rust, this process takes 20 to 40 hours. Once complete, remove the parts from the derusting vat and rinse them well with plain water to neutralize any continuing effect of the derusting solution. When this process is complete, the dipped pieces are covered in a thin layer of phosphate coating, which retards the rust somewhat. However, you should rinse the part clean and coat it with an epoxy primer as soon as possible.

PANEL ALIGNMENT

One of the many things that I have noticed at car shows is that the judges insist that the vehicle's doors, hood, and trunk be open. This of course gives them free access to judge the interior, engine compartment, and trunk area. That is all well and good, but I absolutely hate it for a few reasons. One in particular that relates to this book—with all of these movable panels open, you cannot tell how well the body man aligned the panels. I have literally seen local car show winners brag about their great paint, even though their fenders and doors had uneven surfaces and inconsistent gaps. You may not care about panel alignment, but if you are going to the trouble to paint your car, I think it is worth taking at least some time to get the panels aligned the best you can.

Aligning Panels

OK, now that you have every door, hood, fender, and deck lid perfect, how do they fit with each other when installed on the vehicle? Are the gaps between each panel consistent in width? Are the panels in line with one another, or does one stick out farther than the one adjacent to it? Some vehicles have better panel fit from the factory than others do, no doubt about it. How well

USING PAINT STRIPPER ON SMALL JOBS

For my current hot rod project, a 1955 Chevrolet pickup, much of the sheet metal will be replaced, but I was not sure about the hood. The former owners sprayed gray primer over the entire vehicle before I purchased it, so I was not surprised by the condition of much of the body. However, the hood was in decent condition, with just a couple of small dents apparent on the lefthand side. Since I'm planning on keeping this truck, I will have the cab media blasted or chemically dipped by a professional. Before buying a replacement hood, some detective work was in order; I stripped the hood myself, so it cost me only the price of the stripper and other consumables (and my time), while sending it to a commercial stripper would have cost me more than that. Because I stripped the hood myself, I discovered that it is not in as good condition as I thought, yet I didn't spend a bunch of money to find out.

To strip small parts yourself, you will need aircraft stripper (it is available in different size containers), some disposable paint brushes, a putty knife or something similar to scrape the paint off with, and a paint roller tray or similar receptacle to pour the stripper into and to brush from. You should also wear rubber gloves, eye protection, and a spray mask. You should wear long pants, a long sleeve shirt, and whatever else you need to cover all of your skin. Since this stripper is a chemical, it burns as it works, and it becomes quite hot on your skin. If/when you do get some on your skin, simply flush the area with water as the water neutralizes the stripper. Avoid getting this stuff in your eyes, as I'm sure it would burn quite a bit and could damage your vision.

To use paint stripper, work outdoors if possible, but indoors is suitable as long as there is adequate ventilation. Get as much air flowing through the work area as possible. If you have access to a fan, use it, but do not have it blowing directly onto the surface you are attempting to remove paint from as this will dry out the paint stripper. Situate the panel being stripped so that it is at a convenient height and where no paint stripper will drip onto or be spread anywhere you do not want it. After scuffing the area as mentioned previously to allow for better penetration of the paint stripper, use a paint brush to slather the paint stripper onto the surface. Like a good fishin' story, it works better the thicker and heavier you lay it on. After coating the entire surface, simple give the paint stripper some time to do its job.

After five to 10 minutes, you will begin to see the paint start bubbling up. Resist the urge to start scraping the paint right away and let the paint stripper continue doing its job. If the bubbles quit rising or the paint stripper begins to dry out, simply spread more paint stripper on. Thinner layers of paint and primer will begin bubbling faster than a thicker or oven-baked finish.

When it looks as though the paint stripper has stopped working, use a putty knife or similar tool to scrape away the bubbled paint. If existing paint remains intact, apply more paint stripper and repeat the process. When you are finished using the paint stripper

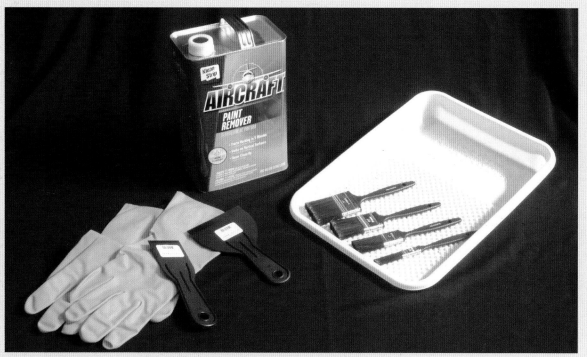

When using paint stripper, you need a pair of rubber gloves to protect your hands, some paint brushes, a small container of some sort, and a putty knife or similar scraping tool. All of these items can be found in the paint department at your local hardware store. For automotive quality paint stripper, you go to an auto body paint and supply store or an auto parts store.

and all of the loose paint has been scraped away, thoroughly rinse the panel (inside and outside) with clear water to rinse away any residue and to neutralize the paint stripper. Verify that all of the paint stripper is rinsed away. Remove any remaining intact paint by hand-sanding with 100-grit sandpaper or by using an orbital sander at a slow speed for more stubborn paint. Remove any plastic body filler that has been coated with paint stripper prior to applying any paint/primer products. Upon completion of the paint stripping process, apply two or three coats of epoxy primer to protect the bare sheet metal until further priming and painting work begins.

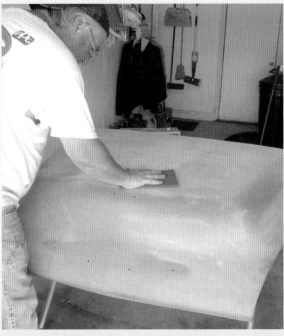

After removing the hood ornament, I scuffed the hood with a gray Scotch-Brite™ pad to loosen the surface and allow for better penetration of the paint stripper. We can see that the gray primer is very thin as it is coming off already, but the turquoise paint below will prove to be another story.

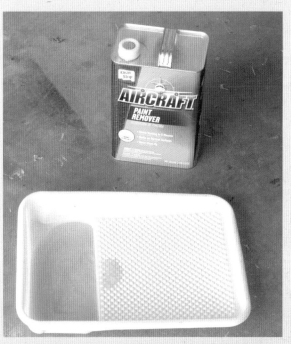

I poured the paint stripper into a disposable paint roller tray liner so that it could be brushed on. Most any type of flat container could be used, just make sure that you dispose of it when the task is completed.

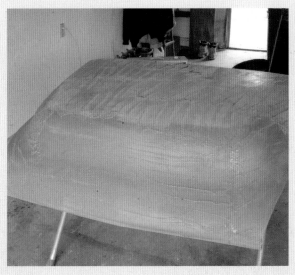

After brushing the paint stripper onto the surface, be patient and give the paint stripper enough time to work. While the Scotch-Brite™ pad worked well enough to loosen the gray primer, using some 100-grit sandpaper prior to applying the paint stripper would have been a good idea.

(continued)

SURFACE PREPARATION

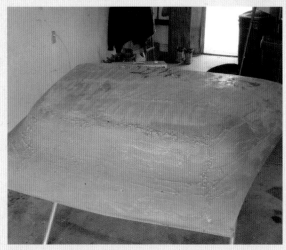

After five to 10 minutes, the loosened paint begins to bubble up from the surface. As the paint stripper begins to dry out, simply brush on some more.

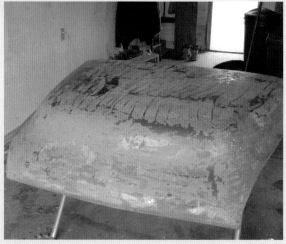

Although the original paint is 57 years old, it still adheres to the surface very well. After taking this photo, I scraped off the loose paint and used a Scotch-Brite™ pad to scuff the entire hood surface again.

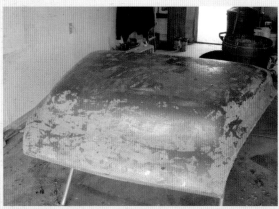

After applying another, thicker layer of paint stripper and waiting a bit longer, the original paint is finally loosening. It is probably safe to assume that the original paint is thicker on the front and sides of the hood because they are easier to reach, and 57 years of sun and washing have probably wiped away a portion of the paint from the middle of the hood.

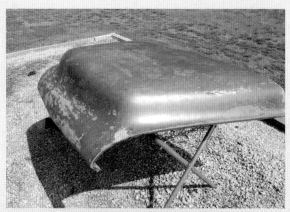

I applied more stripper to remaining areas of paint with mixed results until I finally decided that all of the original paint was not going to come off this way. When finished using the paint stripper, any residue must be removed and the effects of the paint stripper neutralized. To do so, flush the surface completely with water, both inside and outside.

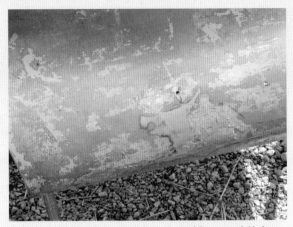

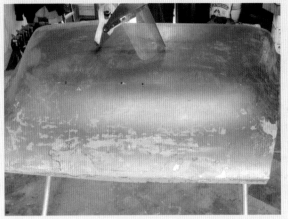

All of this paint should be removed prior to applying any paint/primer substrates. However, the main purpose of this exercise was to uncover any plastic body filler if any, and yes, there is some. It will need to be removed completely by using a grinder, then the imperfections in the sheet metal will be reworked. Once body filler has been covered with paint stripper, it (the body filler) must all be removed as it is no longer a stable surface for applying paint products.

An orbital sander with 100-grit sandpaper takes off the remaining paint and makes short order of removing the plastic body filler.

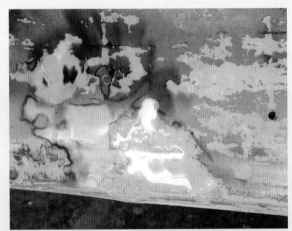

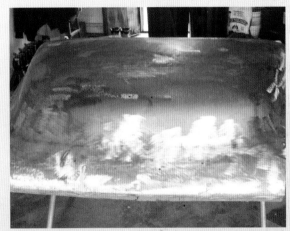

The white area in this photo is a thin layer of plastic body filler that still needs to be removed. The black line appears to be outlining the area that was "worked" prior to applying filler. The area inside the black line was probably primed and painted, while the area outside probably received some color (but no primer) while making this repair.

After just a few minutes with an orbital sander, most all of the paint is gone. Removing all of the paint with an orbital sander would have created too much heat and would have warped the hood.

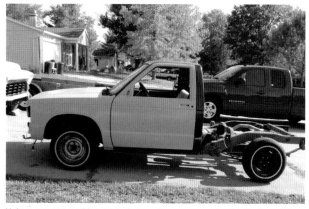

Unless you are working on a custom show car, you should aim for getting the body panel gaps within the factory tolerances, if not better. The next goal is to get them consistent. Adding cheap reproduction panels to a near 30-year-old truck yields less than perfect gaps.

they fit after you have painted the vehicle is up to you, and will be a great testimony to your attention to detail.

Whether they were present originally or not, it may be necessary to install shims behind some panels to get them to align properly with adjacent panels. Doors may have to be moved on their hinges somewhat to align the door latch mechanism or make the bodylines match. Most doors have a slight amount of adjustability built into accommodate for normal wear.

Hoods and deck lids may present the biggest problem, as any gap problem needs to be evenly split between the two sides. Doors and fenders should be fit as accurately as possible; however, slight variations from one side to the other are not as noticeable as a hood or deck lid that is biased to one side or the other.

Obtaining consistent gaps may require removing or adding material to a panel. Body shop professionals commonly shoot for a gap between panels that is as wide as a paint stir stick is thick, although this is not always possible. New vehicles generally have consistent gaps, but are two or three times the thickness of a paint stir stick. Consistency is the prime objective, while factory tolerances or tighter make a good target.

Any panels on which body filler has been applied are suspect when gaps are too tight. Getting the surface smooth may have required too much buildup. This usually happens when a portion of the area being filled was actually higher than it should have been and the surrounding area is brought out to an incorrect surface height.

Fitting Gaps

Now that the panels are all straight and in perfect alignment, are you ready to spray paint? That depends. Are any minor door dings or other blemishes present? Do the doors have a series of vertical lines in them, indicating where another car door may have struck yours? Is the overall texture of the vehicle somewhat rough? If the answer to any of these questions is yes, then you still have work to do before spraying any paint. You need to break out some more sandpaper and block sand the entire vehicle until all such imperfections are eliminated.

Getting Your Panels Straight

When doing bodywork to a vehicle, your main objective is to get the body, fenders, hood, doors, etc., as straight as possible. No, this does not mean removing all of the original recesses, bulges, or character lines so that all you have left is a slab-sided box. What it does mean, however, is that panels that are meant to be straight are like arrows and panels that are meant to be curved are smooth curves. Any and all imperfections to the vehicle's sheet metal, aluminum, or composite body skin have been eliminated. Any imperfections that you can find now will be greatly magnified after applying a new coat of paint.

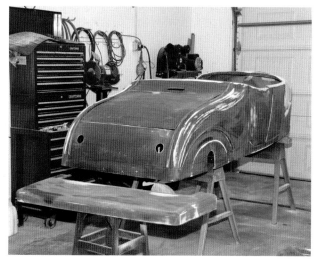

While some fiberglass bodies are better than others, you can bet they all require a fair amount of block sanding to get them as straight as possible. The way to do it correctly is labor intensive, but it makes the difference in a paint job. Using a sanding block (the largest that is practical to use in the area you are working on), sand the surface in an "X" pattern using 220- or 240-grit sandpaper, then apply filler primer. Then repeat the process using 320- or 400-grit sandpaper, followed by another coat of filler primer. In most cases, you will sand off all of the filler primer.

By the time you finish any necessary bodywork, prepare the surface for paint, and wet sand the finished painted surface, you will be intimately familiar with your vehicle's body. Don't worry—you cannot sand too much, or get your car too smooth. You can, however, sand too deep (into the layer below), or in a pattern (leaving a wavy panel). When you are sanding, you should use the largest sanding board or block that will fit into the area that you are sanding. You should also sand in every different direction that you can think of to avoid sanding grooves or other deformities into your vehicle. Anyone can sand, but not everyone does it correctly.

Using Body Filler

Even if you don't have to use a body hammer to remove a dent, or so much as a piece of sandpaper to remove a spec of rust, there may still be some imperfections to the body. If the vehicle has ever been in a parking lot or a two-car driveway, there is bound to be at least one minor door ding. You may not notice it now, but after you have applied a fresh coat of paint, it will stick out like the proverbial sore thumb.

Eliminate most minor door dings (less than ⅛ inch deep) by filling them with body filler. Scuff the dented area down to bare metal or epoxy primer. Mix the appropriate amount of body filler—and you always mix too much or too little—with the appropriate amount of hardener, and then apply the mixture to the dented area with a body filler spreader. Read the instructions for the particular filler that you are using to determine when and how to begin working it. Some fillers require

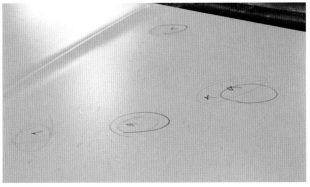
It is much easier to determine areas that may need a little bit of attention with a hammer and dolly and/or a bit of body filler after applying epoxy primer to media blasted, chemically stripped, or sanded sheet metal. I first circled these areas with a pencil to make them stand our better in the photos, but they still didn't show up very well, so I circled them again with a permanent marker.

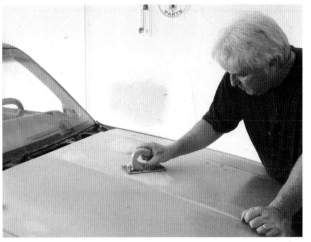
After applying body filler to the slight divots, use a stiff sanding board with 80-grit sandpaper to sand them smooth on flat surfaces such as a hood. For a rounded surface, use a more flexible sanding board.

a cheese grater for rough shaping while the filler is tacky, while others are allowed to fully harden before sanding.

If necessary, apply a second coat of filler to completely fill the area. After rough shaping with a cheese grater or coarse (80 or 100-grit) sandpaper, sand the entire area with finer sandpaper until it blends into the surrounding area.

Sanding Body Filler Repairs

Some sanding is required regardless of the type of surface you plan to paint over, whether it's over a body filler or an existing paint finish. This phase of any automobile paint operation is just as critical as any other. Paint coats only magnify every blemish or surface flaw.

Top layers of body filler are initially sanded with 80- to 150-grit paper to smooth and flatten rough spots and to get the surface close to an even texture. Then, use 240-grit paper to make that finish even smoother and flatter. Use a sanding board or block when sanding. After every two minutes or so, feel the surface with your open hand to judge your progress. Any irregularity you feel will be visible once it's painted, so keep sanding and checking the area until it's smooth, flat, and perfectly blended with surrounding surfaces.

Operate sanding boards and blocks in all directions. Do not simply maneuver them in a back and forth direction from the front to the back. Move them up and down and crossways diagonally, rotating the board or block as necessary for ease of operation. This multidirectional sanding technique will guarantee that all areas are sanded smooth without grooves or perceivable patterns.

MIXING AND APPLYING BODY FILLER

Mixing body filler, quite honestly, will take several tries before you get the proportions figured out just right for your local weather conditions. Too much hardener (catalyst) for the amount of filler and it will begin to set up right there on your mixing palette, or worse, on the body panel that you applied it to, but before you have time to spread it out. Not enough hardener and it will take forever to set, with the worst case being that it never completely cures. In either of these worst cases, you need to scrape off the filler and try again.

If you think about it a day before you are ready to use body filler, turn the can upside down to help the material remix. This is also a good idea for primers. The filler is heavy, so it naturally settles to the bottom of the can. If there is still some separation of the material when you are ready to use it, stir it to mix it correctly. Spoon out the desired amount of filler onto a piece of flat plastic, glass, or sheet metal with a plastic spreader or spatula. Knead the tube of hardener lightly, then squeeze out a line of hardener onto the glob of filler. The hardener should be approximately 1 inch long for every golf-ball-sized amount of filler. A golf ball's worth of filler won't get you very far, but that is about the only description I have ever heard in 40 years of reading and writing automotive magazine articles, so it must have some amount of merit.

The next step is to thoroughly mix the hardener within the filler. The method that seems to work best is to slide a spreader underneath the material to be mixed and fold it over onto itself. Then cut down vertically through the mixture with the spreader and fold half of it onto the other half. Continue this two-step process until there are no streaks of color in the filler, just one uniform color throughout.

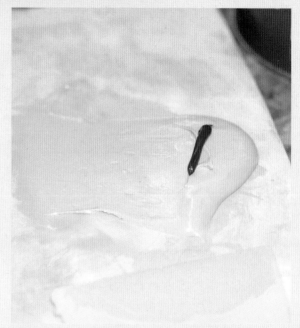

Some body filler labels' instructions say to mix the filler and the hardener proportionately, i.e., one tenth of a tube of hardener to one tenth of the container of filler. That is probably correct, but why do they have extra tubes of hardener available at the auto paint and supply store? Honestly, just work with it a little bit and you'll get a better feel for what works in your shop's conditions.

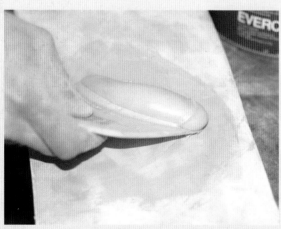

Slide a filler spreader beneath the mixture and fold it over on itself. Continue doing this, along with slicing through the mixture and folding half of it onto the other half . . .

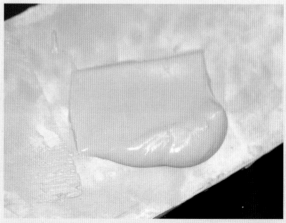

. . . until the mixture has no streaks of color in it. Different fillers are different colors and have different colors for their hardeners. You'll know the filler and hardener are completely mixed when they show the same color throughout, regardless of what color it may be.

To apply the filler, again slide the spreader beneath however much filler you want to spread in one general area and then wipe the filler across the surface. Hold the spreader mostly parallel with the surface to allow the filler to spread onto the surface. If you are spreading filler over a large area, continue in this fashion until the entire desired area is covered with filler. If you are filling localized low spots, you should then hold the spreader more perpendicular to the surface to wipe off excess filler. For best results, remember that filler should not be any deeper than 1/8 thick in any one spot, and thinner would be much better.

For larger areas of filler, you can use a cheese grater file or 80-grit sandpaper to knock off the high spots. The exact time to begin using either one is difficult to describe, but you will quickly learn if you sling much body filler. If the filler starts moving when you touch it, it is not ready yet. However, you don't want it to fully cure prior to sanding it either. With the cheese grater, the filler will peel off in strips when the time is right. If you were able to apply the filler pretty smoothly, you can jump right in with the sandpaper. If you have some ridges, you will be doing yourself a favor by knocking those of with a cheese grater before switching to sandpaper. Use an air hose to blow the filler buildup out of the sandpaper as often as necessary, and use as long of a sanding board as possible.

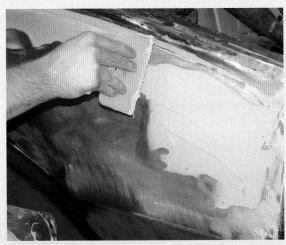

When the filler is mixed thoroughly, scoop some up with a plastic spreader and spread the filler onto the area to be filled by pulling the spreader toward you roughly parallel with the panel. Then go over the area a second time to better refine the levels of the filler.

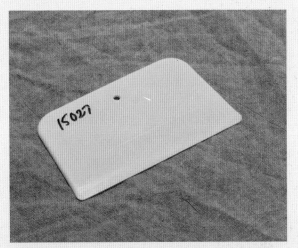

Plastic body filler spreaders come in a variety of sizes. This one is in about the middle of the sizes I have seen at about 5 inches wide. Smaller spreaders are available for adding filler to intricate spaces. Using the largest spreader that will fit into the area helps to get the filler spread in one pass, as the spreader allows the filler to fill the low spot, yet scrape excess material off the higher spots in the same pass.

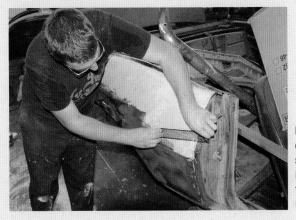

If you are filling a large area that yields an uneven surface, use a cheese grater–type file to remove the excess ridges. When the filler is still slightly tacky (stays in place when you touch it with your finger) but is still slightly soft, using a cheese grater file allows the filler to come through the file in long strips like cheese. This is the ideal time to do the most shaping of the filler.

(continued)

SURFACE PREPARATION

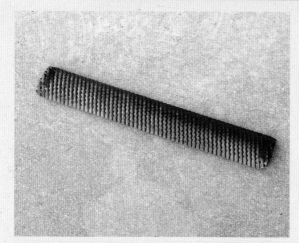

This particular cheese grater file has a semi-circle profile, making it good for roughing in body filler in concave areas. Other similar files are flat, making them more appropriate for flatter surfaces. These files are also known as Surfoam files, but that is a specific brand name that may or may not still be in existence. These files have small brackets on each end for attachment to a handle-type device, but most body men that I have seen use these files without the handle.

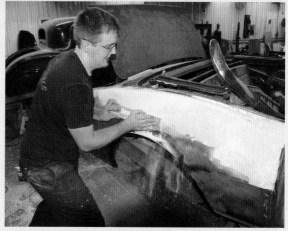

After shaving off ridges with a cheese grater file, get after the rest of the filler with a long board sander to get the shape to what it needs to be. Most fillers can be sanded with 80-grit, then 120-grit. After using the 120-grit sandpaper to get the filler all smooth, look for any areas that require additional filler. Apply the filler as needed, then repeat the sanding with 80- and 120-grit until no additional filler is required. Then you can move on with the finer sandpaper as with the rest of the vehicle.

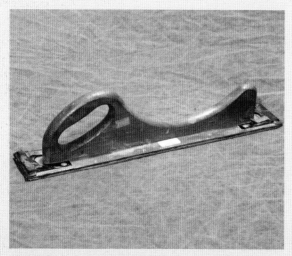

When it absolutely has to be flat—no crown whatsoever—use a traditional long board sander like this one. An aluminum plate affixed to a hardwood handle and the correct grit sandpaper gets the surface flat and smooth. This particular long board is about 14 inches long.

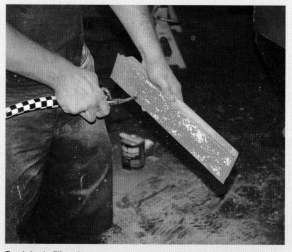

Fresh body filler clogs up your sandpaper if you let it. Use an air hose to blow out the accumulated filler dust as often as necessary.

Once you've made the area flat with 240-grit paper so there are no remaining high spots, wrinkles, grooves or ridges, use 320-grit paper to remove lingering sanding scratches and other shallow imperfections. Up to this point, you've been shaping the body filler until it is flat, and it blends with panel areas adjacent to it. Now, focus on texture smoothness with finer sandpaper grits.

Use a small DA sander for much of this sanding. If you're not experienced using this device on an auto body, practice before you go to work on your vehicle. Although DAs may not appear to be moving at all, they remove a lot of filler material in a hurry.

When satisfied that your filler repair has been sanded to perfection, use 320-grit paper to gradually develop a well-defined visual perimeter around the entire repair area. This "ring" around the repair should expose a band of bare metal about an inch wide, and then successive bands of equally wide exposed rings of primer, sealer, primer-surfacer, and paint. Because undercoat and paint products consist of different-colored materials, you will be able to see your progress clearly. The object, in essence, is to develop sort of a layered valley of smooth walls between the top surface of the body filler area and the top surface of existing good paint. This allows fresh applications of undercoat material to fill to the same thickness as those same materials existing on the rest of the car's surface.

This approach will allow you to apply final color coats in thickness equal to the rest of the paint finish for the best possible blend, color tint and texture identical to surrounding paint finishes. This process is referred to as "feathering in." Subsequent coats of primer-surfacer material will also be sanded to a point where the only depth difference between an existing painted surface and a repair area will be the actual thickness of the existing paint.

Sanding Existing Paint Surfaces

Applying new paint over old paint without properly scuffing up the old surface is a mistake, especially when dealing with factory paint jobs that were baked on at 450 degrees Fahrenheit. Situations like this commonly result in new paint flaking off because it does not have an absorbent base to adhere to. The super hard baked-on paint jobs do not always allow new paint to penetrate their surfaces.

Although painting over a perfectly good paint job might appear to be unnecessary or foolish, some

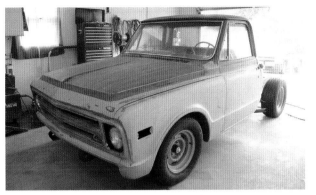

The paint on this 1968 Chevy pickup was fairly new when I acquired it, yet it was full of sins. Poor coverage, runs, improper masking, and other problems too numerous to mention called for a repaint. Since I wanted to get as much of this "new paint" off as possible, I block sanded the entire truck with 220-grit sandpaper. This accomplished two things: it took off most of the paint, and it flattened the surface.

enthusiasts may want to change a solid color scheme into a two-tone blend, or business owners may need to add certain bands of particular colors so new vehicles match the rest of the fleet. No matter the reason, scuff the paint surfaces before painting them.

Fine grade Scotch-Brite™ pads work great for scuffing baked-on paint finishes. The comparatively rough finish left behind makes a great base for coats of sealer. You could also use 500- to 600-grit sandpaper to scuff shiny paint finishes. The overall purpose is to dull all shiny surfaces so that new layers of material have something to grab onto. There is no need to scuff or sand in one direction only. You can, and should, sand in all directions to be sure all surface areas have been roughened up satisfactorily.

Cleaning Sanded Surfaces before Undercoat Applications

Once you've sanded or scuffed the surface as required, you'll need to clean it thoroughly to remove all surface contaminants. Painters normally use air pressure to blow off layers of sanding dust from body surfaces, as well as between trunk edge gaps, door edges, and doorjambs.

Next, they use wax and grease remover products to thoroughly wipe down and clean body surfaces. Each paint manufacturer has its own brand of wax and grease remover that constitutes part of an overall paint system. You should use only those wax and grease remover products deemed part of the paint system you will be using.

Dampen a clean cloth (heavy-duty paper shop towels work great) with wax and grease remover and use it to thoroughly wipe off all body surfaces in the area to be painted. The mild solvents in wax and grease removers loosen and dislodge particles of silicone dressings, oil, wax, polish, and other materials embedded in or otherwise lightly adhered to surfaces. To assist the cleaning ability of wax and grease removers, follow the damp cleaning cloth with a clean, dry cloth in your other hand. The dry one picks up lingering residue and moisture to leave behind a clean, dry surface. Use a new towel on every panel, wipe wet, and dry thoroughly.

To ensure super clean and dry surfaces, go over finishes with an aerosol glass cleaner after a wax and grease remover. The ammonia in such glass cleaners helps to disperse and evaporate moisture, as well as to pick up missed spots of wax or dirt residue. Instead of wetting a cloth with glass cleaner, spray the material on surfaces and wipe it off with a clean, dry cloth.

In the paint booth, as a final cleaning chore just before spraying any paint product, wipe off body surfaces with a tack cloth. As mentioned earlier, these specially made cloths are designed to pick up and retain very small specks of lint, dust, and other particles. Although wax and grease removers work well to get rid of contaminants like wax and grease, tack cloths work best for removing tiny pieces of cloth fiber and other items that could easily cause imperfections in paint finishes. Take the tack cloth out of the package, open it fully, and let it air out before use.

Go over every square inch of body surface that will be exposed to paint product application to be certain that all traces of lint are removed. This should guarantee that debris is not blown over onto painted surfaces during the paint process.

Tack cloths have a limited lifespan. Therefore, you need to refer to product instructions to determine how many times you can use them effectively. Do not try to get more out of them than recommended. Once lint, debris, and residue saturate tack cloths, they're no longer useful. In fact, they may spread accumulated materials absorbed from other cleaning jobs.

USING PRIMER-SURFACER

Primer-surfacer products are generally saved for those body parts that have undergone repair work or suffer very minor or shallow sheetmetal scratches. Primer-surfacers are not a replacement for body filler. Layers

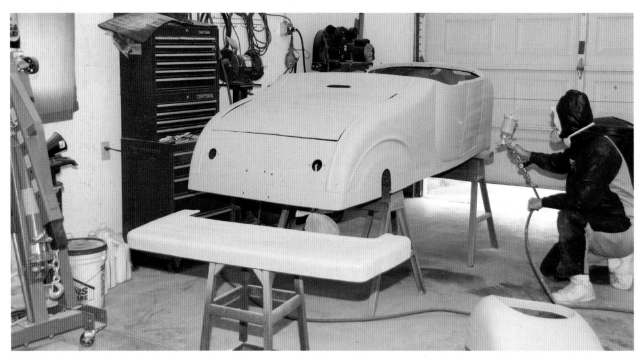

Apply primer-surfacer after all of the bodywork is finished, the body is as straight as possible, and you are working toward getting the sheet metal (or fiberglass) as smooth and flat as possible. Getting the surface as "flat" as possible goes a long way toward obtaining the best gloss from the finished paint. If the surface is not flat, it reflects light in various directions. However, if the surface is flat, such as a perfectly still lake, it reflects light more accurately.

that are applied too thick will shrink to accentuate sanding scratches and other imperfections.

After you have successfully sanded and smoothed a top coat of glazing putty filler material, spray two or three coats of primer-surfacer onto the repair area. Then use 320-grit sandpaper to smooth that surface initially. After that, finish sanding with 400-grit sandpaper. You might find that the first three coats of primer-surfacer did not produce the results expected. Very fine sanding scratches or a shallow low spot may remain. In those situations, apply a couple more light coats of primer-surfacer and re-sand with 320-grit and then 400-grit sandpaper.

Older primer-surfacers were rather heavy, so overspray was not much of a problem, but, with the new high-build primers, that is no longer the case. It is necessary to bag or otherwise mask any area of the vehicle that is not going to be painted. On the bright side, because primer-surfacer will be sanded, there is no need to spray the job in a spray booth. A clean, dust-free area should be sufficient.

Because the high solids content in primer-surfacers can easily flake off masking paper onto work surfaces, it is best to remove masking sheets used during primer-surfacer applications. Sanding dust accumulates on the vehicle's surface and in gaps between doors and trunk lids anyway, which requires a complete cleaning with air pressure, wax and grease remover, an aerosol glass cleaner, and tack cloth before any color coats are applied. After applying and sanding primer-surfacer materials, you can begin definitive masking for sealer applications and actual paint spraying.

Epoxy primers and sealers do not have to be sanded, unless runs or imperfections develop when you apply them. In those cases, use a fine-grit sandpaper to smooth blemishes. Then touch up spots with a new coat of material. As previously described, epoxy primers are sprayed onto bare metal finishes to waterproof and protect them. Most auto restorers apply epoxy primer products, like PPG's DPLF40, to bare metal items once they have removed old paint and rust. Others prefer to apply body filler directly to bare metal and then seal repairs after they've applied and sanded primer-surfacer products.

Spray primer and sealer materials in a paint booth after masking for those body panels or vehicles scheduled for complete new paint jobs. Because those items receive no body repair or body filler applications, their surfaces are essentially ready for paint. Therefore, treat this paint phase as you would a normal top coat application. After masking, clean surfaces with wax and grease remover, aerosol window cleaner, and a tack cloth. Then, mix the primer or sealer product according to label instructions, don appropriate painting attire, and begin.

For those jobs requiring only a part of a vehicle to be shot with primer or sealer, you should lay large strips of masking paper over unaffected areas such as hoods, roofs, and trunk lids to protect them from overspray. Use the minimum recommended pressure and fan the spray gently to cover bare metal spots. Feather them into adjacent areas by slowly releasing the paint gun trigger toward the end of the passes. Practice this technique on something other than your car first.

Complete repaint jobs, in which no bodywork has been performed and existing paint has been scuffed, are also considered ready for paint. They need to be masked and then shot with a sealer, as recommended by your auto body paint and supply professional or by the information in the paint manufacturer's application guide. These sealers will not have to be sanded, unless you botch a spot and have to sand out runs or other imperfections. Once the sealer has cured according to label directions, you can apply paint.

GETTING IT FLAT

When you have completed all the bodywork or rust repair and have all the panels straight and with the proper gaps, you are not necessarily ready to start spraying paint. The body panels all need to be smooth as well. Walk around the entire vehicle, looking closely at its surface. Any and all imperfections that you can see now, while it is in primer or scuffed paint, will be magnified by the new paint.

Even if there are no imperfections, does the entire vehicle feel as if it has a texture to it? A coat or two of paint is not going to smooth out the finish. The only way to eliminate this rough feeling is to block sand the area that still feels rough, whether it is a small area or the entire vehicle.

Sanding with a Long Board

Like a short wheelbase vehicle (such as an ATV) on a rough road, a small sanding block simply rides over an already wavy panel. The panel becomes smoother, but it stays wavy. A long wheelbase vehicle, like a limousine, bridges the high and low spots in the road, smoothing out the ride for the occupants; the same effect happens when you use a long sanding board instead of a short

APPLYING AND SANDING PRIMER-SURFACER

Whether you have already applied epoxy primer or have merely sanded down the existing finish on your vehicle, primer-surfacer is what you will now spray on and sand off until you are convinced that the sheet metal is perfect, and therefore, ready for sealer and then paint. Since most of this will be sanded off anyway, it is not necessary to spray the primer-surfacer in a spray booth, unless of course, your local authorities say so. As long as your garage is reasonably free of dust, you will be fine. Most primer-surfacers are lacquer based, so you don't have to worry about isocyanates getting into your bloodstream either. Just be sure to wear a spray mask and follow the instructions for the primer-surfacer that you are using.

After allowing the proper drying time for the primer-surfacer, break out your favorite sanding boards/blocks and a supply of 320-grit sandpaper. Begin with the 320-grit sandpaper and sand the entire area, using a criss-cross pattern. When you have sanded the entire area, look for any places that might need just a bit more filler. Apply the filler as described previously, then re-sand this newly filled area with 320-grit sandpaper. When all of these low spots are filled and sanded smooth, apply a couple more coats of primer-surfacer to the affected areas. Sand the entire area that has received additional primer-surfacer with 320-grit sandpaper. When you have sanded the entire vehicle with 320-grit sandpaper and there are no more high or low spots visible by eye, apply a guide coat.

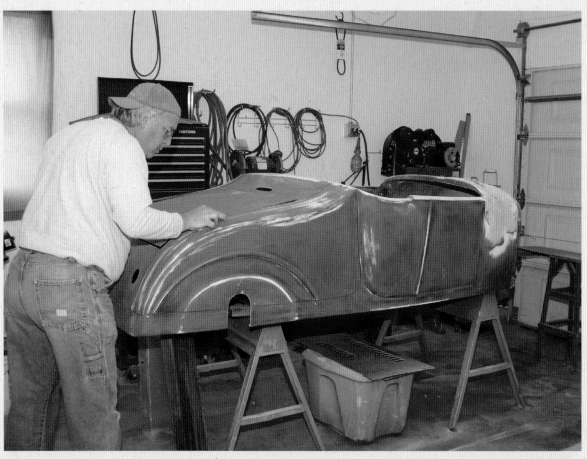

The primer-surfacer stage is the time to get the bodywork as smooth and flat as possible. No amount of paint is going to fill in low spots, dents, or sanding scratches. If you need to use a hammer and dolly to get it right, do that now. If it needs filler, apply it now.

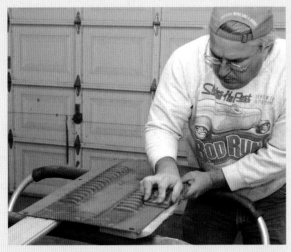

Sand and sand again until the surface is perfect. Yes, each of those louvers need to be sanded as well. When you are sure the sheet metal is as smooth as you can get it, apply another coat or two of primer-surfacer. Then look at it again to make sure you didn't miss anything. Turn on more lights or use a flashlight to closely scrutinize every square inch of body surface. Now is the time to fix it, not after you have applied sealer or paint.

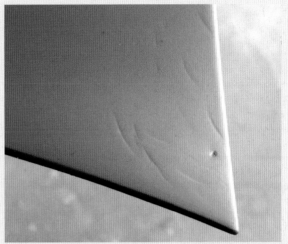

This is the type of thing you are looking for and ultimately eliminating as you block sand filler primer. The lines are where the edge of an orbital sander bit in a little more than necessary while sanding down the original paint. The round hole is simply a small stone chip that I had not noticed previously. With these marks being this obvious with flat primer, you can only imagine how ugly they would be if left unrepaired and covered with glossy paint.

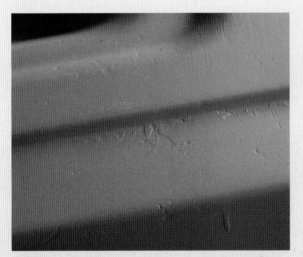

This is a portion of the inside of the tailgate of a pickup truck seen elsewhere in this book. At the top of the photo are some sand scratches, with body filler and low spots that weren't yet sanded flat near the middle.

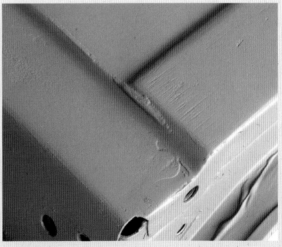

This is some more of the unfinished inside of the tailgate. Some additional sanding and some spot putty will have this looking much better. At the least, make sure that all excess filler is sanded away prior to painting.

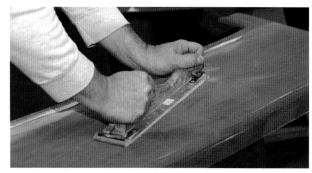

Sanding boards and sanding blocks both must be flexible enough to conform to the body panels they are being used on to get the panel flat. A short sanding block simply rides over the waves in a panel, while a long sanding board works down the waves. The rigid long board in the photo is excellent for smoothing out big, flat surfaces. However, it is not be the best choice for sanding intricately curved panels.

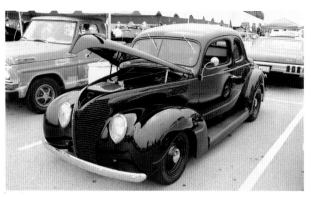

Although most every sheetmetal panel on this 1939 Ford coupe has some amount of curve to it, that sheet metal is optically flat, as proven by the near perfect reflections of the surrounding automobiles. You simply cannot get those high quality reflections with a body that is not smooth and flat.

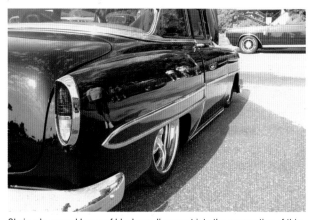

Obviously several hours of block sanding went into the preparation of this early fifties cruiser as noted by the mirror-like reflection. To obtain this type of perfection, the body must be as straight and flat as possible prior spraying any paint. Any imperfections of the paint must be eliminated, and then the clear color sanded to eliminate any imperfections. It is time consuming, but the results are worth it.

sanding block. Using the longest sanding board or block available with progressively finer sandpaper is the key to achieving the straightest and flattest surface upon which to apply paint.

Guide Coats

Properly using a guide coat is one thing that makes a big difference when it comes to block sanding. To aid in detecting the progress of primer-surfacer sanding, spray a light layer of SEM's Guide Coat over the surface. Sanding immediately removes this coating from high spots and highlights low spots. In place of the guide coat, apply flat-black paint (or actually any contrasting color) in very light coats. The key is to mist the guide coat on so that it is uniform. You are not trying to cover the primer beneath it, just apply an even coating. Applying the guide coat on too heavy gives a false indication that the sanded area is low, while not covering an area adequately enough provides a false indication of the area as being too high.

Finer Paper

If you have block sanded the entire vehicle with 400-grit sandpaper, you may still have some sanding scratches that will show when painted over. You will need to go over the entire vehicle with 600-grit sandpaper to eliminate them.

Using Spot Putty (Glazing Compound)

There may still be some slight imperfections. Slight pinholes in body filler, or extremely minor scratches, may be filled with spot putty. This is a substance somewhat thicker than primer-surfacer, but thinner than body filler. Mixed with a cream hardener, it comes in a squeezable bottle and can be applied with a small body filler spreader. Use it for only the tiniest imperfections; only a small amount is needed. After allowing the spot putty to dry according to the product directions, you can sand it with 600-grit or finer sandpaper.

Finer Yet

If you are working on a restoration or show car project, you may choose to block sand the entire vehicle with 800-grit sandpaper. Depending on how elaborate you desire your paint job to be, you could also graduate to 1,000-grit sandpaper, but only after you have used the 800-grit on the entire vehicle—jumping too quickly to a much finer paper leaves you sanding much longer to remove scratches.

APPLYING SEALER

Do not apply sealer until you are sure that all of your bodywork is complete. You can scuff the sealer and do additional bodywork if necessary (it's still better than painting over a less-than-perfect body prep). If you have additional bodywork to do, do it before you spray the sealer. One of the jobs of sealer is to seal and protect body filler and primer from the harsher solvents used in paint and clear top coats.

Sealer is the last coat of anything that goes on prior to actually applying color, so it needs to be as perfect as possible . . . no drips, no errors, no excuses. If you end up with some drips or runs, you should sand them out and respray the sealer, but don't sand the sealer otherwise. Providing a uniformly colored base for the paint to be applied is another use of sealer, so you should be as consistent in your application thereof as well. Additionally, if given the choice, use a light colored sealer beneath a light finish color. This will require less paint to achieve full coverage. Some sealers can even be tinted in a similar color as the finish paint. This makes future, minor scratches in the finished paint less noticeable.

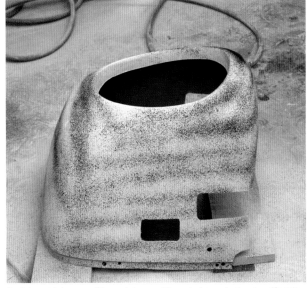

Applying paint as a guide coat does not have to be perfect, yet, uniformity is a key to making the most of the process. All of the guide coat is eventually be sanded off, so use whichever color you happen to have, with the cheaper grades from a spray can being as good for this purpose as the more expensive brands.

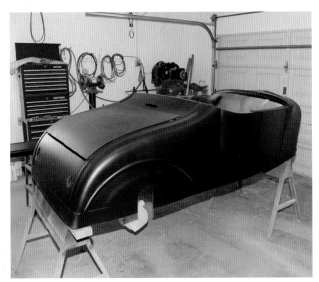

Sealer is what ultimately covers all of the bodywork, body filler, various layers of previous primers, and top coats to provide a uniform canvas to apply the paint and/or graphics of your choice. If it were not for sealer, darker body fillers and primers would not cover as easily as the sheet metal that has not been affected or altered.

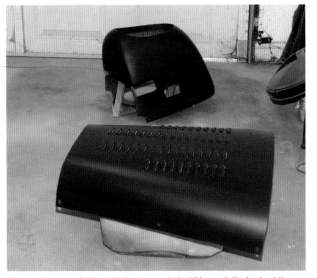

Most sealers are designed to be top coated within a relatively short time, so you should consult the instructions for the products you are using prior to spraying sealer. If you are required to top coat the sealer within a certain time frame that does not meet your schedule, you should put off spraying the sealer until you have time to do both. As seen in this photo, the sealer looks almost like the finished paint, just in a different color and with an eggshell finish.

Chapter 6
Masking

To prevent unwanted paint from landing on body sections adjacent to those being painted, they must be protected with masking paper and tape. Although an initial estimate of the masking needs for your vehicle may appear to be rather limited and easy to accomplish, you must understand that less than meticulous masking will almost always results in obvious spots of overspray.

Some paint overspray can be cleaned off or painted over, but trim pieces and other assorted body items marred with thin strips of paint on their edges may not fare as well. Remember, a conscientious buyer or detail-oriented judge quickly notices small lines of paint on windshield moldings, key locks, door handles, emblems, lights, and reflectors. To them, overspray on any item proves that an automobile has been repainted. They may wonder whether it has also seen extensive bodywork, from a collision or advanced rust. Was this paint job something a conscientious owner did to make the car look its very best, or is it an effort to hide serious flaws? And if the former, why did he or she settle for sloppy work?

Next to color matching, masking is perhaps the most meticulous and exacting chore required of an auto body painter. Since your auto body paint and supply store will mix paint blends and tints, your most precise work revolves around masking. To make the job as simple as possible, be sure to use only those tape and paper products designed for automotive paint masking. Devise and follow a systematic masking plan, and then allot enough time to complete those tasks with strict attention to detail.

Outlining

It is not always easy to lay down a perfect strip of ¾-inch masking tape along edges of trim or other body parts. Around curves, especially tight ones, this kind of tape tends to bunch up and fold, causing flat spots instead of smooth and evenly flowing contours. Masking rounded items is even more difficult when sheets of masking paper are attached to tape strips. In fact, placing paper and tape together along exact edges in one move is not easily accomplished on any body part.

Professional painters rely on quality workmanship and effective time management to make money. It is foolish to waste a half-hour masking trim when only five minutes is necessary to remove the part. Likewise, rather than hassle with a piece of tape and sheet of paper to mask along a section of window trim, they lay down a thin strip of Fine Line brand masking tape first and then attach wider strips of tape and paper to it—a much less meticulous task.

Placing a thin ⅛- to ¼-inch strip of plastic Fine Line masking tape right along molding or trim edges is easy because of its manageable size and texture. It gently follows curves without bunching or folding, and its smooth edges are easy to match along body part edges for perfect masking every time.

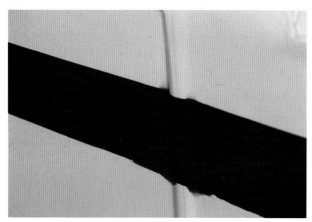

This scallop crosses the edge of the nonopening door panel. It is painfully obvious that the masking tape was not pressed down fully around the contour of the raised area. Instead, it pulled loose, spanning the high spots, allowing the dark paint to mist into the uncovered area. Avoid this by pressing the tape down fully along its entire surface. Rough tape edges are likely part of the reasoning for pinstriping the edge of flames and scallops.

The only function of Fine Line tape is masking those part edges next to body panels slated for new paint. Next, attach additional strips of regular masking tape and paper to Fine Line. This yields a wide margin to work from instead of the precise line of the part's edge.

Although most professional auto painters prefer to use Fine Line for outlining intricate masking jobs, you could also use ¼-inch paper masking tape. It works very well along straight sections, but tends to bunch up and fold around corners. In addition, the slightly rough texture of this material sometimes allows tiny gaps to form along masked edges, which allow paint materials to build up and form spots of overspray.

Another benefit of Fine Line plastic tape is that it is very thin. Painting along thick paper leaves a definite lip of built-up paint when you remove the paper. But Fine Line is so thin that the edge is minimal, allowing you to blend it into surrounding paint work easily.

Windows

It's difficult to paint around windows without getting overspray on belt moldings and trim pieces surrounding the glass. The surest way to avoid overspray is to remove the glass and trim. Barring that, use plastic tape to outline outer molding edges next to those panels to be painted. Attach strips of wider masking tape and paper anywhere along the plastic tape's width; just make sure there are no gaps between the inside edge of the Fine Line and the wider tape.

You only need one strip of masking paper to cover windows, as long as it is wide enough to reach from top to bottom. Fold paper as necessary to make it fit neatly along the sides. Use strips of tape to hold the paper secure and to cover any resulting gaps. A single sheet of automotive masking paper prevents paint from bleeding through to underlying surfaces. If you choose to use a masking material other than recommended automotive masking paper, you might have to apply two or three layers.

Masking paper does not always come in widths that fit window shapes exactly. Most of the time, especially with side windows, you end up with a tight fit along edges and bulges in the middle. To avoid bulges, fold excess masking paper so that it lies flat. Not only does this make for a tidy masking job, but it prevents bulky paper from being blown around by air pressure from a paint spray gun. All you have to do is lay one hand down on an edge of the paper and slide it toward the middle. With your other hand, grasp the bulging paper and fold it over. Use strips of tape to hold it in a neat fold.

Whenever masking, always remember that paint covers everything it touches. Small slits between tape and masking paper allow paint to reach the surface below. Lightly secured paper edges blow open during spray paint operations and allow mists of overspray to infiltrate underlying spaces. Therefore, always run lines of tape along the length of paper edges to seal off underlying areas completely. This is especially important when the edge of one piece of masking paper overlaps another.

Windshields and rear windows are generally quite big. You might have to use two or three strips of paper horizontally placed in order to cover all glass. If you leave trim pieces in place, consider applying Fine Line tape around their outer edges before working with wider tape and paper. You must remove rear window louvers or side window air deflectors when painting body areas next to them.

Rubber moldings that lap against body panels—rubber windshield moldings along roofs, A-pillars, and cowlings—present difficult masking challenges. To make the job of placing tape directly over the molding's outer edge easier, consider putting a length of thick, nonscratching cord under it.

The Eastwood Company carries a Weatherstrip Masking Tool designed to insert long strips of plastic cord under the edges of molding and weather stripping. It raises these edges up off body surfaces to allow complete masking under them. This way, paint can reach under molding edges, instead of just up to them, ensuring good paint coverage and eliminating distinctive paint edge lines next to moldings.

If you've removed the windows and moldings, you'll have to mask off the interior compartment. Generally, exterior paint colors are applied to the middle of window openings. You could lay down strips of wide tape inside these openings and fold it over toward the inside for side windows. Along the spot-welded metal edge of windshield openings, simply apply perimeter tape and paper from the interior compartment side.

TAPING AND MASKING WINDOWS AND WINDSHIELDS

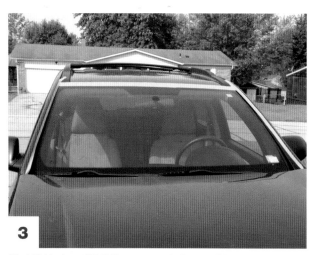

1

This type of windshield installation is common on many contemporary vehicles. There is no rubber molding to contend with, yet there is more than glass to be covered. Begin by running a piece of masking tape along the edge of the body, covering what should not be painted, but leaving the part to be painted exposed.

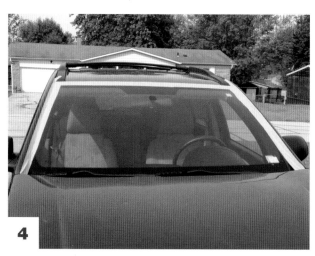

2

Using 1-inch-wide masking tape (narrower tape is a little easier to work with in areas that are not straight), cover both A-pillars and across the top of the windshield.

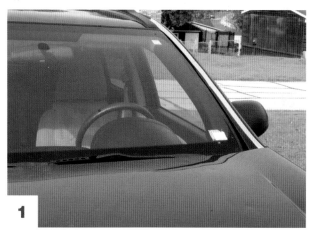

3

Windshield wipers fit into the recess at the bottom of the windshield and behind the hood, but you don't want to paint them. You can remove the wiper arms, but you still need to mask the recess that they fit into, so in this case the wipers were left on.

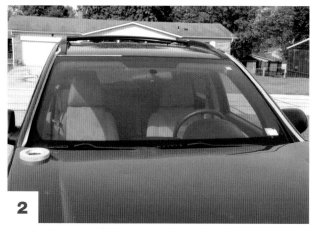

4

Since the masking material is transitioning roughly 90 degrees on each side of the windshield, secure a second strip of tape onto the first piece along the A-pillars over to the glass. Using the widest tape you have available will make this easier. Also attach a piece of masking tape to the back edge of the hood (if it is not going to be painted) or to the underneath side of the hood or the plastic trim. This first piece of trim along the back edge of the hood provides an attachment point for the masking paper to follow.

MASKING

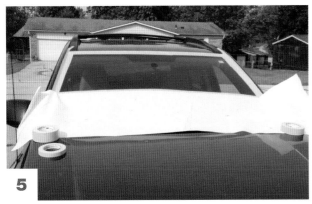

5

Cut a piece of masking paper long enough to span the lower portion of the windshield. Since two pieces are required to fully cover this windshield, position the first so that it reaches the tape at the back of the underneath side of the hood. Then tape it in place across the windshield so it doesn't move.

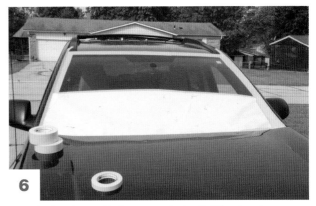

6

Now trim the edges and bottom as required so that they do not cover any portions of the body to be painted. Press the paper as flat as possible, refold if required, and tape it securely in place.

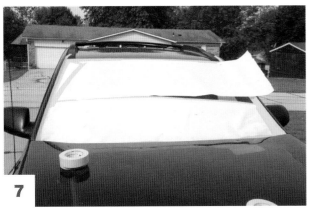

7

Following the same general principles, apply a second piece of masking paper to cover the top of the windshield. Tape the paper to the tape already along the top of the windshield, then fold the excess on one end to fit the windshield, and tape it down.

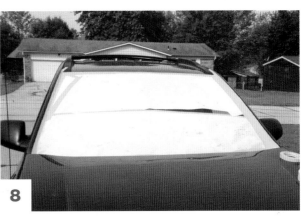

8

Press the paper flat against the windshield and trim or fold the excess to fit. Then tape down the end of the paper, along with any flaps that may remain.

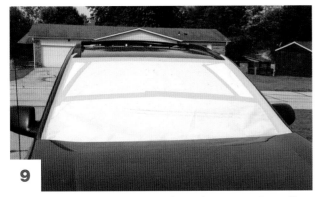

9

If there are any gaps between the two pieces of paper, cover them with another piece of paper or the required number of strips of masking tape if the gap is a relatively small area.

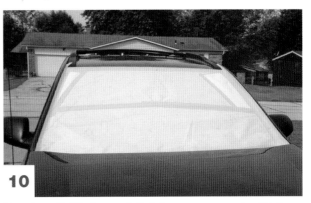

10

Press down all of the tape, verify that all seams are covered, and that there are no gaps. If you follow this procedure, it makes removing the masking simple. Begin at the first corner where the first piece of tape was applied and pull firmly but gently. The masking can often be removed in just two or three pieces.

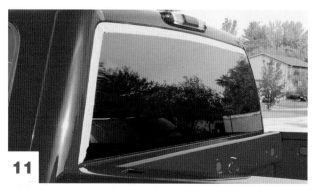

11 The author's 2008 Chevrolet Silverado rear window is among the type of vehicles where the rear window is glued into place without any weather stripping around it. This makes it fairly easy to mask should the need arise. It doesn't really matter where you start, but the edge of the glass should be masked off first. I used 1½-inch-wide masking tape, wrapping it inward over the edge and then flat onto the surface of the glass.

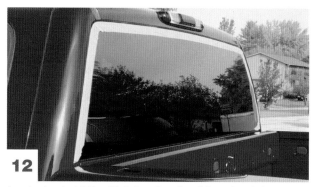

12 A professional might be able to tape the edge of the entire window with one piece of tape, but I did the sides and top with two pieces. It doesn't really matter how many pieces of tape or masking paper you use as long as you get the job done.

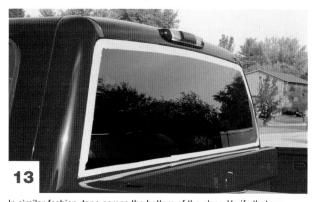

13 In similar fashion, tape across the bottom of the glass. Verify that you have not covered any of the area on the cab that will be painted. Rub your fingers over the edges to ensure that the tape is stuck to the glass. This perimeter of tape makes it easier to secure masking paper.

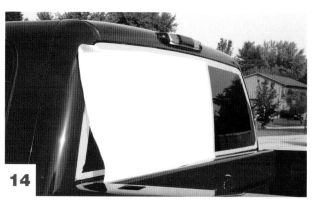

14 Having a masking paper rack that automatically adds a strip of masking tape along one edge as it dispenses makes masking much easier, but I do not have one. So, I cut a piece of 18-inch-wide masking paper long enough to cover a little more than half of the back glass. With a couple of short pieces of tape, I attached it to the tape along the top edge of the glass so that covers the end of the glass.

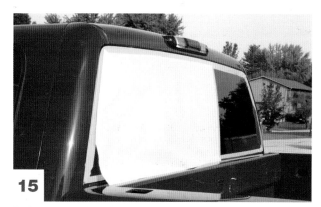

15 As shown in this photo, the 18-inch-wide masking paper is more than adequate for this rear glass. Wider paper is available if necessary, or you can use multiple rows across the glass. Fold the end of the paper as required to cover the shape of the glass on the end.

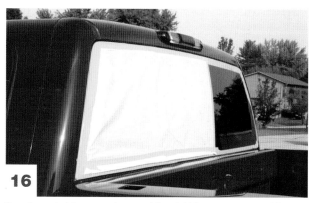

16 Tape the end of the paper down and then fold the excess paper at the bottom upward. Rub your hand over the folds to crease the paper (making them easier to tape over). It is unnecessary to keep the paper precisely flat, but you should attempt to avoid bubbles or bulges that could easily be ripped open and ruin your masking job.

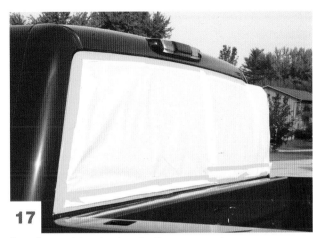

17 Cover the remaining glass by using the same procedure.

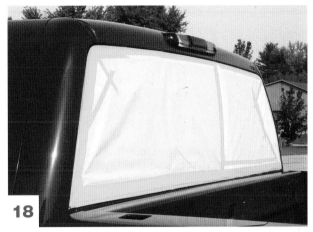

18 Now that paper covers all of the glass, apply another row of tape over all of the paper edges and the seam in the middle.

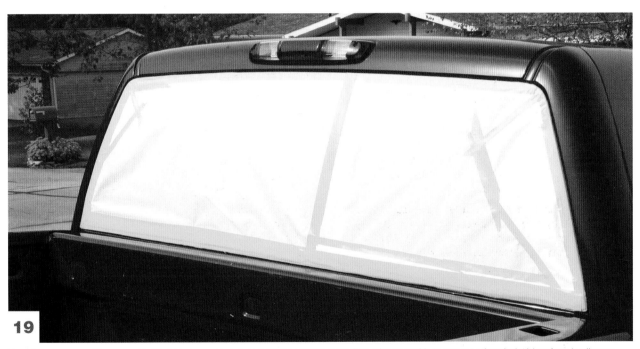

19 Even the excess masking paper that is folded over at each end must be taped down. The primary goal is to prevent primer/paint/clear from landing on the glass. However, a secondary goal is to remove any chance of forming pockets that collect dirt or debris that could fall onto your fresh paint when the masking is removed.

Emblems and Badges

As with trim pieces, it is best to remove emblems and badges before painting. They are secured by clips, pins, screws, adhesives, or double-backed tape. Be extra cautious while attempting to take these items off any vehicle. Too much prying pressure causes them to break. Unless you can see that their protruding support pins are secured from inside a trunk space, inner fender area, or other locations, you will have to carefully pry open an edge to determine just how they are mounted.

If you are not sure how to remove those items, consult a dealership service representative, auto body paint and supply professional, or professional auto body painter. Should an emblem or badge break during dismantling, don't despair—even professional auto body technicians occasionally break these plastic items.

Although most painting jobs call for removing emblems and badges, there are two occasions where they can be left in place—when you're spraying only clear coat paint or spot painting work with only a light melting coat close to their edge. In those cases, carefully mask to ensure that no overspray builds up along their edges.

To ensure that emblem and badge edges are completely covered, mask carefully around their edges, allowing no part of the tape to extend onto the painted surface. Tape over the edges first, before masking their faces. Again, Fine Line tape may be the best material for this meticulous task. After attaching the tape's end to a corner of an emblem, maneuver the roll with one hand while carefully placing and securing the tape with your other hand. Practice is essential, so do not expect to accomplish this kind of unique masking on the first try.

Some painters make this job easier by covering emblems with wide strips of tape first. They then use a sharp razor blade to cut tape along the emblem edges at the exact point where they meet the painted body. You must use a very delicate touch to avoid cutting into paint or missing the mark and leaving an open gap along the part being masked off. If you should decide to try this technique, opt for very light passes with the razor blade, even if it takes two or three attempts to cut completely through the tape. This will allow you to avoid a deep scratch in the paint, should your hand slip.

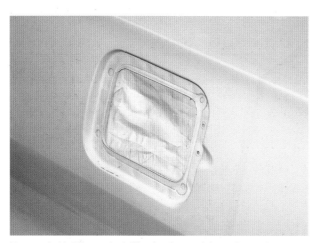

The area behind the gas tank filler door is one of those places where you can quickly tell the pros from the amateurs when it comes to masking. The amateurs may not bother masking this area, instead leaving an uneven coat of paint on the gas cap and whatever else is beneath the filler door. The pros will remove the door so that it can be painted separately and mask the opening so nothing behind it shows signs of overspray.

About the only way to mask vinyl decals, like those under gasoline filler housings that say "Unleaded Only," is to cover them with masking tape and then cut off excess with a *sharp* razor blade. Dull razor blades, even those used to make only three or four cuts, tear masking tape instead of cutting it cleanly. Again, use light pressure to prevent unnecessary damage to underlying paint.

Door Locks and Handles

Because door locks and handles are secured right next to painted door panels, the same kind of meticulous masking is required for them as for emblems and badges. The best approach is to remove them, unless you're doing only clear coats or light paint feathering or melting in up to their edge.

Door handles are best masked using tape for the entire process. Paper, even in 4-inch widths, is just too cumbersome to work with. Use ¾-inch tape to mask the perimeter edges and then 2-inch tape to completely cover the unit. If your car presents a rather unique handle, employ whatever means necessary to cover it. Use your imagination. Tape can be applied initially from the back to offer sticky edges that can extend out past upper and lower edges and can be folded over to cover the front. Remember, the most critical part of masking is along the edge, where items meet painted panels. Wide strips of tape can easily cover faces and other easy-to-reach parts.

Key locks are easiest to mask by simply covering them with a wide strip of 1-or 2-inch-wide tape, and then cutting the excess from around the lock's circumference with a sharp razor blade. Before cutting, though, use a fingernail to force tape down along the circumference to be sure coverage is complete and that the tape is securely in place.

Doorjambs

Many novice painters forget to mask doorjambs before spraying undercoats or top coats. This oversight always results in overspray in doorjamb areas, including the inner side of door edges. As paint enters the gaps between doors and jambs, it bounces off surfaces to land anywhere it can. The same problem exists inside the gaps along the tops and bottoms of doors. The mess created by this kind of overspray can be difficult to remove.

Painters commonly prefer to coat doorjambs and edges first when they are to be painted along with the body. After those areas have cured, you can close

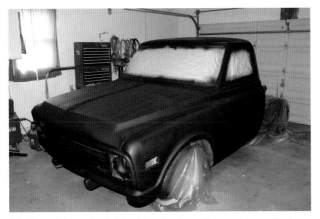

Prior to applying sealer to this pickup truck, multiple masking methods were completed. First, the truck bed was completely removed to provide access to the back of the cab and the front of the truck bed. A large piece of plastic film sheeting was cut off a larger roll to cover the exposed chassis and rear wheels/tires. Smaller pieces of the same material were used to mask each front wheel and tire. Masking tape and masking paper was used to protect all four windows and the headlight bulbs. I should have masked the side marker light opening as well.

the doors and paint their exterior portions without overspray concerns. You may choose to mask the doorjamb areas after they are cured to avoid overspray; however, same-color overspray in doorjamb areas is not uncommon among new vehicles. To paint doorjambs, door edges, and outer door skins all at the same time, you must move the doors so you can reach their front section, which swings inward past the rear part of the fender. This movement damages wet paint on hinges.

It is much easier to paint the interior side and perimeter edges of doors while they are off the vehicle. Once that has dried, assemble the window and latch mechanisms, install the doors, and spray their exteriors in one sequence. When painting the exterior surface, you must still mask the jambs, even those freshly painted with the same color applied on the outside. This keeps the jamb coat even and smooth.

Some painters like to apply 2-inch tape along the edges of rear doorjambs with the sticky side facing out. Only about half of the tape strip actually goes on the jamb; the rest is folded over, so that it is perpendicular. Place another strip on the rear door edge in the same manner; half of it sticks out, with the sticky side facing out. This way, when the door is closed, the two strips of tape are attached to each other to effectively seal the gap between the door and jamb.

Use the same technique along the lower door edge. For front doors, apply tape to the front edge of the rear door to match the rear edge of the front door when it is closed. It takes a little practice and some patience to perfect these maneuvers. Tape does not always stick the way you want it to, and sometimes the air movement caused by the door closing will throw off the alignment with the corresponding strip.

You can use 2-inch tape and 4- to 6-inch paper to mask doorjambs and edges, but be careful where you place the tape edges. If you set them too far out, they may allow a visible paint line between the door and the jamb. This will be especially apparent if you paint the jambs a different color from the exterior. You will have to decide where the dividing line will be and make sure you position the tape symmetrically.

Trim

Body side moldings and other trim pieces do not look their best when painted over or marred with thin strips of paint overspray along their edges. Remove them for painting and reinstall them later, after the paint has dried, and you've performed all rubbing out or buffing operations. By waiting until you're done polishing, you avoid compound buildup on trim and along its edges.

Drip rail trim is generally snapped over the welded drip rail edge and then screwed tight at each end. Avoid bending or creasing these pieces by dismantling them carefully, employing a helper on long pieces. Pay attention when masking the top inner side as well as the facing portion. Place tape of adequate width on the inner side first and then lay it down over the face. Should another strip be needed, apply it to the bottom edge first and fold excess over the front to overlap the previous strip.

On many cars, metal trim around windshields and rear windows sticks up just above the vehicle body. Take advantage of this gap to insert masking tape with the sticky side facing up. Gently slide the tape strip back and forth until you can no longer force it any deeper into the gap. Then, fold it over on top of the trim section. You may need to stand on a sturdy stool to reach top trim pieces, and you might need a helper to assist you from the opposite side. Employ the same technique for the side and bottom sections.

Applying tape to other types of trim does not require any special skill other than patience and attention to detail. Cover edges next to body panels first and faces last. Hold a roll of tape in one hand and position the extended strip with the other hand directly on top of trim sections. Be absolutely certain that trim edges are covered and that tape does not extend onto the body. Small pieces of tape that do touch body parts will block paint reaching from the surface and cause a blemish.

Always inspect your masking work after you've positioned the tape. Use your fingernail to secure tape firmly along edges. On the bottom sides of bodyside trim, you may have to lie down to place masking tape properly.

OTHER EXTERIOR FEATURES

Remove the radio antenna if it protrudes from a panel you're going to paint. They often unscrew from their bases, leaving large gaps between the car body and remaining antenna unit. If you decide to leave the antenna in place, don't wrap it barber pole style from top to bottom. Instead, sandwich it between two vertical strips of tape—they'll cover it just as well and be much easier to remove.

Taillight and side light units are usually easy to remove by loosening four to eight nuts on their housings' back sides. Should you decide to mask them instead, use overlapping strips of 2-inch tape. Be sure to overlap each strip by at least ¾ inch to prevent paint seepage into seams.

Bumper designs range from out-in-the-open pickup truck step bumpers to closely fitted wraparound urethane-faced models. You must remove them to paint surrounding areas.

If you're not painting the surrounding surfaces, mask bumpers with regular masking tape and paper. If possible, insert a strip of tape between body panels and those parts touching them. Fold it over and then attach paper and tape to it. Fold paper over the top and face of bumpers. If the part requires more paper coverage, start from the bottom and fold over the top to overlap with the preceding piece.

If you intend to touch up only a quarter panel, and only the side-mounted bumper guard is in your way, consider dismantling the guard alone. These are attached to bumpers with nuts and bolts. They are flexible, for the most part, and bending them out of the way should give you enough room for dismantling them. If not, maybe that piece can be pulled away and secured with tape so you can paint below and around it.

License plates and their holders are very easy to remove. If set into a housing, remove the entire unit if possible. Masking these units requires the same

techniques described above for complete coverage with good overlap to prevent seepage.

Vinyl graphics, stripes, and decals are not easy to remove or store. The procedure for removing them typically destroys them. If you can't replace them, you'll have to mask them off when painting near or around them. Use thin Fine Line tape for a precision line with low paint buildup along its edge.

Meticulously mask the outer perimeter edges of vinyl graphics, stripes, and decals first. Be sure to place Fine Line tape directly on top of the item being masked and perfectly in line with its edge. When touching up or spot painting a body section below such items, you need only to mask the bottom edge. Cover the rest with paper and regular masking tape.

However, should you need to paint areas between vinyl graphics, be sure to outline the entire scheme and then fill in with wide tape or paper, whichever is most appropriate. With a two- or three-step paint system, where clear paint will finish the job, you could remove masking after applying color coats and then cover everything, including the graphic, stripe, or decal, with clear. This effort will fill in the gap between color paint layers and vinyl to make the entire panel smooth, with no distinguishable paint edge or lip.

Be sure to confirm the effectiveness and compatibility of this procedure with your auto body paint and supply professional, as various vinyl graphic, stripe, and decal materials may not be compatible with the paint system you employ. In addition, be 100-percent certain you want that vinyl adornment to remain on your car or truck for a long time. Once you spray clear over it, you will have to remove the clear coat before you can remove what lies beneath.

Grille

If you don't need to remove the grille, mask it with wide strips of paper. Attached to the top of the unit first, paper will hang down to cover most of the assembly. Use ¾-inch tape to secure paper on the sides. There is no need to mask individual contours or sections. If you have 12-inch paper and need to cover a grille that is 20 inches top to bottom, simply tape the paper edge to edge and attach the extra-wide sheet as a unit.

Remove the grille for intricate nearby paint work. No amount of masking allows you adequate spray gun maneuverability. However, if all you need to do is paint the front parts of your ground effects system, then start masking from the bottom of the grille and work upward. When masking, always keep in mind the painting requirements for the job and the sequence you plan to follow.

The most important part of a masked area is the section adjacent or perpendicular to the area to be painted. It is the edges of those items that will expose overspray and the paint buildup edge so predominant with repaint efforts. Be sure the first piece of masking tape placed along the edges of those items is secure, adequate, and accurate.

Wheels

Many hot rods, as well as other specialty automobiles, have painted fender wells and special wheels. It would be a shame to mar them with overspray. So, for paint projects that include fender wells, remove the wheels. Support the vehicle on sturdy jack stands.

On those vehicles that demand a new paint job or spot painting and already have painted fender wells, take time to cover them with masking paper and tape. Do not mask cars with normal everyday driver fender wells covered with undercoat unless you want to. On those, you can cover overspray imperfections with new layers of undercoat or black paint. The choice is up to you.

Most paint shops have covers designed just for wheels and tires. In addition, there are packages of plastic tire and wheel covers available. They fit easily and quickly over tires and wheels to protect them from overspray. If you do not have access to such items, plan to mask tires and wheels as you would anything else. Should some paint land on the tires, use thinner or reducer, whichever is appropriate with the paint system employed, to scrub them clean.

Wheels are a different story. Polished wheels do not look the same after you overspray them with harsh solvents, number 0000 steel wool, or other abrasive. Chances are you will have to get them polished by a wheel restoration service. To save the expense and hassle, take a few minutes to mask them appropriately. Use enough paper to cover them completely, and use plenty of tape to make sure paper seams do not open from the pressure of the spray paint gun. The best protection against overspray is to remove the wheels and stow them away from the painting area.

Tape does not stick to dirty, oily, or dusty surfaces, including grungy tires and filthy fender wells. Even if tape does stick initially, air pressure from your paint gun quickly blows it off. In that instant, paint overspray settles on the area and mars the surface. So, before you bring your car or truck in for masking, make sure you spend plenty of time washing those areas where you need to place tape.

UNAFFECTED BODY AREAS

Even the best HVLP system produces overspray. Therefore, before you begin your project, plan to mask every part of your car that will not receive paint.

This doesn't mean you have to mask individual trim items on the driver's side when all you will be painting is the passenger side quarter panel. You will need to mask the driver's side of the car, however, or overspray will settle on it.

At most body shops, painters use large sheets of plastic to cover everything beyond the immediate painting area. They hold the plastic in place with tape so that air pressure doesn't blow it around and knock it loose or stir up particles.

In lieu of large plastic sheets, you will have to use masking paper. Think of your car as a large present. Using large sheets of paper, cover the roof, hood, and trunk lid, and secure it with masking tape. Overlap successive sheets by an inch, and seal the seams along their full length with tape. You can never mask too much.

Individual panel painting requires masking at the edge of each panel. This is a simple process. You can place a strip of tape down first and attach paper and tape to it. Or, if you have the means, roll off a section of paper with tape attached and secure it as necessary.

Paint feathering or melting requires a little different technique. Mask off panels by applying a taped sheet of paper over the area to be painted, then fold it over toward the area to be masked. This forces tape to roll over backward. So instead of a clean edge, the curved tape contour forces paint to bounce away to create a soft, gentle edge. After applying all coats, empty the paint from your spray gun except for about ¼ inch. To that, add about ¾ inch of reducer, creating a 3:1 mixture.

Remove the section of masking paper that was rolled over itself and spray the over-reduced paint mixture onto that newly exposed area. The extra reducer melts old paint and allows just a hint of new paint to infiltrate the surface. The result is a perfect blend and feathering of new paint edges into old.

Chapter 7
Paint Application

I t's show time! You've spent many, many hours preparing your car to receive a first-rate, beautiful, smooth paint job that will last for years and prove what you can do when you put your mind to it. But, just as we didn't rush earlier steps, we're not going to hasten things now with the finish line close at hand.

How you apply the paint is every bit as important as the quality of the paint itself. Before you start spraying on your carefully prepped vehicle, get a used door, hood, or trunk lid, and practice the art of laying on paint smoothly and evenly. You're not just developing your own skills, you're also learning how your equipment performs its job. Leave the runs, drips, and irregularities on your practice panel and shoot your vehicle like a pro.

Another thing to consider before mixing the paint and filling your gun is to highlight certain time-frame

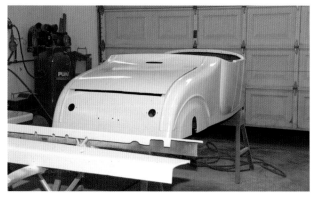

Prior to painting, position everything to be painted so that you can actually get to it. You sure don't want to bump into a freshly painted quarter panel or drag your air hose across the hood. When done spraying, avoid doing anything that stirs up dust collects on the fresh surface. If the outside climate is calm, open the garage door a foot or two to exhaust your garage. However, you don't want to do this on a windy day when who knows what might be blown in to ruin your new paint job.

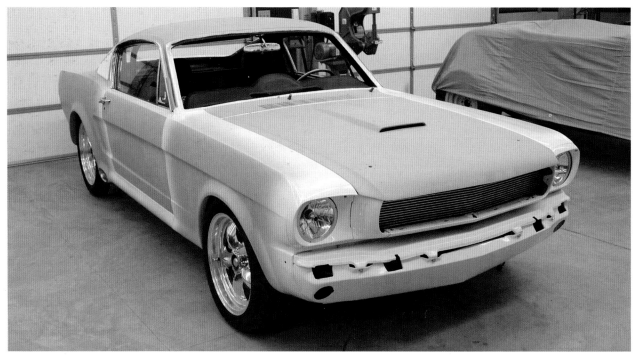

This Mustang is awaiting final paint in Jack and Donnie Karg's amazingly clean garage. While some paint each piece of a vehicle separately and then assemble it, running the risk of scratching or otherwise damaging the paint in the process, Donnie has a better idea; after applying the gray sealer, he has painted the insides and edges of each panel prior to assembly. The vehicle is then assembled, masked off, and then the entire vehicle painted at one time. This provides for more uniformity in the overall paint job and minimizes damage to painted parts.

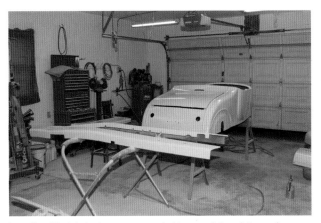

Less than ideal, but a two-car garage is big enough to paint a car in . . . of course, a Track T is a small car. The body is situated on a pair of sturdy sawhorses. Body aprons are on the tubular framework, while the three-piece hood and nose (outside the photo) are hung or are supported by something that does not obscure the edges. When situating the various pieces in the workspace, make sure to leave enough room in between everything to ensure that you can get to them. If weather permits, leave the garage door open a bit for ventilation.

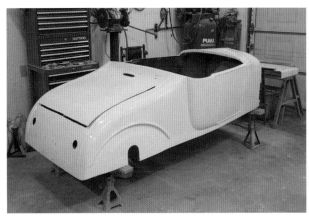

In addition to having a place to paint your car, it needs to be a place where the car can stay long enough for the paint to dry sufficiently. While this Track T body was painted closer to the middle of the garage, it was light enough for four guys to each pick up the end of one of two 2x4s supporting it while someone else moved the jack stands.

recommendations and other important data that came with your paint system so you can refer to it during your job. If you prepare a small outline, including all of the painting and drying steps in sequential order, you can check off each step once you've completed it. If you like to multitask, or have kids, a cell phone, or other distractions, this approach will help you to remember what you have done, what you need to do, and how much time you have to do it. Try using something other than a typical sheet of paper for this—like an off-size piece of light cardboard, or a colored sheet—and you'll be able to distinguish it quickly among any other notes or papers.

Mix your paint products according to label instructions and apply them at the recommended air pressure. Try painting with different fan patterns and pressure settings to see which combinations work best for intricate work in confined spaces, and which perform better on large panels. Practice holding paint guns at perpendicular angles to work surfaces; see what happens when you don't. Use cans of inexpensive paint, and practice until you become familiar with the techniques required for good paint coverage. When the paint has dried, practice wet sanding, rubbing out, and buffing.

Practice with your new dual-action sander to remove those coats of paint. Put a deep scratch in your practice panel and repair it, instead of practicing on your favorite car or truck. Become proficient with the tools and materials that you expect to use while fixing your special car before attacking its precious surface with power tools and harsh chemicals. Practice, practice, and practice some more. Once it looks good on your practice panel, you know you're ready for the big time.

PAINT MIXING

Because there are literally tens of thousands of different automotive paint colors, mixing the correct shade for your car is a precise science. Following stock vehicle color codes or those selected from paint chip catalogs, auto body paint and supply personnel measure drops of color tints to the tenth of a gram to create the prescribed colors. They do this work for you as part of your paint system purchase.

Paint materials are shipped in concentrated form, which helps keep the heavy pigments and other solid materials from settling. Painters then add solvents to make those products sprayable. Remember that the atmospheric conditions at which you spray the paint also affect the thinners or reducers you need to add. By shipping the paint in concentrated form and allowing end users to mix and dilute it as necessary, according to suppliers' instructions, manufacturers help to ensure that painters in any region and climate can get precisely the paint and mixture they need for best results.

In most cases, you will have to dilute concentrated paint with solvent (thinner or reducer) to yield a sprayable mixture. You must also add specific quantities

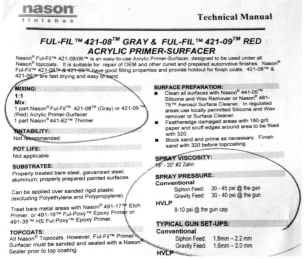

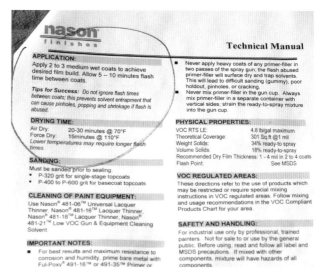

Information sheets (available from your paint dealer or the Internet) provide ample information about the various products used during a paint project. Some of the info may not be of interest to you, but the mixing information and the spray pressure are very important. I typically print one of these for the product I am using and then tape it on the wall near where I mix the primer or paint. All products vary somewhat, but the info is readily available, so there is no reason to attempt to remember all of it.

Just like the mixing and air pressure info, I usually tack a copy of the application info on the wall closer to where I am spraying. Knowing how many coats to apply and how much time to allow between coats is very important to success, whether you are spraying primer, sealer, color, or clear.

of hardener to those products that call for it. Be careful—once you mix in hardener, the hardening process begins. Catalyzed paint has a limited shelf life, which your paint system's instructions will explain.

Take the following steps to be sure you get the right paint mixture. First, read the instructions that came with the paint system. Next, read the instructions that came with your spray gun and air compressor. These two sources should give you a strong sense of the mixture ratio you'll need. Then, before you mix, run any questions you may have past the paint supplier from whom you got your paint. By checking and crosschecking in this manner, you'll be sure you have just the right mixture for your application, climate, and equipment.

For the mixing process itself, paint manufacturers have designed calibrated mixing sticks. According to the mixing directions, pour an amount of paint into a clean, empty can with straight sides (not a spray gun cup) up to a certain number located along one vertical column on that paint system's designated mixing stick. Then pour solvent in until the fluid level in the can rises to a corresponding number on the next column over on the same stick. Clear mixing cups with calibrations printed on them are used in the same manner as mixing sticks.

If you need a one-to-one ratio of paint to solvent, for example, pour paint into an empty mixing cup up to the number one or to the number one on a mixing stick. Then add reducer until the mixture reaches the number one on the next column over. If you need more paint for a large job, simply mix the ingredients up to a higher number—again, following the ratios your particular system and circumstances indicate.

If your paint system requires mixing paint, solvent, and hardener, it will use a mixing stick with three columns instead of two—one for each ingredient. Pour paint up to the desired number on the paint column, solvent to the appropriate number in that column, and hardener to its corresponding number.

Not all paint systems are based on a one-to-one ratio. By looking at a paint-mixing stick or mixing cup, you will see that sometimes the numbers on the reducer or hardener are not twice as high up the stick as those in the paint column. Measuring sticks and cups provide a very accurate way of mixing paint, solvent, and hardener. You must follow the manufacturer's recommendations and instructions to be assured of a quality blend.

Once you've blended your paint product, use the stir stick to swish the contents around in the mixing cup. Pointed tools, like screwdrivers, don't work well for stirring. You want something flat-bottomed, and rather

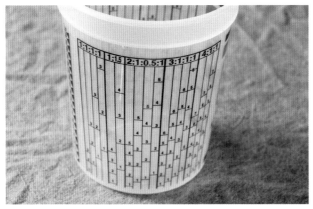

Most mixing cups include the most common primer and paint product mixing ratios on them, as shown between the bold lines. Determine the proper mixing ratio from the product's information sheet and then find that particular ratio on the cup. For instance, the product may say to mix two parts primer to one part reducer to 0.5 part hardener. Pour the first part (primer in this example) into the cup. You are going to have a total of 3.5 units of sprayable components, so don't pour in too much for the cup you are using. Note which line the primer comes to and then pour reducer in until the total rises to the same numbered line in the next column. Finally, add the hardener until the total rises to the corresponding number in the third column. Then stir until all components are thoroughly mixed.

wide—hence the stir stick. Stir for at least two minutes. Then place a paint filter over the opening of your spray gun cup and pour in the mixture. It is important that you never, repeat, *never*, pour paint into your spray gun cup without using some type of filter. An impurity passed into your gun could cause it to misspray or clog, creating a lot of extra work fixing the paint surface and your spray gun.

Your paint product is now ready for spraying. Be sure to put the caps back on containers of solvent and hardener, as well as paint. This will prevent unnecessary evaporation or accidental spillage.

In the paint booth, tack off your car or truck's surface immediately and then start painting. Some paint products and colors are designed with many heavy solids that could settle to the bottom of paint cups in just 10 to 15 minutes. If you were to take your time tacking and get distracted while your paint gun sat idle, solids could settle, possibly causing the color to change. This would be a catastrophe, especially with spot paint repairs.

SPRAY GUN MANEUVERING

You've secured two essential components for your project: good paint and a quality spray gun. But those essentials alone won't get you a great paint job. How you apply the paint is just as important. Spray paint

guns typically work best when held perpendicular to the surface being sprayed at a distance of 6 to 10 inches; check the recommendations for your particular spray gun. PPG's Refinish Manual has this caution for painters: "If the gun is tilted toward the surface, the fan pattern won't be uniform. If the gun is swung in an arc, varying the distance from the nozzle to the work, the paint will go on wetter (and thicker) where the nozzle is closer to the surface and drier (and thinner) where it is farther away." Should the outer layers of the thick, wetter paint dry before the inner layers, the solvent evaporating from within will cause defects in the finish. At the far end of the arc, the paint will go on too thin to provide adequate coverage, or may be too dry by the time it hits the surface, resulting in something more like overspray than a proper coat of paint.

About the only time painters do fan the paint gun is on small spot repaints. These spots call for full coverage in the center and less paint around their feathered perimeter where it blends with existing paint. This is done with wrist action to lightly blend edges only. Practice this technique on a test panel before attempting it on your car or truck.

Because automobile roofs, hoods, and trunk lids lie in a horizontal plane, you must hold the paint gun at a horizontal angle and make smooth, even, uniform passes. To prevent paint from dripping on the body, many painters tie an old tack cloth or other absorbent and lint-free rag around the top of the cup where it makes contact with its support base. Even with paint guns that are reported to be dripless, this is not a bad idea.

Holding the paint gun so that the nozzle is perpendicular to the surface is very important. Lock your wrist and elbow, and then walk along panels to ensure a right-angle position. Do not rely solely upon your arm to swing back and forth. Move your body with your arm and shoulder steadfastly anchored. Again, this takes practice, especially when you have to move from one panel to another in a smooth, steady, and even walk.

Even fan spray should overlap the previous spray by half. In other words, the center of the first pass should be directed along the masking line: half of the paint on the masking paper, the other half on the body surface. The second pass should be directed in such a way that the top of the fan rides right along the masking line. Then, each successive pass should overlap the previous one by half. Maneuver each pass with the same speed and at the same distance away from the surface: 6 to 10 inches.

Look at your painting results. If you have practiced with your equipment on an old hood or trunk lid, chances are good that your efforts are proving worthwhile. If not, you might be experiencing runs or other gross abnormalities. Runs are generally caused by too much paint landing on the surface at one time. You may be holding the gun too close or walking too slow. Whichever, you have to adjust. Keep practicing until the paint appears to go on smooth and even without running.

SPOT PAINTING

Whether your project involves a minor body repair or complete repaint, the rules of right-angle application and controlled spraying remain in effect. The difference is in the amount of paint needed and the technique for blending new paint into old finishes.

What you want to avoid when spot painting is a raised line separating the section you painted from the old surface. One way to get around this problem is to mask along a definite edge, groove, vinyl graphic, or stripe. Depending upon the type of paint you use and the prominence of the lip or raised paint edge, some delicate wet sanding could make the scar almost invisible. Professionals opt for a different method. First, they mask an edge or stopping point with tape rolled over upon itself.

Let's say that you want to spot paint a ding repair near the driver's side taillight on the quarter panel. You've masked along a piece of body side molding on the bottom of the panel and a design groove on the top. But, toward the front and back there are no definite breaking points. To solve this problem, lay a piece of masking paper at both the front and rear ends of the repair area as if they were going to cover more of the paint surface than needed. You affix the front tape edge of the piece toward the front, and the rear tape edge of the piece toward the rear.

Now, roll the paper over the tape edge so that only the sticky side of the tape is exposed. In other words, roll the front section of paper toward the front of the car, over the secured tape edge, and roll the rear section of paper toward the rear of the car. This leaves the repair area clear and both the front and rear areas masked with a strip of tape that has been rolled back over itself.

The purpose of this technique is to create a curved section of tape that paint can bounce off of and become overspray, with only a portion of it actually adhering to the surface. This prevents the paint from forming a well-defined line along the tape and helps it to feather into a great blend.

Now, to help that kind of situation even more, painters like to reduce paint to about a three-to-one ratio for melting. Once they've painted the spot, they will remove those rolled over strips of paper and tape, and then empty their paint gun cups to about ¼ inch full. To that, they add ¾ inch of reducer. This makes for a very hot mixture, a blend that will loosen earlier paint and allow just a tint of the new paint to melt in. The results are great, as it is difficult to find where the new paint starts and the old paint leaves off. If any nibs remain, you can wet sand them smooth, unless you've used uncatalyzed enamel paint.

The most important thing to remember about spot painting is that a valley has to be filled from where you removed the old paint and sealer. It might only be one to three mils deep, but nevertheless, it has to be filled if the overall surface is to be flat, even, and smooth. New sealer and primer-surfacer will fill up most of the valley, with paint filling in the rest and then blending with the adjacent surface.

The reducer-rich paint mixture literally opens up the existing paint to let a touch of new pigments fall into place and blend with the old. This is the very last step of a paint job, after the appropriate flash time has passed for the final spray paint pass for the center of the repaint.

Warning! Before attempting this kind of spot repair technique on your car, confirm its value with your auto body paint and supply specialist. It works great for some urethanes and lacquers, but may not fare so well with certain enamels. It all depends on the brand and type of product you use, the paint currently on your car, the color, and what additives, like metallic or pearl, are involved. There is no clear-cut rule to follow and each case is unique.

FLASH TIMES

Paint dries as its solvents evaporate and its pigments cure. You cannot spray additional coats until the solvents from the first coat, and each successive coat, have had adequate time to evaporate. This is critical! If you spray a new coat of paint over one that has not had time to flash (dry), you'll trap solvents underneath the new layer. But they will not remain harmlessly in place. Instead, they will pass through the overlying material causing blistering, checking, crazing, cracking, dulling, lifting, sagging, or other such imperfections on the top coat.

Flash times are clearly indicated on all information sheets and application guides for all paint products. Second and final coats may require longer flash times than initial coats. Read and follow the directions for the individual paint system employed. They are not all the same. This goes for undercoats, top coats, and clear coats.

FULL PANEL PAINTING

Automobile and paint manufacturers advise auto painters to repaint complete sides of certain cars, even if the only problem area is minor body repair on a single panel. As ridiculous as this sounds, there is a method to the madness. This type of overkill repaint involves those vehicles factory-painted with pearl or other special additives. Tri-coat or candy finishes are also extremely difficult to match with new paint because of the complex interplay of coatings that produce the finish's unique look.

To find out whether your finish is amenable to spot painting—new-style paint schemes are more likely to be difficult—check with your local auto body paint and supply store.

Painting just a panel or two is generally no big deal with noncustom paint products. Masking can begin and end on definite body design breaks. You can see what has to be painted and know that virtually everything else has to be masked. But, what if your car or truck is a little on the old side and you are concerned about matching the new color with the old? Who wants a door and fender to look like new, while the quarter panel, hood, and roof look old and oxidized?

Many times, a complete buff job on old paint surfaces makes them look as if new paint was just sprayed onto doors and fenders. In other cases, you must spray a blend to feather in between the new paint and the old.

Feathering-in is similar to the melting-in process described earlier: melting-in describes this process on a single panel, whereas feathering blends surrounding panels to match the one that was repaired or refinished. After a panel is completely painted, remove the masking from surrounding panels and spray a light coating of heavily reduced paint and reducer onto the existing paint. This works well for certain products, but not at all for others. Check with your auto body paint supplier to see if your new paint can be feathered into the existing paint in this manner.

To blend in panels with compatible paint finishes, painters complete their main job and then take off strips of masking from adjoining panels. With a heavily reduced paint mix, they gently melt in a feathered edge. These edges may extend out to 6 inches. When the paint finishes are incompatible for melting, painters must rely on a perfect color match between adjacent panels.

If you want a multicolor paint job, or custom touches like flames or scallops, refer to Chapter 8, Extra Details. Although they can be added later, you may be better off including them as part of the original paint scheme. Pinstriping, lettering, and other graphics are also discussed in Chapter 8.

CLEAR COAT FINISHES

Along with offering better protection for metallics and other paints, clear coats reduce the amount of color material needed for a good finish, thus reducing some of the overall solvent needed and helping manufacturers stay within governmental guidelines. Clear coat finishes are also good for smoothing out sharp paint lines left

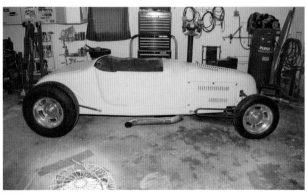

After waiting the proper amount of time for the base coat to dry, a couple of coats of clear were applied to the Track T components. It was then reassembled so that the scallops could be laid out and applied. It's difficult to tell in the photos, but even after just a couple of coats of clear, the paint was noticeably glossier. The real shine will come after wet sanding and buffing.

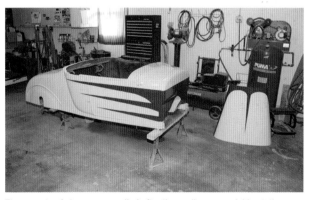

Three coats of clear were applied after the scallops were laid out, the vehicle disassembled, and the scallops painted. Make sure you allow the proper flash time between coats and the proper amount of time between the last coat and the taping process (a.k.a. time to tape).

SPRAYING COLOR

When spraying color, the main goal is to obtain even and complete coverage. If you do much painting, you will find that some colors "cover" better than others, requiring only one or two coats, while others may require three or more coats. Whether you are spraying single stage, base coat/clear coat, or tri-stage, even and complete coverage will be important. To obtain this, you may have to bend over, get down on one knee, or perhaps even roll around on a creeper to access all panels that are to be painted. Having adequate light in your workspace will help to ensure that you can see if everything is covered adequately.

Make sure that you stir the paint adequately during mixing and then again prior to pouring it into your paint cup. Stir each refill as well. Spray a test pattern on a piece of cardboard or masking paper and adjust your spray gun as necessary. Keep your spray gun nozzle perpendicular to the surface and about 8 inches away.

I was always taught to paint the edges of a panel first, and then paint the middle of the panel. If you paint the middle first, it will end up with overspray on it when you paint the edges, but if you do the edges first, you will quickly blend in the little bit of overspray that may have landed on the middle. This applies to spraying primer, color, or clear.

Color of any type will go on with a shine, but will dull down as the paint flashes. For this reason, it is imperative to develop a systematic method for painting all of the pieces and parts, whether they are apart to be assembled later, or already on the vehicle. However, you should not always stop and start in the exact same place. If you are using base coat/clear coat or tri-stage, apply as many coats as it takes to achieve coverage, but don't worry about gloss. That will come with the clear.

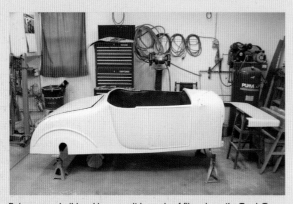

Being a new build and because it is made of fiberglass, the Track T body was easy enough to remove from the chassis for primer and paint, requiring very little masking. This also made it easy to move after painting. If you are painting a vehicle that is still drivable, park it as close to the middle of your workspace as possible. If it is a low-profile vehicle, consider driving it up on ramps or setting it on jack stands so that you can more easily see and access the lowest portions of the body. You can always stand on a ladder if necessary to paint the roof.

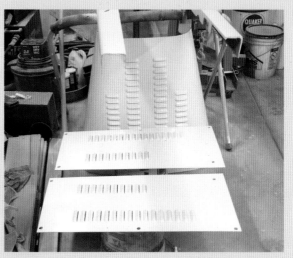

Having as much light as possible and plenty of room for maneuverability is important toward achieving complete and even coverage. These pieces have already been painted and moved (carefully) out of the way to fully cure.

behind along custom graphic paint edges. Painters also use clear to help feather in repaints along adjacent panels and old paint perimeters.

Applying clear is no different from applying other paints. You have to maintain a close eye on your work so that each pass is uniform. Exterior body parts, like door handles and key locks, can be masked for clear paint applications without as much concern about overspray blemishes as with color coats. This is because it dries to a clear, invisible finish. Beware not to spray clear until the last color coat has dried for the recommended period. Spraying clear too early will trap the color coat's solvents and lead to the same finish problems described in the Flash Times section.

TRI-STAGE FINISHES

Originally reserved for custom jobs or high-end vehicles, tri-stage paint systems are becoming more common. Whether custom or original, tri-stage finishes include a base coat, color coat, and clear coat. The base coat gives the color coat a compatible base and also influences its appearance. For example, a purple coat sprayed over a silver base has a different tint than the same color sprayed over a white base.

As you would with any other paint, apply base coats to cover all intended new paint surfaces. After the recommended flash time has elapsed, spray on color coat using the techniques described earlier. When you've sprayed the correct number of color coats and the proper flash time has passed, proceed to the clear coat stage. Be sure to clean your spray gun according to the methods described earlier, and the paint and spray gun manufacturers' instructions.

Once the final coat of clear has dried for the recommended period, you will be able to wet sand blemishes and buff areas that need extra polishing. The clear coat finish will prevent wet sanding or polishing from distorting the blended color achieved between the base coat and color coat.

PLASTIC OR FLEXIBLE ASSEMBLIES

A great many different kinds of plastics are used today on all types of automobile parts and assemblies. They range from Acrylonitrile Butadiene Styrene (ABS) to Thermoplastic Olefin (TPO) and Sheet Molded Compounds (SMC) to Reaction Injection Molded Plastic (RIM). Each has its own place, from rigid grillework sections to flexible bumper covers.

If you use lacquer or enamel paint, such as on a vintage restoration, spray any flexible components with paint containing a special additive that allows it to flex along with the part. You may also have to use special undercoats in addition to top coat additives. The only way to be certain that the products you use are compatible and designed for painting the parts you intend to spray is to check with your auto body paint and supply specialist. If you are using a base coat/clear coat paint system, however, flex additives are no longer necessary due to the flexible characteristics of today's urethane products.

The same caution applies to rigid plastics. Some materials are compatible with normal painting systems, while others may require specific undercoats. By using the designed paint system and proper additives, along with the recommended preparation techniques, you will be assured that newly applied paint coats will not peel, crack, or flake off. In rare cases, you cannot repaint certain solvent-sensitive plastic or urethane parts when the factory primer seal has been broken. In those situations, you have to replace the parts.

AFTER SPRAYING PAINT

Once you've painted the vehicle to your satisfaction, you need to complete several further tasks to ensure the overall quality of the job. Once the paint has dried sufficiently, you must wet sand nibs smooth and carefully remove the masking tape to prevent unnecessary paint edge peeling or other accidental finish damage. Read the sections on wet sanding and buffing before removing any masking material.

Uncatalyzed enamels cannot withstand wet sanding or polishing. With this kind of paint system, what you see is what you get, unless you later decide to sand a completely cured but blemished panel down to the substrate and repaint it to perfection.

Certain lacquer and urethane paint finishes can be wet sanded and polished to remove nibs, flatten orange peel, and otherwise smooth small blemishes. This work is normally done on clear coats, as opposed to actual color coats, and may require additional light applications of clear. For this reason, professionals seldom remove masking material until they are pleased with the entire paint job and are satisfied that they've remedied all imperfections.

Drying Times

Automotive paint has to dry. If not allowed to do so in a clean environment, the wet finish can be contaminated by dust, dirt, or other debris. Professional painters always leave freshly sprayed vehicles in paint booths until enough time has elapsed for the material to cure completely, according to the paint manufacturer's recommendations.

PPG recommends their DCC Acrylic Urethane paint systems be allowed to dry 6–8 hours at 70 degrees Fahrenheit, or be force-dried for 40 minutes at 140 degrees Fahrenheit. Force drying requires portable infrared heaters or high-tech paint booths equipped with heating units. For its Deltron Base coat and Clear coat systems, PPG lists specific drying times for air drying, as well as force drying, each of the system's components. As stressed earlier, proper drying is essential to prevent trapped solvents from damaging future coats.

Factory paint jobs with urethane paint products and those that are suitable for force drying are baked on body surfaces at temperatures around 450 degrees Fahrenheit. This can be accomplished only while cars are in a stripped condition. Otherwise, plastic, rubber, and vinyl parts melt. Cars still equipped with these items cannot be force-dried at temperatures above 160 degrees Fahrenheit. Excessive heat can also damage the vehicle's computer.

There are other factors you must consider when using heat lamps and other force-dry methods. Initial flash times are extremely important. Most paint products must air dry for 15 minutes or longer on their own to let the bulk of their solvent material evaporate. Too much heat too soon will evaporate this solvent too quickly, causing blemishes.

Some paint finishes have a window of time during which you must wet sand or recoat. Wait beyond that period and you may have to scuff sand and clean the surface again, before applying touch up coats to get proper adhesion.

Wet Sanding

You must confirm ahead of time that the paint system you use is compatible with wet sanding. Your auto body paint and supply professional can do this while you are discussing your paint needs at the time of purchase. Each automotive paint manufacturer has its own set of recommended guidelines it advises painters to follow. What may be good for PPG's Deltron system may not be so good for a BASF or DuPont system. In fact, you might even be advised to completely disregard wet sanding and opt instead for polishing to guarantee a perfect finish with the type of product that you have chosen to use.

Not every type of paint system can be wet sanded. Enamels, for example, cure with a sort of film on their surfaces, which becomes damaged if broken by sandpaper or harsh polish.

Sand lacquers and some urethane products with fine sandpaper soon after they have cured. Although it is not recommended that you wet sand color coats, you might be able to lightly sand off nibs, providing you are prepared to touch up the spots with a light color coat. Wet sanding yields its best results on clear coats that are then polished.

Base coat/clear coat paint systems generally call for a number of color coats and then clear coats. Especially with candy finishes, sanding directly on the color surface distorts the tint and causes visible blemishes. Wet sanding for them is done on clear coats only. Your wet sanding efforts should be concentrated on clear coats in order to not disturb the underlying color coats. Wet sanding clear coats will bring out a much deeper shine and gloss when followed by controlled buffing and polishing.

Painters use very fine 1,500- to 2,500-grit sandpaper with water to smooth or remove minor blemishes on cured paint finishes designed to allow wet sanding. Only sandpaper designated wet or dry must be used, however. Those kinds that are not waterproof will fall apart and be useless.

As with all other sanding tasks, you have to use a sanding block. Since nibs of dirt or dust are small, fold sandpaper around a wooden paint stir stick instead of using a large hand block. Their 1-inch width is great for smoothing small spots. Use only light pressure for this type of delicate sanding. Be sure to dip sandpaper in a bucket of water frequently to keep the paint surface wet and reduce the amount of material buildup on the sandpaper. Add a small amount of mild car washing soap to the water bucket to provide lubrication to the sandpaper. Allow the sandpaper to soak in water for 15 minutes before wet sanding.

If certain blemished areas need a lot of sanding, you may need to apply new coats of clear. This is why you should leave masking material in place during wet sanding.

In some cases such as on show cars, the entire car body may be wet sanded to bring out the richest, deepest, and most lustrous shine possible. Because they anticipate extensive wet sanding and polishing operations, painters of these cars make sure that they have applied plenty of clear coats.

Removing Masking Material

To many enthusiastic automobile painters, removing masking paper and tape to reveal a new paint job or quality spot paint repair is like opening birthday presents. It is always a pleasure to see a finished product, especially after viewing it in primer for any length of time. However, unlike the wrapping paper on presents, masking materials must be removed in a controlled manner to prevent finish damage.

As we've discussed, paints have solids in them that build up on car bodies. Especially on jobs where numerous color and clear coats were applied, the thickness of the paint can bridge the lips along masking tape edges. What will occur, in some situations, is the formation of a paint film on a car body that continues over to include the top of the tape. If you pull the tape straight up, it could tear flakes of paint from the body surface.

To prevent paint flaking or peeling along the edge of masking tape strips, painters pull tape away from the newly painted body area (as opposed to straight up off the panel), and back upon itself to create a sharp angle at the point tape leaves the surface. This sharp angle can cut extra-thin paint films so they don't cause flakes or cracks on the finish.

When they've applied several color and clear coats along a masked edge, meticulous painters often use a sharp razor blade to cut the paint film between the panel surface and tape edge. If you damage the paint while removing the masking material, you will have to sand and repaint as needed.

As a basic rule of thumb, most paint products that are catalyzed (has hardener added when the paint is being mixed with reducer just prior to application) can be wet sanded and buffed. As some products can be buffed after just 24 hours and others require 90 days, you should verify the necessary requirements with your paint supplier.

To remove evidence of wet sanding, finishes are rubbed out or buffed with fine buffing or polishing compound. This work also brings out more shine and luster as well as flattening slight hints of orange peel. For spot painting or single-panel jobs, polishing adjacent body sections may be desperately needed to bring their lightly oxidized surfaces back to the point where they shine as brilliantly as the new paint.

As meticulous as you were while masking, there may be a few body parts that exhibit signs of overspray. Before putting all of the dismantled exterior body parts back on, you might consider removing obvious overspray and then repaint those affected areas with a proper color. In some cases, such as on fenderwells, you could get away with just new coats of black paint or undercoating material. A task of this nature would be easier to accomplish while masking is still in place on the vehicle.

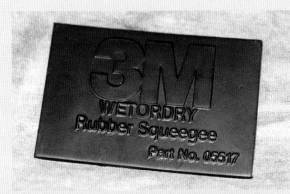

When wet sanding after applying clear, it is still important for the sandpaper to have even pressure, so a sanding block of some type is still necessary. Rather than using a long board or other large sanding block, use a rubber squeegee such as this. Because it's flexible and only about 3x4 inches, it works well for surfaces of most any contour.

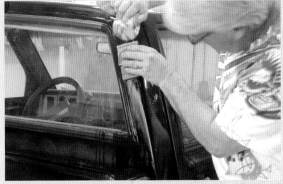

If you do not have access to a DA, or for areas that are too small for using a DA, use a squeegee with 1,000-, 1,500-, and 2,000-grit sandpaper, with lots of clean water to wet sand the newly painted surface smooth. Verify that you have waited the appropriate amount of time for the paint to cure prior to doing this. Refer to the instruction sheets for the specific top coats you are using to determine this information.

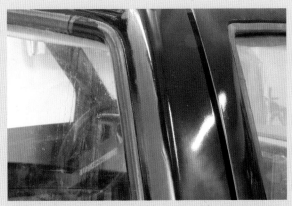

The gray area in this photo shows where the B-pillar has been wet sanded. It looks very gray, but is very smooth at this point. Buffing and polishing will bring back the color. You must verify that you do not sand through the clear, however.

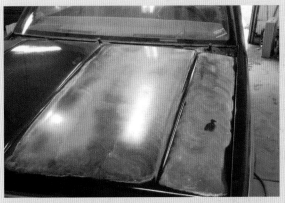

If you are fortunate enough to have access to a DA (Thanks, Bones), the wet sanding process will go much easier. Unless you are using 3,000-grit or finer sanding material, water is not required for this process. Simply use a light touch with the DA and 1,500-grit paper. Do not run the DA at full speed and be careful sanding on edges or curves, so that you do not burn through the clear, into the paint.

PAINT APPLICATION

Rub Out and Buffing

As with wet sanding, not every type of paint system can stand up to vigorous polishing or rubbing out. With single-stage urethane, for example, buffing with a gritty compound only dulls the surface and ruins the finish. In contrast, polishing a catalyzed urethane (base coat/clear coat) or cured lacquer makes the finishes much more brilliant, lustrous, and deep shining.

A wide variety of polishing compounds are available for new paint finishes. Auto body paint and supply stores carry the largest selection. Some are designed to be used by hand, while others can safely be polished with buffing machines. Foam pads work best with prescribed compounds and buffing machines limited to slower rpm, while pads made with cloth material are better suited for other compounds and machine speeds. Be sure to get what is appropriate for your paint.

PPG manufacturers its own brand of rubbing and polishing compounds for its paints. In addition, companies such as 3M and Meguiar's produce several varieties of polishing products, all of which carry labels with specific instructions for their intended use and application.

Basically, rubbing compounds include relatively coarse polishing grit material. They are designed to quickly remove blemishes and flatten paint finishes. Because these compounds contain grit, they will leave behind light scratches or swirls. Therefore, after using compound to flatten orange peel or produce a higher surface luster, you will need to buff or polish the paint finish with a very fine grit material. Especially with dark colors, this may involve exceptionally soft finish-buffing pads and wax.

As refinish products have changed over the years, some ideas that seem like common sense are no longer valid. Manufacturers of the new urethane paint products often suggest polishing with 2,000-grit compound using a foam pad. This should minimize swirls and yield a satisfactory finish the first time around. If swirls are still present, return to a slightly coarser compound to remove the swirls, then use the finer 2,000-grit again. With older technology, painters began with the coarse rubbing compound, then worked up to the finer stuff, instead of this seemingly backward procedure.

Although paint finishes may appear dry, especially those that include a hardening agent, they may not be ready for buffing right away. You must allow sufficient time for all solvents to evaporate before smothering them with polishing compound. Application guides and information sheets will generally list the recommended time. The information sheet for PPG's Polyurethane clear, for example, states, "Allow 16 hours before polishing either air-dried or force-dried DCU 2021."

By hand, use a soft, clean cloth for rubbing out and polishing and follow directions on the product label. Many auto enthusiasts apply polish in straight back-and-forth movements from the front to back of vehicles, instead of circular patterns. They profess that polishing panels in this manner greatly reduces their chances for creating swirls.

You need experience practicing with a buffing machine before using it on your car's new paint job. Practicing helps you avoid a paint burn—polishing through the paint finish down to primer or bare metal. Buffers with maximum speeds of about 1,450 rpm are best for novices. Machines with faster revolutions require more experience. Be aware that even the slower 1,450-rpm buffers are quite capable of causing paint burns if you don't pay close attention to what you're doing.

To use a buffer, first spread out a few strips of compound parallel to the floor about 4 to 6 inches apart. Cover an area no bigger than 2 square feet. Operate the buffing pad on top of a compound strip and work it over that strip's area, gradually moving down to pick up successive strips. The idea is to buff a 2-square-foot area while not allowing the pad to run dry of compound. Keep buffing on that body section until the compound is gone and all that remains is shiny paint.

Buffing pads can be operated back and forth, as well as up and down. Always keep them moving. Just as with power sanders, a buffer left in one spot can rub through the paint. Be exceptionally careful buffing near ridges, gaps, and corners. If you hit those surfaces with the buffer, all of the buffing force is expended on a very small, focused area and it will burn through the paint very quickly. Instead of running the buffing pad on top of ridges, run it just up to their edge and stop. Some painters prefer to mask edges, ridges, and corners with strips of masking tape to protect them against accidental buffing burns, and then remove the tape and buff them by hand. This might be a good idea for the novice.

If you have to buff in tight areas, such as near door handles, throttle the machine on and off to lower the rpm speed. Slowing the pad in this way will help to reduce the possibility of paint burns. Be sure to spread plenty of compound over the area. For extra-confined spaces, apply compound by hand with a soft, damp cloth.

Make sure you don't drag power cords for electric buffers and air hoses for pneumatic models over the paint finish. A good way to keep them under control while buffing roofs, hoods, and trunk lids is to drape them over your shoulder. Wear an apron to prevent buckles, zippers, snaps, or rivets on your clothing from scratching the car as you move alongside it. A long sweatshirt may also work. If possible, simply avoid clothing with these hard, sharp features.

Power buffers throw spots of compound all over your car, clothes, and nearby surfaces. Be prepared for this kind of mess by covering adjacent cabinets or workbench items with tarps or drop cloths. Always wipe buffing compound thrown by the buffer off the paint as soon as possible, as it can damage the new paint if it is allowed to dry.

As cloth buffing pads become covered with compound (or every three passes—whichever comes first), use a pad spur to clean them. With the pad spinning, gently but securely push a spur into the pad's nap. This breaks loose compound and forces it out of the pad. You will be surprised at how much material comes off of pads, so be sure to do your pad cleaning away from your car and anything else that you don't want covered with compound or pad lint. You cannot clean the buffing pads too much.

Overspray

Polishing and buffing efforts usually work well to remove very light traces of overspray from hoods, roofs, and trunk lids. Extra-heavy overspray residue may require a strong polishing compound for complete removal. For severe problems, consult your auto body paint and supply professional.

If you've been meticulous with your masking, most overspray problems, if any, will involve items such as tailpipes, fender wells, horn units, and other low down pieces. You could spend a lot of time removing overspray from painted items, like fender wells, or spend a lot less by simply covering overspray with black paint or undercoat. If this won't work for some reason, e.g., a show car with matching-color fender wells, you'll have to sand, polish, or possibly even repaint affected areas.

Overspray on chrome is easily removed with a chrome polish, like Simichrome. Heavy concentrations may require number 0000 steel wool with polish. Chrome items commonly prone to overspray include

tailpipes, wheels, bumpers, grille pieces, and trim. The best way to avoid overspray problems on these accessories is to mask them properly with plenty of tape to secure paper edges so puffs of paint spray cannot infiltrate the masked space.

Remove paint overspray from glass using the solvent appropriate to the vehicle's paint system. Dab some solvent on a clean cloth and rub off overspray. If that does not work, try using number 0000 or finer steel wool and solvent. In extreme cases, you might have to use a razor blade and a delicate touch to scrape overspray off glass.

Caution: Some newer windshields are made with acrylic ingredients that even fine steel wool may scratch. If you are not sure whether your car's windshield is solid glass or an acrylic, check with a dealership service department, auto glass business, or your auto body paint and supply professional.

OVERVIEW

The way the paint looks on your vehicle depends on what happens before you spray it, and afterward. To get the results your hard work deserves, make sure the surface is perfectly flat, smooth, and free of dirt and particles before you spray. Have the painting steps and drying times within reach throughout the process so you can keep track of what you've done, what comes next, and how much time you have to do it.

Take your time to smooth nibs with fine 1,200-grit wet sandpaper. Use a sanding block with plenty of water. Be prepared too, in those wet sanding instances, to buff out or polish the spots smoothed with sandpaper. Polish will remove sanding scratches to leave the surface blemish-free and looking crisp.

Practice with a buffing machine and avoid ridges and other surfaces that concentrate the machine's power over a very small area. Be sure to remove spattered rubbing compound so it doesn't create blemishes when it dries. With masking paper still in place, you can add light coats of clear as necessary, or touch up spots that need that kind of attention. This is essentially your last chance to fix mistakes or repair blemishes.

By all means, take your time removing masking paper and tape. Be certain to pull tape at an angle away from the newly painted surface and also at a sharp angle over itself to prevent damage to the adjoining paint. Where paint coats are numerous and consequently thick, have a sharp razor blade handy to cut paint that may look like it is ready to peel off with the tape.

If you are using buffing compound that can be applied by hand, use a back-and-forth motion. This will help prevent swirls and when you are buffing by hand, you should do whatever you can to minimize your work.

Power buffers will throw spots of compound all over your car, clothes, and nearby surfaces. Be prepared for this kind of mess by covering adjacent cabinets or workbench items with tarps or drop cloths. Always wipe buffing compound thrown by the buffer off the paint as soon as possible, as it can damage the new paint if it is allowed to dry.

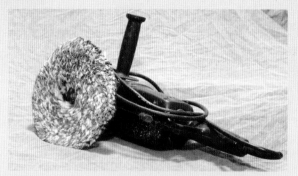

This buffer is the same electric sander seen elsewhere in this book. With the sanding disc removed and a polishing bonnet installed, it serves two purposes. When shopping for a buffer, look for one that is variable speed.

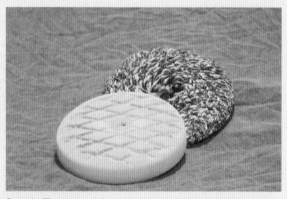

Some buffing compounds are designed to be used with foam pads (typically as a higher speed), while other buffing compounds are designed to be used with cloth pads (typically at a lower speed). Be sure to read the directions for whichever compound you are using so that you can select the correct type of buffing pad.

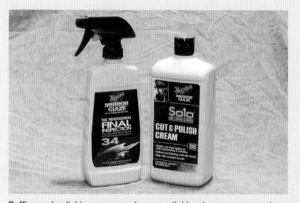

Buffing and polishing compounds are available wherever you purchase your painting supplies. With the ever-changing paint products and buffing compounds on the market, an auto body or paint supply employee should be able to suggest the best buffing and polishing products for the paint products you are using. These products from Meguiars are what I used on the Track T and were easy to use.

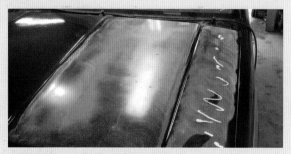

After wet-sanding the clear (with or without a DA), it must be buffed to bring out the shine. Use your favorite cut-and-polish-type cream to remove any remaining scratches from the painted surface. Apply the polishing compound as directed by the specific product, then use the specified type of pad on your buffer to spread the compound.

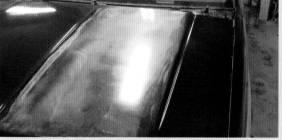

Some products may call for a final glaze to be applied after the compound. Each product will usually require a different type pad. In this photo, we see the final painted and cleared surface of the hood on the left. It has been wet-sanded in the middle, and finally buffed and polished on the right. After about 30 days, the entire vehicle will be washed and waxed for protection from the elements. Waiting 30 days allows the paint to continue to breathe and cure completely.

PAINT APPLICATION

Chapter 8
Extra Details

It's best to decide whether you're going to paint your vehicle in one color, multiple colors, or with flames or scallops before you buy your paint, yet nothing says you can't add these extras later. Either way, you should concentrate on getting the vehicle painted properly before you add additional colors or graphics.

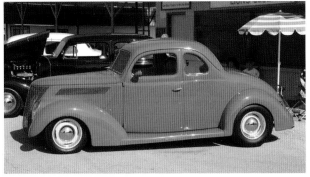

This orange 1937 Ford features a simple but tasteful paint job using one color, but then contrasting it with a neutral color for the wheels. If this were a monochrome paint job, the door handles, wheels, and wheel trim (caps and rings) would be painted the same color as the body. This example seems to be significantly more stylish and less likely to become a vanishing trend.

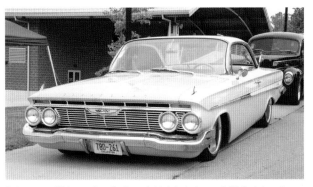

Not every vehicle needs a flashy paint job to look great. While I do not know if this is a stock color for this particular vehicle, it projects that image when combined with the stock trim intact. The paint job is fantastic, and proves that subtlety sometimes is the way to go.

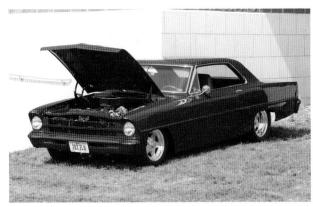

Contrary to the previous two examples, this red hot Nova is quite noticeable due to its eye-searing paint. On a true monochromatic paint job (somewhat popular in the 1980s), even the wheels would be the same color as the body. This example is certainly more tasteful by having the polished wheels to provide a little sparkle.

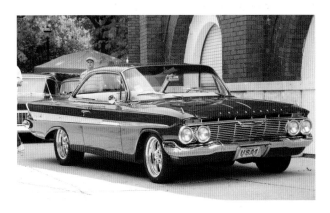

Looking much like something that would have been seen on the showroom floor in the early 1960s, this Chevrolet captures the essence of those mid-century days when new automobiles were exciting. Shiny paint, lots of chrome trim (that was real chrome), and American muscle under the hood.

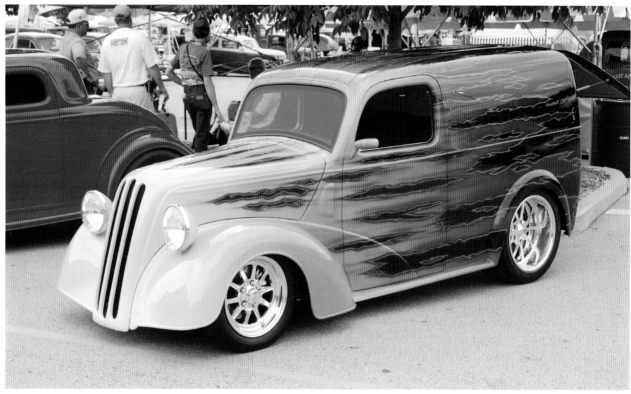

This paint job is a little more complicated than the one in the previous photo. There are multiple ways to go about laying this out, and they all require quite a bit of masking and potentially some labor-intensive airbrush work. No doubt about it, though—this 1948 English Ford Thames grabs your attention.

Realize that anything other than a monotone (one-color) paint job will require more work. Except when doing detailed airbrush work, you'll have to mask the entire vehicle for each color of paint you spray. If you have masked the vehicle properly one time, you can do it again, but this may be more than the first-time car painter wants to try.

I highly recommend a base coat/clear coat paint system if you choose a paint scheme of more than one color. That way you can apply two coats of clear over the first color. If you get any overspray from the second color on the first, you can sand it out of the clear without damaging the underlying color coat. After applying the second color (and third, if applicable), apply two or three additional coats of clear over the entire vehicle.

Flash and drying times are also critical to a successful multicolor paint job. Applying masking tape or masking paper to freshly painted surfaces that have not yet dried adequately will cause you much more work. Product information sheets will provide a specified time to allow the paint to dry before taping. Likewise, clear coats must be added within a specified time, or the base coat will need to be scuffed and additional base coats added.

PART OF THE PAINT SCHEME

Flames, scallops, or a multicolor paint job, such as the tri-color paint schemes from the 1950s, are usually considered part of the overall plan. Although any of these can actually be added after the initial paint application, they would still be considered part of the paint scheme when describing the car to someone. Graphics, on the other hand, are often added later. Even when graphics

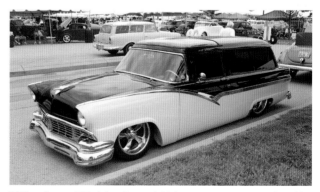

While yellow and black two-tone paint jobs were very common when this station wagon was new, these colors are certainly more vibrant than the originals. Notice how the combination of dark-tinted windows and black paint on the upper body accentuate the low stance.

are painted on, their application is somewhat different from the main body surface paint.

Multicolor Paint Schemes

If you are repainting a vehicle that originally featured a two-tone paint scheme, it may seem natural to include the second color this time around as well. If that is the case, you should study your vehicle very closely before removing or priming over any of the existing paint. Where does the primary color stop and the secondary color start? Is there a piece of trim that covers this seam, and will that trim piece still be used after the paint job? Does the trim cover all of the paint seam, or is some of it left out in the open? Which color are the doorjambs? How well you duplicate the original color transitions

will have a great impact on your overall paint job. It is better to have a high-quality monochrome paint job than a mediocre two-tone finish.

Whether you are duplicating a stock paint scheme or developing one of your own, look at other vehicles that are two-tone to see where the paint colors change. Graphics are a different story, but on a normal two-tone paint scheme, the colors almost always change underneath a piece of trim, or at a body line, rather than in the middle of an otherwise uninterrupted body surface.

Think about how you would mask the area that is to be a different color and realize that it should be the same on both sides of the vehicle. This will help you realize that you need to take advantage of body lines and

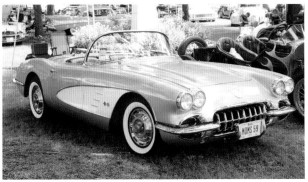

Some cars just beg for the stock look more than others. For one of these early Corvettes, the cove area really needs a second color to set the car off. Not all Corvettes have the second color, which is fine. Still, when you are looking for a way to make your car stand out, this will do it.

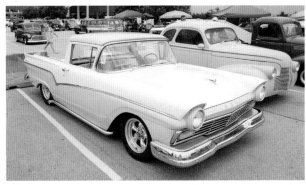

This Ford Ranchero makes good use of the stock-style trim to conceal the edges of the different paint colors. That is the main reason that the trim was there in the first place, so avoid trying to buck the system. Breaking the colors on this car anywhere but under the trim simply doesn't make sense.

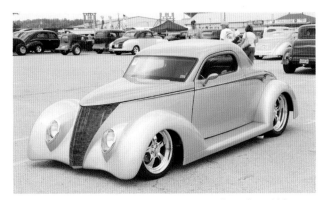

Chrome and stainless trim was not as common on the earlier vehicles, such as this 1937 Ford. That allows the painter to be more creative with paint breaks; however, making those breaks along body lines usually provides the best results. You should work to accentuate the vehicle's body lines, rather than fight them.

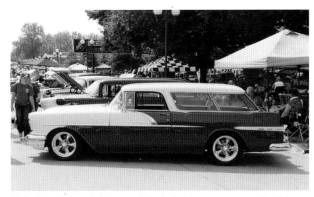

While the colors probably are not stock, they are a good example of the types of combinations of paint schemes common in the 1950s and 1960s. Back then, paints were simply solid colors. Now they can include metallics, pearls, and candies to make those once boring multicolor paint jobs exciting again.

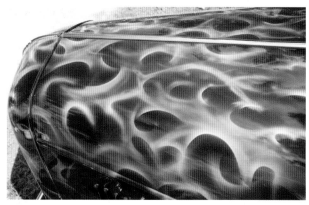

Red, orange, and yellow flames on a black hot rod have always been traditional. However, these flames are known as "realistic flames" as they more closely resemble an actual fire. Any style of flames takes some practice to look good, but these realistic flames are far more difficult than traditional flames.

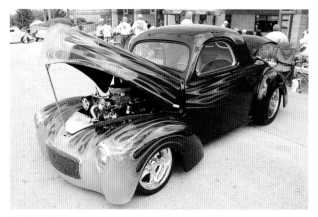

Traditional flames also include warm colors on a dark background and, with the right combination, can be applied to most any background color with good results. Having a good eye for compatible colors and for layout makes a big difference in the appeal of any set of flames or other graphics.

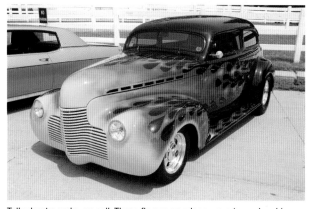

Talk about a wake-up call. These flames go a long ways toward making this otherwise black sedan become a standout. Many people would not look at this rod twice if not for the flames. They are tastefully done, use traditional colors, and transition well.

natural breaks when designing a two-tone paint scheme. If you are going to be hiding a paint seam under a piece of trim, be sure to split the width of the trim evenly with each color. If the trim is an inch wide, this leaves a half-inch for each color. You should be able to align the trim accurately enough to cover this; however, if the trim is narrower, you will have less room for error in masking or trim installation.

It doesn't really matter which color of a two-tone paint scheme you paint first, though many painters would paint the portion that's easiest to mask first, so that once it's painted, they can mask it off quickly and proceed to the second color. For example, if you were painting a large four-door sedan maroon, with a dark gray secondary color below a body line that runs approximately through the middle of the doors, it might be easier to paint the lower area, mask it off, and then paint the rest of the car, rather than painting the top, hood, trunk, and half the doors, and then masking all of that off to paint the lower portion. While painting the gray area, you would mask the color boundary with masking tape and the bulk of the car with plastic masking material. Once painted, you would mask the gray area with masking paper and tape.

A couple of other situations may call for a multicolor paint job performed after the initial paint application. Commercial vehicles, for example, have custom paintwork on top of the manufacturer's paint. For large national accounts, vehicle manufacturers usually paint the vehicles as required by the purchasing company; however, smaller companies are required to make their own paint additions. For this type of job, you must first identify the original paint. Clean the area to be painted with wax and grease remover, then scuff the original paint with 1,000–1,200-grit sandpaper; clean again with wax and grease remover. Masking is as required for the company scheme, sprayed in a paint compatible with the original finish.

Another sort of multicolor paint job involves repainting only one of the two colors to freshen up the finish. For example, the lower color might be chipped and dinged, while the upper color remains virtually flawless.

Flames

On the right vehicle, flames that are laid out properly, utilize the right colors, and are applied properly look great. However, there are probably more flamed paint jobs that don't look as good as anticipated. Some flames look good, some don't, while others are purely hideous.

If you are having any doubts about the proper flame layout or colors to use, avoid them completely . . . or at least until you feel that you can't live without them any longer. There is simply no reason to deface a great paint job by applying a mediocre set of flames.

If you are contemplating flames for your hot rod or road rocket, it is a good idea to check out vehicles similar to yours that have flames. The first goal is to find a pattern or layout that you like. Although flames are not required to be perfectly symmetrical, they should be balanced from one side to the other in their layout and intensity.

Flame patterns can be long and narrow, or big and bold with short tips. Choose what looks best to you and flows with the lines of your vehicle. Remember that real flames would naturally be progressing upward if the burning object were sitting still, or toward the back if moving. Therefore, don't aim flames downward

or toward the front of your car—you laugh, but there are examples of both cases!

When flames will extend across more than one body panel, assemble the panels prior to painting in the exact spots where they'll remain after final assembly. If you don't do this, your final panel adjustments—to get everything to open and close smoothly and the panel gaps even—will pull your paint scheme out of alignment. You don't want to have to choose between a misaligned paint job and a hood that won't shut right.

To balance the flame layout from one side to the other, you must find the centerline of the vehicle. Run a strip of ⅛ inch Fine Line tape down this centerline from the front to the back of the vehicle. If the flames will be extending in multiple layers across a large area, such as a hood or roof, this large panel should be sectioned off with tape running from side to side. The length of the flame tips can be balanced in this manner.

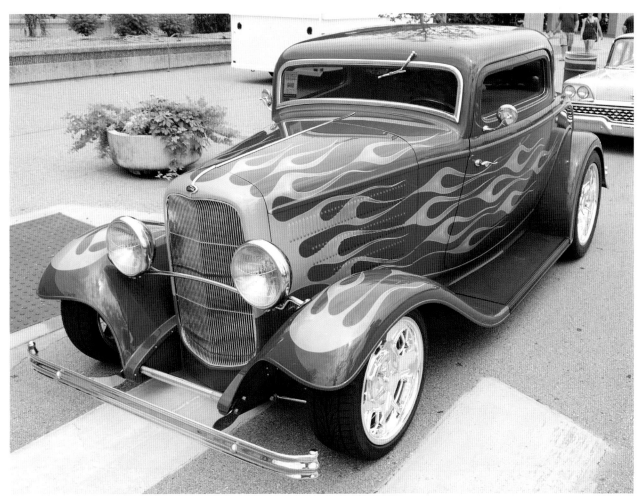

Any time flames, scallops, graphics, or even multiple colors are used to paint a vehicle, panel alignment becomes so much more critical. With all of the opening panels closed, all paint lines should be aligned from one panel to the next. All the more reason to get the panels aligned before painting.

Before beginning the layout procedure, you must decide if you want merely balanced flames, or if you want them to be symmetrical. For symmetrical flames, the flames should be laid out on one side of the vehicle in ⅛-inch Fine Line tape. Then spread a large piece of pattern paper (or several pieces taped together) over that flame layout. There must be no bubbles or pockets in the paper. Tape down the pattern paper and mark several reference points that can be identified on each side of the vehicle. Next, trace over the flame layout with a pounce wheel, which will poke tiny holes in the pattern paper. A pounce wheel is like a small pizza cutter, except that the pounce wheel has teeth.

When you've traced over the entire flame pattern, carefully remove the pattern paper, flip it over, and position it on the other side of the vehicle. Use the reference points marked earlier to align the paper on the vehicle. With the pattern paper aligned and secured to the vehicle, spread drafting pounce, carpenter's chalk line chalk, or talcum powder over the paper and lightly brush it into the holes made in the paper by the pounce wheel. When you've dusted all of the holes with powder, remove the pattern paper. Then, using ⅛-inch Fine Line tape, lay out the pattern by connecting the dots.

More experienced flamers may choose to lay out the flames freehand. As long as balance from side to side is maintained, this method works just as well. Using ⅛-inch Fine Line tape, lay out the first flame that intersects the centerline of the vehicle. Start at the tip of the flame, work forward to the belly, and then across the centerline. Form a pattern that is a mirror image of the first side. The overall style of the flame pattern begins to take shape as you lay out the mirror image of the first flame.

With the layout phase completed, the masking can begin. Overlap the original outline with ¼-inch masking tape, applying the excess to the area to be masked off. The ⅛-inch Fine Line tape will serve as the actual edge for the flames. Use masking tape in ¾-inch or larger sizes to mask the remaining area. Overlapping the masking tape in a continuous fashion will make the tape easier to remove as a sheet later, rather than removing each strip of masking tape. Use the largest tape available to cover the area to be masked; however, be sure no masking tape enters the flame area and that all of the area to be masked is covered. After the entire flamed area has been masked, the rest of the vehicle can be masked using masking paper and tape. Be sure to extend the masking paper down below the bottom of the vehicle to avoid getting any overspray on the underside.

To ensure that the painted flames adhere well, you will need to scuff the area to be flamed. Consult with your paint and supply professional to determine the best procedure for the paint system you are using. Next, use an air nozzle to remove any dust or dirt that may have accumulated, wax and grease remover to clean the surface once again, and finally a tack cloth to pick up all remaining lint or dust prior to spraying.

With the vehicle masked and the surface prepped, apply the flame colors you've selected. Depending on the area (size) of the flames, you may use a full-size production gun, a detail gun, or an airbrush. Fading is done by varying the air pressure and applying less than full coverage, and is definitely a practiced art. You simply aren't going to get it perfect the first time out.

If you have doubts about what colors will work best with your vehicle, consult a few pros and other

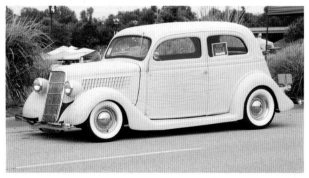

These are outline flames, as they are not painted a different color than the surface they are painted on. The flame outline could be the final and desired finish, or they could simply be a way to get used to having flames or checking the layout on the vehicle before going to the effort to paint them on.

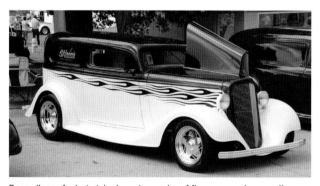

Regardless of what style, layout, or color of flames you choose, all (except realistic) look better when the edge of the flames (or scallops) accents approximately 1/8-inch-wide pinstripes of complementary or contrasting colors.

enthusiasts whose paint jobs you admire. Red, orange, and yellow flames are very traditional for a black vehicle. Ghost flames, which appear only from certain angles, have become popular on some newer vehicles, such as the PT Cruiser. There is really no limit to the style and colors to choose from—just be sure the combination you settle on complements your vehicle's existing paint and is something you'll be happy to look at for many years.

Once you've applied the flames and they have dried, remove the masking paper and tape with the same care you used on the rest of the vehicle. Properly clean the surface one more time and then give the whole car two or three coats of clear. For traditional flames, apply a pinstripe over the junction of the flame colors and body color. Without this pinstripe, traditional flames simply aren't complete.

Scallops

Scallops, like flames, date back to the early days of hot rodding. They have become slightly more common than flames among the custom car crowd, yet their popularity tends to rise and fall more frequently.

Generally, though not always, scallops are one solid color. Since they are also more of a geometric shape, and therefore easier to lay out, scallops are probably easier than flames for the first-time painter.

There are two main layout questions as you plan your scallops. First, how many points should there be, and should the bellies of the scallops be pointed, rounded, or square with rounded corners? Second, should the tops or the bottoms of the scallop be parallel, and what should they be parallel to? How to answer these questions depends on the vehicle you're painting. What looks good on a 1982 Chevrolet Malibu may not work as well on a 1949 Buick.

Just as with flames, when scallops extend across multiple body panels, you must assemble the panels to their final position when you lay them out to be sure the scallops don't get pulled out of alignment through later panel adjustments. Don't lay out the scallops until all your panel gaps are even, and moving panels open and close smoothly and properly.

To balance the scallop layout from one side to the other, locate the vehicle's centerline. When you've taken appropriate measurements to determine the centerline, run a strip of ⅛-inch Fine Line tape down it from front to back. Additional guidelines may be applied in similar fashion to provide reference points from which to measure as you add the scallops.

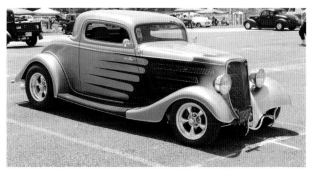

Like flames, scallops vary in layout, color, and style. These purple/blue scallops on a silver coupe actually fade from one color to another, have equal length tails, and round bellies.

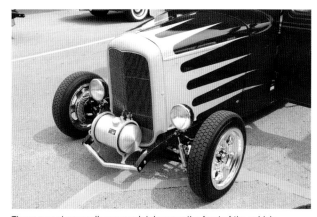

These monotone scallops completely cover the front of the vehicle, stretch back farther as they go lower, and are finished with a contrasting pinstripe. It appears as though the top lines of these scallops are parallel with each other and the bottom lines are parallel with each other. Since scallops are significantly more geometric in design than flames, consistency during layout is crucial.

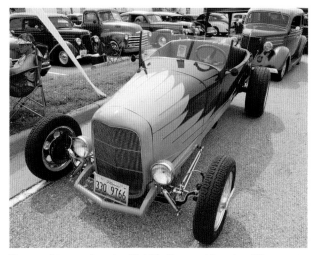

These scallops are shaped as birds' feathers, and there is nothing wrong with that. Most paint on hot rods is meant to personalize the vehicle in one way or another.

LAYING OUT AND PAINTING SCALLOPS

Early on in the process of building my Track T roadster, I made the decision to paint and apply scallops to it myself. I contacted Steve Gilmore of Stilmore Designs to provide some possible layouts. To provide a bit of a vintage look to the Track T, I went with Harvest Moon (almond) for the body and Medium Mocha (dark brown) for the scallops, wheels, chassis, and various other components. After making a photocopy of the chosen layout, it was time to begin the process.

You need at least two rolls of 3M ⅛-inch Fine Line tape, a water soluble marker, a tape measure, and a flexible ruler. You also require a French curve, circle template, or some sort of pattern for making the bellies of the scallops similar. Verify that any marker that you use for making reference marks is water soluble so that those marks can be removed from the painted surface easily. There are other ways to lay out scallops, but this method worked for me.

Begin by positioning the vehicle on a level surface and so that you can back away from it to see how your layout really looks. If the vehicle is not parked on a reasonably level surface, it will be difficult to layout the scallops correctly as your brain will be trying to

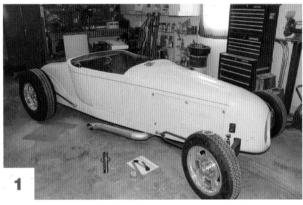

Establishing a baseline for the scallops was the most difficult part of the job. Flame layout usually begins in the middle of the hood and works outward, but with the geometric pattern of scallops, it made more sense to start with the sides first.

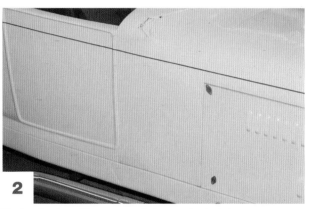

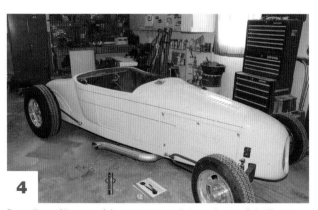

The baseline (top of the upper scallop) seemed to look the most appropriate when roughly centered between the top of the hood side panel and the top edge of the door. With the rounder shapes of older car bodies, finding similar locations to measure from to determine a set of parallel lines can be difficult. This makes stepping back to take a look at the overall picture even more critical.

Now that a baseline has been established, there is something to measure from to establish parallel lines. Two more evenly spaced points were marked on the cowl and near the back of the passenger compartment. These marks establish the top line of the middle and lower scallop. A flexible steel ruler with a cork back is being used in the photo, but a seamstress' cloth tape would be less likely to scratch any paint.

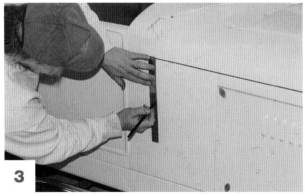

Regardless of how careful you measure, what may be parallel still may not look correct, so don't hesitate to step back every so often to verify that everything "looks" correct. Most likely, no one is going to be measuring the scallops on your car, but they sure may be vocal about it at times.

compensate for level. You need to be able to step back from the layout so that you can gain a better perspective, rather than forcing yourself into a skewed view from being too close.

Establish a baseline, which can be difficult if there are few parallel lines in the body. While you may not be able to find any distinct bodyline to be parallel to, your baseline should be roughly parallel to the longest straight edge along the bottom of the body. After determining the location of your baseline, lay down a line of ⅛ inch Fine Line tape. Place one end of the tape on the body, holding it with one hand, and then

pull the tape roll with the other hand to keep the tape straight. Be careful not to stretch the tape, but keep it taut. Press the tape onto the body and especially into recessed areas without pushing it off line. If the tape is not making complete contact with the body, paint will find its way between the tape and the body.

When the baseline (the top edge of the top scallop) looks to be in the correct location, measure down some distance for the top of the middle scallop, and measure that same distance again for the top of the bottom scallop. This measurement varies depending on the shape of your car and the number of scallops,

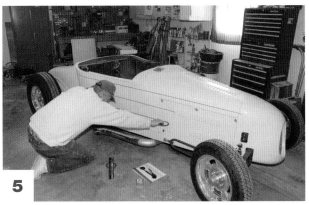

5 With the small size of the Track T, stretching tape is not a big deal, but on a larger vehicle, assistance might be necessary. Even if you can reach both ends of the tape, a second set of eyes is useful to make sure everything looks as desired.

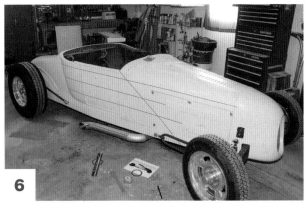

6 The diagonal tape is the baseline for the bellies of the scallops. Its location is arbitrary, but should be located somewhere easy to re-create on the opposite side of the vehicle.

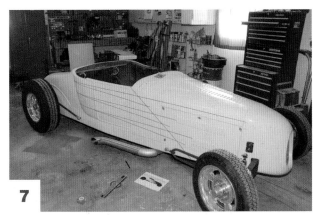

7 Determine the angle of the lower line of each scallop by measuring from the intersection of the top line of each scallop with the belly baseline. For the angle to be identical, each measurement along the upper line must be the same, and each measurement along the belly baseline must be the same.

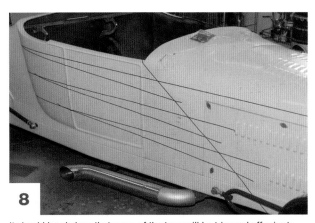

8 It should be obvious that some of the tape will be trimmed off prior to the layout being finished. Just be sure to leave all of the baselines in place on the first side until the layout is re-created on the opposite side.

(continued)

but it will give you a rough idea of the process. Unlike flames, scallops are a geometric design. That does not mean that distances must be equal, but if not, they are usually proportional for the best results. With two sets of points marked, use Fine Line tape to connect the dots, creating the top line of each scallop.

The next step is to establish a baseline for the bellies of the scallops. This line can be straight, a circular curve, or an irregular curve, but it should be something that is easily duplicated on the other side of the vehicle. Using your artwork, sketch, or imagination as a guide, choose two points on the profile of the car and lay down a piece of Fine Line tape to create a baseline between the two. Admittedly, the location of this baseline is quite arbitrary, but like many things, you have to make a decision and move on.

The next steps determine the lines that represent the bottom of each scallop. Where many painters falter is by failing to make the lower edges parallel to each other, even though the top lines are parallel. Begin by measuring along each top line from its intersection with the belly baseline the same distance toward the back of the vehicle and marking a point with a water-soluble pen (using a pen to mark reference points is much easier than using strips of tape that get in the way when you actually start masking). To get the angle the same on each scallop, measure downward along the belly baseline from its intersection with the top line of each scallop some distance. Use Fine Line tape to connect the dot at the baseline with the dot representing the point of the scallop. Since the belly baseline is steeply angle with the top lines, this distance will be quite a bit more than the final width of the scallop. Again, this distance is arbitrary, so you will need to lay it out, step back and look, and then adjust accordingly. On the scallops shown in these photos, the distance along the belly baseline was 5 inches. In this particular situation, that made the scallops about half that distance at their widest point.

Bellies of scallops can come to a single point, be angular, circular, or curved. To match my artist's sketch, I simply used a French curve to define a curve from the lower edge of the scallop to a point being the intersection of the belly baseline and the top line of the next scallop. To make sure that the curve is similar on each scallop, I made reference marks on the French curve so that it was positioned the same on each one. You could certainly use a pattern made from poster board to serve the same purpose. I know of at least one set of scallops on a '32

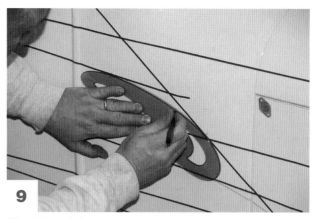

9

Although it would be easy enough to lay out tape along an arc at the belly of the scallop freehand, I did not feel confident in being able to repeat the same shape adequately enough. By tracing around a French curve with a sign pen, I established a guideline for the tape to follow. I used reference marks on the French curve to align it correctly with each scallop.

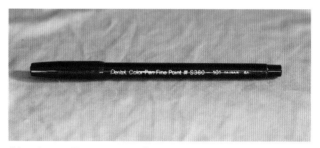

Although you still need to outline flames or scallops with Fine Line tape, being able to draw a design or make reference marks on the painted surface makes the task easier. A water soluble pen (commonly referred to as a sign pen) is available in many colors and can be wiped off the painted surface with a damp cloth (or some spit and your thumb). Just be sure to first test the ability to remove the pen's ink in an inconspicuous location on the car.

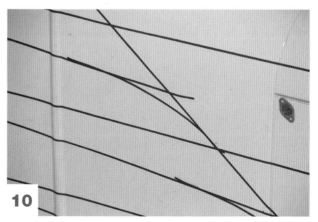

10

After tracing around the French curve with a sign pen, Fine Line tape was applied over the line.

Ford that used a portion of artwork from a case of Bud Light as a pattern.

With the side of the scallops laid out, it is time to move to the hood top. This is one place where the layout will change drastically depending on the type and size of your vehicle. For this vehicle, the intent is to have the edge of one scallop running up the center of the hood and then curve around to blend in with the top line of the side scallop. Another goal is to avoid any louvers passing through the edge of the paint. Additionally, I did not want any painted edges crossing the front portions of the hood and nose area due to fear of vibration induced movement in that area that would result in misalignment of the artwork. The back of the hood is secured to the body, so movement is minimal there, but the front end of the hood and nose are not as static. After multiple attempts, I was able to freehand a line that blended into the side adequately and meet the requirements that I had imposed.

After stepping back and looking at the layout for a while, decide if your work is satisfactory—you can always make changes now, and then duplicate it on the other side. At this point, it is your decision, so take some time to look it over before moving on.

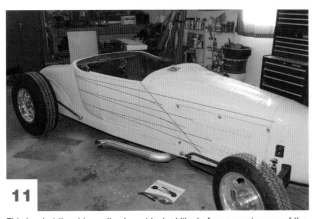

11

This is what the side scallop layout looked like before removing any of the extra tape. Having a drawing to use as a design aid greatly helps when laying out scallops.

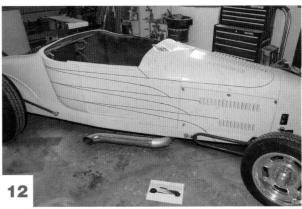

12

One side down, another side to go. I re-created the pattern on the opposite side by using guidelines and measurements. Another method is to cover the artwork with Kraft paper, tape it down, make some reference marks, and then trace over the Fine Line tape with a pounce wheel. The pounce wheel makes a series of small holes in the Kraft paper. After repositioning the Kraft paper on the other side of the vehicle, spread carpenter's chalk over the paper. When the paper is removed, the chalk outlines the masking lines.

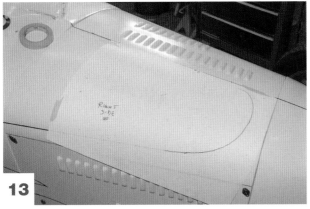

13

I had no feasible way to layout this curve geometrically, so after doing it by hand on one side, I used vellum tracing paper to create a pattern by tracing over the Fine Line tape, cutting out the pattern, and then tracing around it.

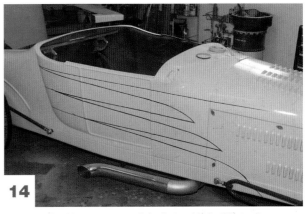

14

With extra Fine Line tape removed, the first real look at the scallops can be seen. Perhaps not perfect, but not too bad. Good, bad, or otherwise, I can say I did it myself. If I can, most likely you can too.

(continued)

Whenever you are ready to move on, make sure that you do not remove any of the extra Fine Line tape used for baselines until you have measurements duplicated on the opposite side.

One method to re-create the design on the hood top is to use a piece of drafting vellum. Tape it down over that portion of the hood top, mark several reference points on the vellum that that match the points on the other side of the hood, and then trace over the Fine Line tape. Carefully remove the tape, and cut along the line just made on the vellum. Make sure that your reference marks are still attached to the vellum when you cut along the line. Now position the vellum pattern and tape it in place. Using a water-soluble pen, trace along this pattern onto the hood. Now remove the pattern and Fine Line tape used to outline the scallop. When the layout is complete, remove any extraneous tape that is not part of the final outline. Press down all of the tape firmly so that it does its job of masking, but make sure that you do not move the tape out of position in the process.

After the layout is complete, use ¾-inch-wide automotive-grade masking tape for most of the masking. Begin by placing one edge of the masking

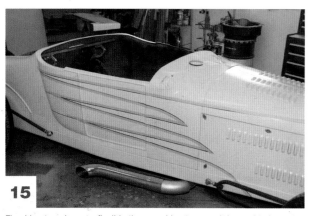

15

Fine Line tape is more flexible than masking tape, so it is used to lay out the scallops and provide the actual masked edge of the painted surface. Whether using more masking tape or using masking paper, the Fine Line tape should be followed by one line of 3/4-inch masking tape. This is flexible enough to stick to the 1/8-inch Fine Line tape, but wide enough to make attaching more tape or paper possible.

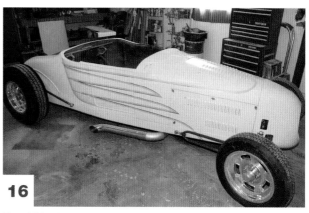

16

The additional application of masking tape also provides a more visible look at the layout. Now is the time to change the layout if anything is amiss.

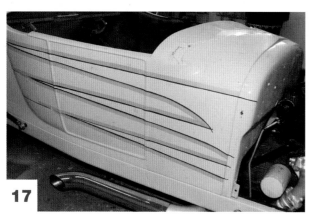

17

Although it looks very white in the photos, the body is VW Harvest Moon, which is a light tan. After buffing and adding an orange pinstripe between the two colors, the Track T should look traditional when sitting in outdoor light. Notice that the squared-off belly between the middle and lower scallop is hidden when the hood side is in place.

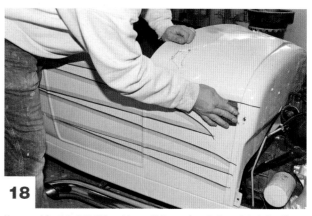

18

Use a red Scotch-Brite™ pad to scuff the surface to be painted. Scuffing allows the paint to adhere better. You should also clean the surface with wax and grease remover prior to painting it.

tape on the Fine Line tape, with the width of the masking tape extending toward the area that is to be masked. The more flexible Fine Line tape is what will actually define the edge of the painted scallops. The masking tape should not extend past the edge of the Fine Line tape; however, you must avoid leaving slivers of unmasked area between these first two pieces (or any other pieces) of tape. Go around the entire outline of the Fine Line with the masking tape. Make sure that you press the tape down firmly. Use masking tape between the scallops, and then use masking paper to cover the larger areas.

Scuff the scallops prior to applying paint. Apply another strip of Fine Line tape just inside of the original line of Fine Line. This allows you to use a red Scotch-Brite™ pad to aggressively scuff the bulk of the scallop area, while providing protection for the Fine Line tape that represents the edge of the layout. When the bulk of the area is scuffed, remove the second line of tape, and carefully scuff the edges of the area that is to be painted.

Whether you mask and then scuff or scuff and then mask is a matter of personal preference. Just make sure that you scuff the surface to be painted adequately so that the paint sticks. Make sure that you mask adequately so that you do not have slivers of paint in the wrong places. However, if slivers of paint appear when everything is said and done, they can be removed with some polishing compound if there is clear between them and the underlying paint.

Begin painting scallops only after double-checking that everything is masked sufficiently, and that you have an adequate workspace around everything that is to be painted. Like with all base coat paint products, apply enough color is to provide complete coverage. The scallops for this Track T are Medium Mocha, which is a dark brown that matches the single-stage color used for the chassis and engine, albeit in a base coat formula. The base coat/clear coat paint system used for the body and scallops proved to be more user friendly than the single-stage paint followed by clear used on the chassis. Whether using a single-stage or multistage paint system, you should always apply multiple coats of clear prior to adding artwork.

After waiting the recommended dry time, apply clear with the proper flash time between coats. As the clear begins to dry, it immediately begins to turn glossy. If the surface is not glossy after the second coat of clear is applied, you are not getting adequate

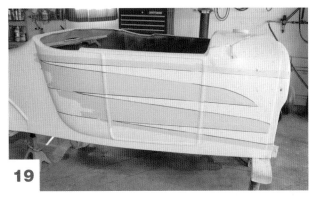

19

Due to the irregular shape, I chose to use masking tape to mask the area between the scallops. My roll of 18-inch-wide masking paper would have required too much cutting and trimming in this area, although I did use masking paper on the back half of the car and along the lower edge.

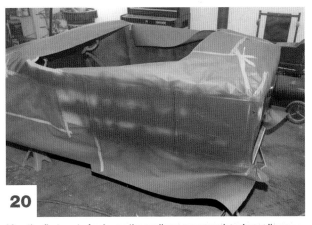

20

After the first coat of color on the scallops, coverage is only mediocre. Remember, add enough coats of base coat to achieve complete coverage, allowing sufficient flash time between coats. The base coat itself will look dull.

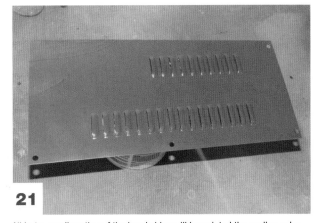

21

All but a small portion of the hood sides will be painted the scallop color. If you look close, you can still see the masked-off area after this first coat of color.

(continued)

coverage. Although the clear has no pigment, it does begin to "gloss" quickly, which tells you if you missed any spots. Apply three or four coats of clear to make sure that you have enough material to work with in the buffing process.

After allowing the paint and clear to dry completely (refer to the instructions sheets for the proper time for the products that you are using), wet sand to remove any orange peel. Then buff, polish, and reassemble as necessary.

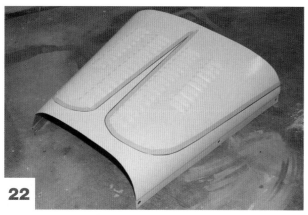

22

It may be a little easier to see the difference between the scuffed and the nonscuffed areas of the hood top. The area on the front, center, and edges has been scuffed and will be painted. The area that will not be painted has had the clear wet sanded, so it is a bit glossier. When all of the painting is done and the entire hot rod buffed and polished, it will all be very shiny.

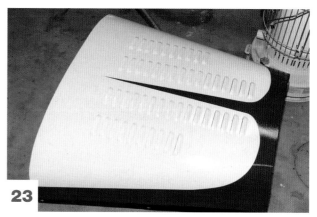

23

After being buffed and polished, a 1/8- or 3/16- inch wide pinstripe (Omaha orange) will finish off the scallops.

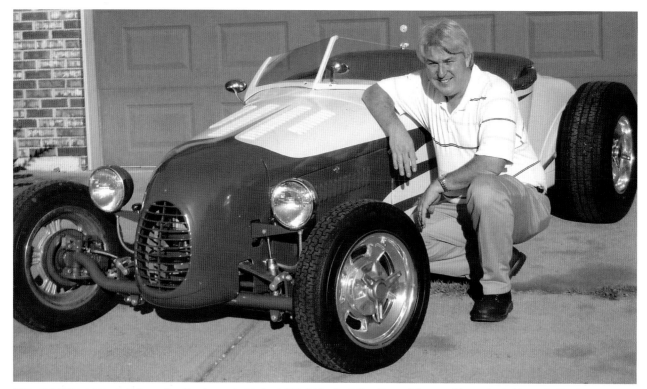

Although I did have some help from a few friends on select tasks, I did build the Track T pretty much by myself for my book, *How to Build a Cheap Hot Rod*. Next to reading books about how to do it, rolling up your sleeves and getting your hands dirty is the best way to learn most any task. Don't say you can't do anything unless you have at least tried it.

As scallops cascade across the hood or down the side of the vehicle, they form a repeat pattern, rather than the free-flowing design of flames. When you're satisfied with the layout on the first side, duplicate it on the other side using the pattern method described in the flames section, or freehand.

With the layout phase completed, the masking can begin. Overlap the original outline with ¼-inch masking tape, applying the excess to the area to be masked off. The ⅛-inch Fine Line tape serves as the edge for the scallops. Use ¾-inch or larger masking tape to mask the remaining area, and then mask the rest of the vehicle. Be sure to extend the masking paper down below the bottom of the vehicle to avoid getting any overspray underneath the vehicle.

You must scuff the area to be scalloped to ensure that the painted scallops adhere properly. Consult with your paint and supply professional to determine the best procedure for the paint system you are using.

Use an air nozzle to remove any dust or dirt that may have accumulated, wax and grease remover to clean the surface once again, and finally a tack cloth to pick up any remaining lint or dust prior to spraying.

Spray the scallops. After the proper drying time, carefully remove the masking paper and tape, clean the surface again, and apply two or three coats of clear.

PINSTRIPING

Pinstriping can be a simple standalone accent to a single-color paint job, or a finishing touch to most any multicolor paint scheme. Before the days of the automobile, painters applied pinstripes to the spokes of covered wagon wheels. They have endured as a design feature ever since, on almost any type of vehicle, from bicycles to children's wagons to cars and trucks. In some contexts, they're virtually mandatory—you should always pinstripe traditional flames or scallops; otherwise they simply are not finished. Pinstriping provides a finished appearance to flames or scallops, covering the otherwise unattractive seam of color where the flame or scallop meets the vehicle's main paint finish. It can also serve to conceal slight irregularities in the edge of the paint.

Pinstriping is common on factory paint jobs, and usually consists of a single or double line approximately ⅛-inch wide running along the beltline of the vehicle in a contrasting or complementary color. Since pinstriping is an accent, painters often choose a bright color, such as orange for a maroon vehicle, or purple on a black

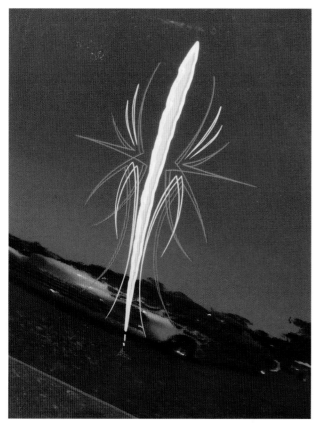

Pinstriping can be used to accent body lines, outline various pieces of trim (hood and deck lid emblems), or to simply break up a large area that "needs something." Most professional pinstripers use very small brushes called daggers to apply their multicolored artwork.

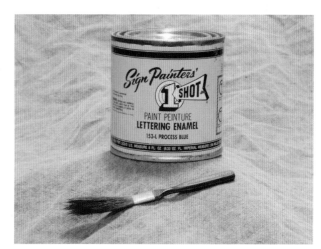

The two basics for traditional pinstriping are a Grumbacher striping brush and 1 Shot Lettering Enamel. Pint-size cans of just a few basic colors and a couple different sizes of brushes (and perhaps a lettering brush or two) are enough to get you started as a pin striper. You add the natural talent and lots of practice.

Problem	Cause	What to Do	
Film that resembles an orange peel.	Film lacks the ability to flow smoothly. Rough substrate transmits irregularities to subsequent top coats.	• Check if defect is on whole unit or in specific area. • Check for low air pressure. • Check for under reduction. • Check for proper film build.	• Check for improper gun distance. • Check reducing solvent and viscosity. • Check smoothness of substrate. • Check if defect is specific to one color. • Check for excessive temperature.
A rough, textured surface often found in a small area.	Paint lacks ability to flow properly.	• Check if defect is on whole unit or in specific area. • Check if defect is specific to one color or many colors. • Check for proper film build.	• Check for excessive film build. • Check for improper gun distance. • Check reducing solvent selection and spray viscosity.
Tiers or curtains of paint on vertical or inclined areas.	Uneven distribution to a vertical or inclined surface producing excessive buildup.	• Check if defect is on whole unit or in specific area • Check if defect is specific to one color or many colors. • Check for excessive film build. • Check for excessive fluid delivery. • Check for improper gun distance (too close). • Check solvent selection (too slow).	• Check for insufficient air pressure. • Check for excessive application overlap. • Check for too short flash time. • Check for low spray room temperature. • Check temperature of paint. • Check temperature of unit. • Check for proper reduction.
Finished panels do not match color standard.	Differences in application and/or paint materials.	• Check for complete hiding. • Check for variables in spray application. • Check lines and equipment for contamination from previous color. • Check for improper mixing.	• Check for proper agitation. • Check gun pattern. • Check gun distance. • Check equipment setup.
Small rounded indentations that resemble fish eyes.	Foreign substances that do not blend with paint.	• Check if defect is on whole unit or in specific area. • Check for oil in air lines and spray equipment. • Check airborne contamination in spray area. • Check for possible contamination in paint materials	• Check for painter contamination, skin oils, perspiration, greasy foods, etc. • Check for any oils or contamination that might get into paint or spray area. • Check for proper cleaning procedures prior to refinishing.
Small pebbles or pebbled ridges deposited in, on, or under the paint film.	Foreign particles entering wet paint film.	• Check if defect is on whole unit or in a specific area. • Check paint mixing/filtration process. • Check spray environment (booth). • Check preparation process of unit, tacking, solvent wash, etc.	• Check painters clothing. • Check spray equipment. • Check used paint filters for contamination. • Check for use of anti-stat wipe or spray products.

Problem	Cause	What to Do	
Top coat peels off when unmasking.	Top coat layer or paint separating because of lack of physical bonding.	• Check if defect is on whole unit or in specific area. • Check film build. • Check for contaminants such as sanding residue, overspray, oil, water, solvent cleaner residue, etc. on substrate prior to top coat application. • Check for nonsanding or primer-surfacer. • Check for case hardening of substrate.	• Check for poor surface preparation prior to topcoat application. • Check for masking tape contacting painted surface. • Check solvent selection (too fast). • Check for thin sealer film builds or no sealer. • Check for incompatible products.
Easy to blemish or penetrate film with fingernail.	Insufficient cure of paint film.	• Check if defect is on whole unit or in specific area. • Check for improper film build. • Check hardener (old, improper, or contaminated). • Check for improper mixing ratio. • Check for improper heat during cure time.	• Check for improper airflow. • Check flash or dry times. • Check solvent selection (too fast). • Check for excessive humidity. • Check for cool temperatures.
Loss of gloss after application.	Improper evaporation of solvent, or poor initial cure.	• Check if defect is on whole unit or in a specific area. • Check for too fast a solvent selection. • Check for cool temperature during cure. • Check for lack of airflow during cure.	• Check for improper film build. • Check for improper flash times. • Check for incompatible products.
A "goose pimple" or funnel-like appearance in paint film, which, on close examination, frequently has small holes in the center of the bumps.	Improper evaporation of solvent from wet paint film during initial cure or force dry.	• Check to determine if defect is on entire unit or just in a specific area. • Check for high temperature in first part of force dry. • Check for correct reducing solvent. • Check if defect is specific to one or many colors. • Check if defect is most prevalent on horizontal surfaces.	• Check for excessive film builds. • Check for high fluid delivery. • Check for low air pressure. • Check for high viscosity. • Check for too much overlapping in film build. • Check for proper flash and purge times.
Spotty, nonuniform, blotchy appearance of metallic paint.	Uneven distribution of metallic flakes.	• Check if defect is on whole unit or in a specific area. • Check if defect is specific to one color or many. • Check for excessively high fluid delivery. • Check atomizing air pressure. • Check gun pattern. • Check gun distance.	• Check equipment set-ups (fluid delivery). • Check solvent selection. • Check reduction, viscosity. • Check flash and dry times. • Check temperature in spray environment (too cool). • Check temperature of unit being sprayed.

(continued)

Problem	Cause	What to Do	
Undesirable sanding pattern imperfections that show through the finished paint film.	Imperfections due to soft primer, improper sanding techniques, and low top coat film build. Excessive film builds with improper flash times.	• Check if defect is on whole car or in a specific area. • Check if defect is specific to one or many colors. • Check for correct sandpaper grit (too coarse). • Check top coat film thickness. • Check for proper featheredge technique. • Check for uncured primer. • Check for poor quality solvent used in undercoats.	• Check flash and dry times. • Check for excessive primer film builds. • Check for proper gun technique and atomization. • Check for under reduced primer-surfacer (bridging scratches). • Check for sanding before primer-surfacer is cured. • Check film builds of sealer or no sealer.
Paint materials from another unit falling on adjacent surfaces.	Misdirected spray droplets or dry spray.	• Check to determine if defect is on entire unit or in specific area. • Check other units to see if a pattern exists. • Check for correct booth air balance and flow.	• Check for sequence of panel application. • Check gun technique. • Check if defect is specific to one color. • Check air pressure (too high). • Check for over reduction.

vehicle. You most likely would not choose a two-tone paint job using equal amounts of these colors, but in the thin width of a pinstripe, it all works well.

Artists of the 1940s and 1950s popularized another type of pinstriping on hot rods and lead sleds. This pinstriping features short sweeping lines, curves, and arcs, rather than one or two long lines wrapping around the vehicle. Intertwined, overlapped, or connected short lines of one or more colors create some interesting artwork. Although they rarely constitute an actual picture, they do invite some fun interpretations on occasion if viewed from different angles.

The most common paint for pinstriping or lettering is One-Shot Sign Painter's enamel, which is available from larger art supply stores or some auto body paint and supply professionals. It is relatively inexpensive, so with just a few primary colors and some extra mixing jars, you can produce virtually any color. Before applying pinstriping paint, clean the surface with a wax and grease remover and a clean cloth, and wipe it off with a second dry cloth.

Sign painter's enamel is compatible with most other paint surfaces. Different reducers are available to speed up or slow down the enamel's drying time. Due to the relatively small area to which it is applied, it is usually allowed to air dry, although a blow dryer can speed up the process.

Brush
Until fairly recently, all pinstriping was done with a brush specifically designed for the purpose. Known as a pinstriping dagger, this brush is normally only about 4 to 6 inches long. By dipping the tip of the brush into enamel, and then slightly squeezing the brush hairs, you can apply the pinstripe at the desired line thickness.

Striping Tool
A somewhat recent development in the art of pinstriping is a mechanical striping tool. It is much easier to apply accent stripes with a striping tool than brush painting. You could do curves or freehand shapes like flames or scallops with it, but you would need to practice a fair amount first.

A mechanical striping tool is made of a small cylinder with variable heads. The cylinder holds the paint while the head applies it to the surface. The heads have either one or two wheels, providing either a single or a double line. The wheels are available in different widths for lines of different thickness, but they will always be parallel or concentric if you use a head with two wheels.

GRAPHICS
Graphics can vary from the adhesive graduated shading from a 30th Anniversary Corvette to checkered flag patterns common on a variety of stock production

EXTRA DETAILS

vehicles, and also to airbrushed murals of any design. As you plan your paint scheme, keep in mind that a body side molding or stainless-steel trim adds the same type of accent as a graphic. Examine each of the design and paint features that catch a viewer's eye and consider whether, taken together, they improve the overall look or make it too "busy" or cluttered.

Painted Graphics

A base coat/clear coat system is best for any painted graphics or artwork, as it allows you to sand overspray or other mistakes on subsequent layers out of the clear without damaging the underlying color coat. Before adding any artwork, clean the entire area with wax and grease remover. Surface preparation depends upon the applied media, so read the instructions provided, or check with your paint and supply professional.

Vinyl Adhesive Graphics

Although diehard hot rodders or customizers laugh at the thought, vinyl adhesive graphics are becoming more popular. A new generation of car enthusiasts appreciates their improved materials, low cost, and versatility. Many enthusiasts prefer to spend a hundred bucks on a vinyl graphic they can remove if they grow tired of it, rather than investing five to ten times that much for artwork that incurs almost as much expense to remove and that can otherwise outlast the vehicle.

Today's computer graphics and vinyl technology make it easy for almost anyone to create high-quality artwork for a fraction of the cost of hiring an airbrush artist. These advances have also made vinyl adhesive graphics more common as an OEM item. To repair a stick-on graphic, you typically purchase a replacement from the dealer's parts department.

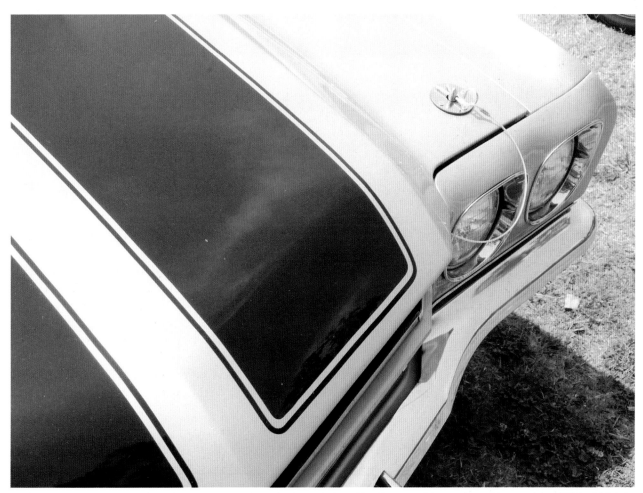

Rally stripes can be masked and painted by hand or applied by adhesive-backed graphics. For many of the popular muscle cars of the 1960s and 1970s, when stripes and other graphics were popular from the factory, vinyl graphics are available from aftermarket sources. If they are not available for your particular vehicle, you can mask off the area as needed and paint your own.

APPLYING VINYL ADHESIVE GRAPHICS

Although trim, emblems, and badges on contemporary vehicles are usually made of plastic rather than the polished chrome-plated metal of years ago, it is still present in some form on most vehicles. Being plastic, adhesive usually backs the trim instead of the trim being bolted to the vehicle. Mike at Jerry's Auto Body makes installing a new piece of trim on the rear quarter of an SUV look pretty simple.

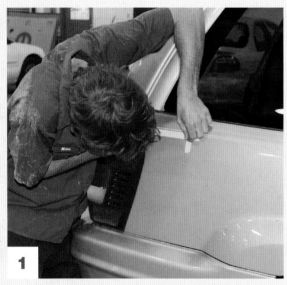

1

By measuring the graphic on the other side of the vehicle, it was determined that the top of the emblem is ¾ inch below the bottom of the silver pinstripe. Coincidentally, ¾-inch masking tape is very common, so this emblem location is no surprise. As a guideline, a piece of ¾-inch masking tape is aligned at the bottom of the aforementioned pinstripe.

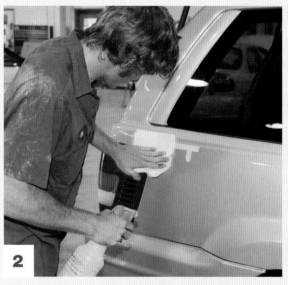

2

To ensure that the emblem adheres properly, spray a bit of wax and grease remover onto the application area, and wipe it off with a clean paper towel. This should remove anything that would prevent proper adhesion.

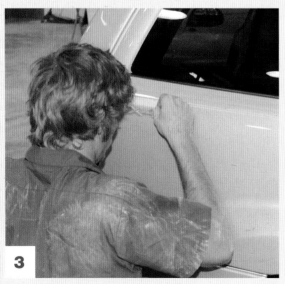

3

Remove the protective backing from the adhesive on back of the "4x4" emblem. Then, align the top of the emblem with the lower edge of the masking tape, and press it into place.

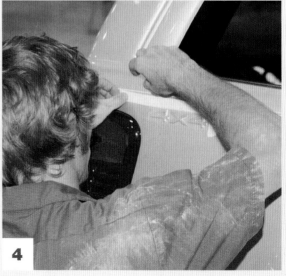

4

Peel away the masking tape used to align the emblem.

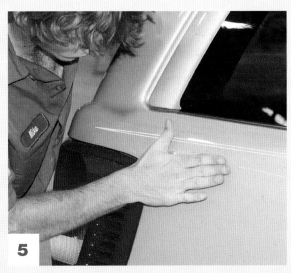

5

Apply firm and even pressure to the emblem to ensure that it adheres to the body surface.

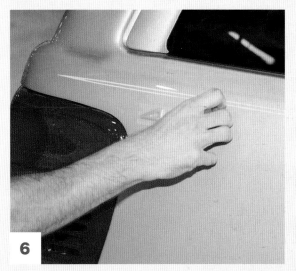

6

Remove the emblem's protective covering.

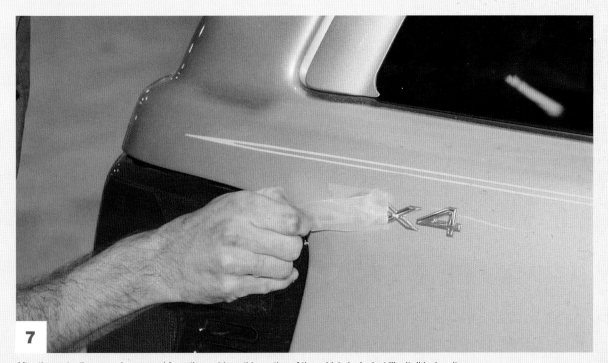

7

After the protective cover is removed from the emblem, this portion of the vehicle looks just like it did when it was new.

Chapter 9
Part Replacement and Reassembly

Now that you've produced a beautiful paint job, you don't want to tarnish it by refitting dirty parts. Unless you cleaned and polished the parts when you removed them, now is the time to detail everything before restoring it to your vehicle's pristine body. Also take the time to clean up the engine compartment, interior, and trunk—including vacuuming out sanding dust—to bring them up to the same high standards. Windows that are clean on both sides, a dust-free dashboard, spotless doorjambs, scrubbed tires, polished chrome, a well-groomed interior, grease-free engine compartment, and a tidy trunk space all work together to complement new body paint and make the automobile look, feel, and smell like new.

Install the clean, detailed parts systematically so you don't have to remove anything again to fit another component. Certain trim sections, for example, are designed to be put on first with an adjacent section covering part of their edge. Likewise, you may need access to the inner side of the door panel to refit trim or a handle; install those items before replacing the interior panel. Look at all of the components that need to be added to a particular panel or section of the car and figure out the proper sequence for fitting them before you start. This way you won't have to redo anything and risk scratching the paint in the process.

GLASS
Glass requires special care because glass is both delicate and heavy enough to dent as well as scratch your vehicle. Since the paint should be cured by the time you begin installing glass, consider laying strips of wide masking tape along window frame edges to guard against accidental bumps that could cause paint scratches or nicks. Be sure to use automotive masking tape because generic tape might leave adhesive residue.

To avoid galvanic corrosion, make sure any metal clips holding glass panels in place are mounted correctly and avoid contact with sheetmetal body panels. Be careful installing the body panels to avoid chipping or scratching the paint. Even the smallest paint chip allows moisture and air to reach the metal and start the rusting process. Once started, especially on areas hidden by trim, oxidation spreads under layers of paint unnoticed until severe metal rust damage causes bubbles, cracks, or other problems.

Along with recognizing the importance of preventing paint chips while installing glass, you should be concerned about watertight seals all around window perimeters. Not only are water leaks annoying, but they create ideal conditions for corrosion damage on metal panels and rot or mildew in upholstery and carpeting.

Fixed glass panels, like windshields, rear, and some side windows, are held in place by various means. These means vary not only by window type, but also by vehicle make and model. Some feature clips, others rely on thick rubber molding, and many call for strips of butyl- or urethane-based sealers. If you are not familiar with auto glass installation, seriously consider hiring a professional to complete the work for you. Most auto glass businesses offer mobile service, sending a specialist to your location to complete the work.

Rear window glass on pickup trucks and hatchbacks oftentimes is set inside grooves along the inside perimeter of heavy rubber moldings. Another groove runs around the outer molding perimeter. Once the molding is fitted around glass, the installer inserts a cord into the outer perimeter groove and pulls it taut. While one person holds the glass and molding unit in place from outside the vehicle, another person starts pulling the cord from inside the vehicle. As the cord pulls away from the rubber, it also pulls its edge back, allowing the molding to fit around the panel edges forming the window opening. Thus, the edges of the window opening gradually replace the rope in the groove. Professionals typically wrap the rope so that both ends meet in the middle of the bottom groove. The inside person pulls one end of the rope, then the other end, easing the bottom lip on first, and then inching up each side and around each top corner, toward the middle of the top groove, at which point the rope pulls free and the last portion of molding pops into place.

Installing fixed glass units with urethane sealer actually adds a degree of structural strength to some automobiles. Continuous beads of urethane sealer often secure windshields and side-mounted fixed glass units on newer cars and vans. In some cases, a bead of butyl material is used instead of urethane. Butyl has a strength of approximately 5 psi, while urethane boasts adhesion strength of approximately 500 psi.

If you performed extensive bodywork by a window opening, you may want to use a butyl bead to secure the glass in case you have to remove it for adjustments to the sheet metal or window. Since butyl is not nearly as strong as urethane, you'll be able to remove the glass again much more easily.

Before installing a fixed-glass unit, ensure that its supportive body opening is completely clean and free of contaminants. Then, lay a bead of butyl material around the window opening. For butyl-only installations, make a full bead. If you also use urethane, slope the butyl bead away from the glass at a 45-degree angle toward the body. Then add urethane material to fill the triangular void left in the butyl bead. For either kind of installation, butyl actually holds the glass in place. It's used with urethane installations because the urethane takes more time to cure.

About the only way to remove fixed glass units secured by butyl or urethane beads is to cut through the beads with a special tool made of wire. Make an opening in the bead, pass the wire through it, then attach a handle to each end. With an assistant—one person inside, one outside—manipulate the wire so that it cuts the bead all the way around the window. Coordinate with your assistant so that you catch the glass once it's cut free. Afterward, loosen the old bead material using a dedicated solvent available from your automotive paint supplier.

The tools and materials needed to remove and install fixed glass units are available at auto body paint and supply stores. Be sure you fully understand all installation instructions for the products that you use. Have a helper available to assist you in removing or replacing glass units, as they can be quite heavy and cumbersome. If for any reason you are hesitant to tackle such a job, consider the services of a professional auto glass installer. Compared to the cost of replacing broken glass units (from $100 to well over $1,000), a professional auto glass installer's fee is minimal.

TRIM

In addition to detailing trim pieces before installing them, you might consider using an artist's fine paintbrush and compatible paint to fill in chips, scratches, or peeled sections in paint lines. Older cars generally feature metal trim pieces with painted lines that run lengthwise along grooved indentations.

Use a soft brush and an all-purpose cleaner like Simple Green to scrub vinyl or rubber trim sections. When they are dry, apply a satisfactory coat of vinyl dressing. Rub the treatment in with a soft cloth or very soft brush. Be sure to wipe off all excess. If you don't want to use a silicone-based treatment, check with the auto body paint and supply store to see if it carries vinyl and rubber rejuvenation products without silicone.

Make sure you have all of the clips and retainers on hand before attaching trim pieces. Also be sure you know where they go and how they fit—to the vehicle and to each another. Have a helper assist you in replacing extra-long pieces. This helps prevent bends or wrinkles in the trim, and also adds more control to the installation, reducing the chance that you'll scratch the paint.

Do not use a screwdriver or other hard object to flip rubber edges over onto painted frame openings while installing belt moldings around windows. Instead, use a plastic tool designed for this procedure. The tools are shaped like medical tongue suppressors and available at auto body and supply stores and some auto glass shops.

Since door handles and key locks attach directly to painted body panels, install them with care so as not to scratch, chip, or nick the finish. In many cases, gaskets or seals separate hardware from the body skin. Do not use the gasket if it is worn, cracked, or otherwise damaged. Wait until you have a new gasket to install that handle or exterior door item.

A defective gasket increases the odds that the handle will come in direct contact with the sheetmetal body panel. Should the two metals be incompatible (like one aluminum panel and one steel panel), their contact point creates a perfect spot for the start of galvanic corrosion. This is an oxidation process produced by the chemical reaction between the two

Remove glass and interior door panels to make the necessary repairs whenever a door is damaged. The key to doing this is finding out how the interior door panel is secured. On newer vehicles, the door panel often snaps into place, and therefore can be pried off. However, there are usually one or a few screws typically located around the interior door latch mechanism. Inside the door pull and other "out of view" locations are typical. With the interior door panel removed, you now have access to the various bolts and screws that hold everything in place. When disassembling the door, make sure that you contain all hardware and make notes of anything that you may not remember when you get ready to reassemble the door.

Reassembling the door, its glass, and weather stripping is typically the reverse of disassembly. Follow along as Mike at Jerry's Auto Body reinstalls these items on an SUV that has both fixed and opening glass in one door.

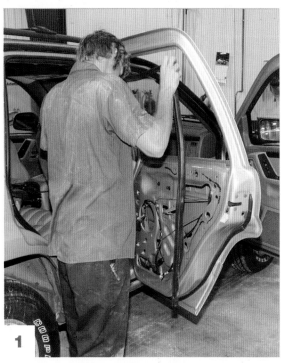

There will be a piece of rubber weather stripping that fits between the glass and all portions of the window frame where there needs to be a weather-tight seal. This particular door will have two pieces since there are actually two pieces of glass. In this instance, a tall, skinny piece of glass is fixed in place, with a division bar adjacent to the front edge to provide a track for the opening section.

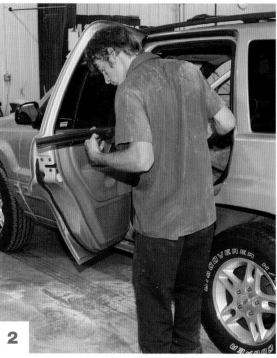

If you are not sure how some of the pieces fit into place, refer to the other side of the vehicle if it was not damaged. If both sides were damaged and therefore require disassembly, you may need to refer to the photos or notes that you took upon disassembly.

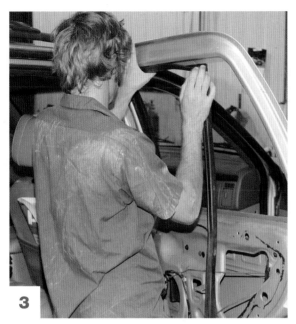

3

Since this weather stripping is made especially for this vehicle, the corners are molded in and therefore provide a hint as to how it fits into place. If you were using "universal" weather stripping, this would not be so evident. Regardless of universal or model specific, push the weather stripping into the opening around the perimeter of the window opening.

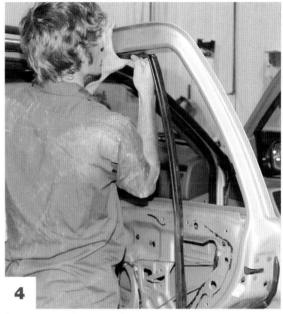

4

There may be notches in the door sheet metal that provide indications of proper alignment of the weather stripping. Just make sure that you get it aligned and seated properly to avoid leaks.

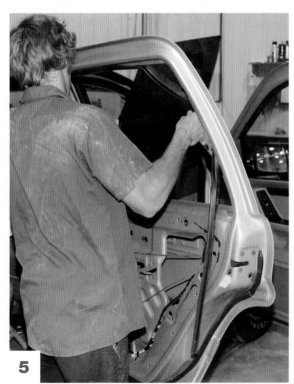

5

Since this Jeep has two pieces of glass in the door (along with a division bar), the operable glass is installed first. Installing the glass can be tricky, but the main thing to remember is to not get it in a bind, which causes it to crack and/or break. Door glass often has a slight curve to it, which may necessitate installing the glass from the outside as shown, or it may need to be slid in at an angle.

(continued)

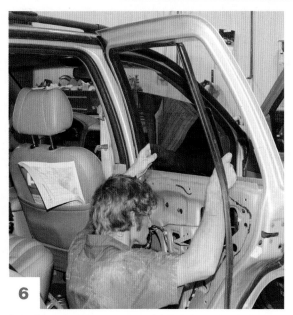

6

By looking through the access panel, it is easier to align the bottom of the glass with its window track and riser mechanism. There will usually be some sort of clips, rather than nuts and bolts, to secure the glass to the riser. However the glass is installed, make sure that it is secure but not over-tightened.

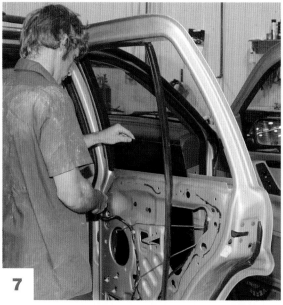

7

With the door glass installed, install the window crank mechanism or connect the power window switch and slowly run the glass through its up and down cycle a couple of times. If there is any binding, stop and correct the situation.

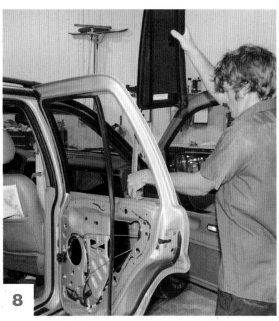

8

Now the fixed glass and its attached division bar can be installed. As seen in this photo, the division bar is much longer than the glass as it also serves as a track for the glass that moves. Carefully insert the division bar into the door opening and continue sliding it downward until it is in position. Be careful not to catch any wires or door latch linkages.

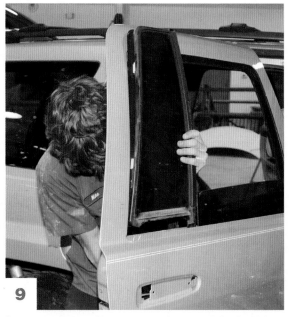

9

Do not use a hammer, but you may need to "bump" the division bar with your hand a time or two to fully seat it in the opening.

PART REPLACEMENT AND REASSEMBLY

132

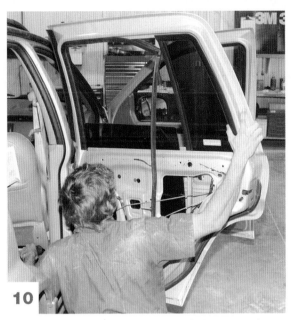

10

With the division bar installed, check and verify correct operation of the opening glass again. If it does not work smoothly, find the problem and fix it. You will see in this photo that there is quite a gap between the opening glass and the division bar where the weather stripping has not yet been installed.

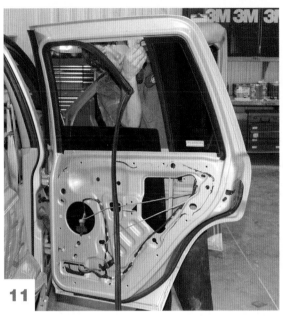

11

Almost forgot to install a screw at the top of the division bar! Pull the weather stripping down as required and install the screw.

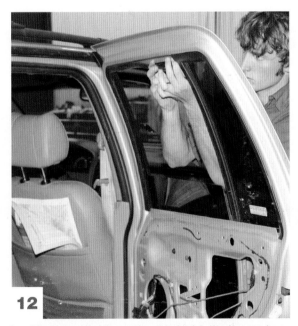

12

Insert the loose end of the weather stripping into the door opening. Now press the weather stripping into place around the top of the window opening and along the front edge of the division bar.

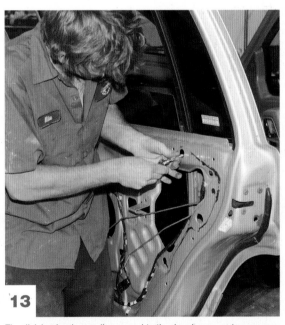

13

The division bar is usually secured to the door by one or two screws. Do not forget to install them.

(continued)

PART REPLACEMENT AND REASSEMBLY

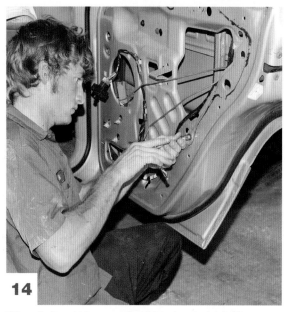

14

This particular vehicle secures the division bar at a total of three places. One is at the top of the window opening, the second is just below the bottom of the window opening, and the third is near the bottom of the division bar. Making sure that the division bar is secure helps ensure that there is no binding in the operation of the window.

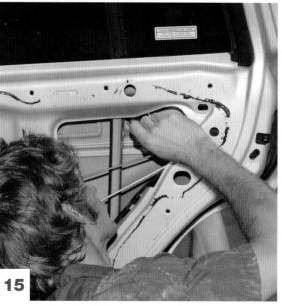

15

Install and secure the exterior door handle to the door. On this vehicle, it is secured with two bolts that pass through the interior of the door and thread into the handle mechanism.

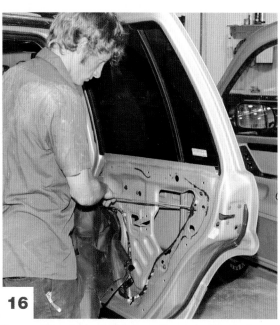

16

Reconnect the actuator rod(s) between the exterior door handle, the interior door handle, and the latch mechanism. You may need to refer to your photos and/or notes taken during disassembly to make sure you get this correct.

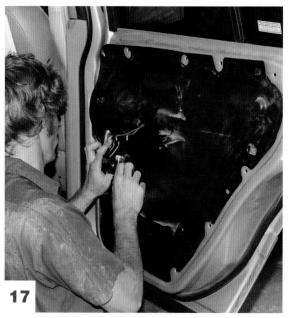

17

Some vehicles have a flexible panel that typically snaps into place between the door and the interior door panel. This is basically a method of insulation/sound deadening. If your vehicle has one, reinstall it and any stereo speakers that are installed in the door.

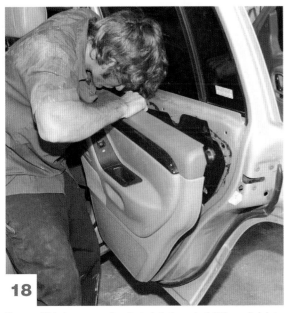

18

If your vehicle has power door locks/windows, install the switch into the interior door panel from the back side. You will find that another couple of inches of wire for these power accessories would have helped. Now reinstall the interior door panel. It may snap in place and/or be secured with small screws.

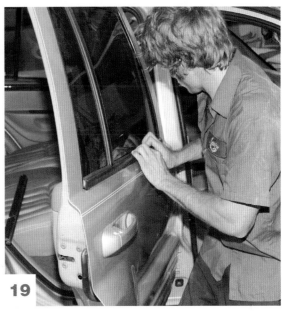

19

Now carefully install the exterior trim that is designed to prevent rainwater and other moisture from running down the door glass and into the inside of the door panel.

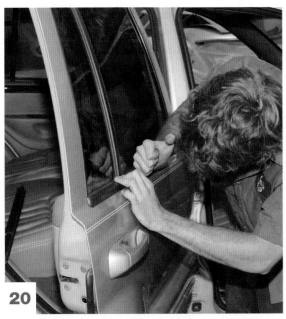

20

You may need to apply some extra effort to seat the trim in place, but be sure that it is aligned properly before exerting the extra effort. A few taps with your fist will usually do it if the panel is aligned properly.

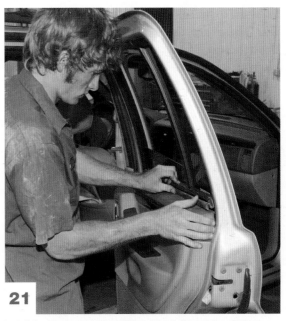

21

Install the interior garnish molding at the bottom of the window. On newer vehicles it generally snaps into place, but it might be secured with trim screws on older vehicles. In addition to the snaps that secure this interior door panel in place, one screw "hidden" away in the door pull secures it.

metals of different composition. The weaker of the two metals will corrode.

The screws, nuts, or bolts used to secure door handles are normally accessed through openings on the interior side of the door. You have to reach through with your hand to tighten the fasteners. Be sure to use wrenches or sockets of the correct size to make this awkward job as easy as possible. After handles and key locks are secured, you must attach linkages or cables that run to the actual latch mechanisms.

GRILLE

Most grille sections are secured by screws of some type. Many screws are tightened into metal clips, as opposed to nuts. These clips have to be positioned correctly in order to support the grille. Pay attention to the way you place clips, as they can slide around to cause scratches along the metal supports to which they fasten. Likewise, screws must line up with the center of these clips in order to work properly. Be sure you've determined the way the pieces fit together so you can install them in the required order.

Headlight buckets, housings, or trim rings are generally separate from grilles. This is so you can change a burned-out headlight without dismantling the entire grille. Remember, there are normally two screws next to headlights that tighten down over springs. These are used only for positioning the headlight beams. If you disturbed these screws, be sure you get them properly positioned again before you need to drive after dark.

As with other exterior trim pieces and accessories, you should take this opportunity to clean, polish, and detail grille assemblies while they are off your car. Touch up paint nicks, clean tiny nooks and crannies, and wax metallic parts as necessary. Use a soft toothbrush and cotton swabs to reach into tight spaces. Should painted parts look old and worn, consider sanding and repainting them. Tiny chips or nicks can be touched up with the proper paint, using a fine artist's paintbrush.

BUMPERS

Older cars and trucks feature bumpers that are relatively easy to take off and put back on. The bolts attaching them are generally in clear view and plenty of room is provided for adequate maneuverability. Newer cars, on the other hand, can require some rather intricate dismantling and installation procedures.

Many newer bumpers are actually combinations of a number of different parts. A basic frame assembly bolts onto supports that are mounted to structural members under the front or rear ends. To that frame, urethane faces, rock shields, guards, and other items may snap into place or attach with a number of screws. Install each part correctly or the entire unit may not be able to sit flush with ground effects or other body designs.

If you are not the person who originally removed the bumpers from your vehicle, or if you have simply forgotten how they are supposed to go back on, take your time during installation and do not cinch bolts or nuts down until you are sure the entire unit is assembled correctly. In some cases, install shields or faces before securing the bumper to the mounts; otherwise they won't fit into place. If that happens, simply loosen the bumper, pull it out, and insert the shield. Then, slip the unit back in and tighten it up.

Some front bumper assemblies are quite large, more or less encompassing the entire nose of the vehicle. To manage their size and weight, plan to have someone help you install them. In addition, most of these units feature many screws and bolts that work somewhat in unison to adjust the bumper from a number of different points. To position the bumper perfectly, move from fastener to fastener tightening them gradually. If you wrench one bolt too quickly, you may find that one side sticks out more than the other, or the gaps are not even around its periphery. Again, this is where a helper proves invaluable by lifting, pushing, or pulling parts of the bumper into their proper position and holding them there while you tighten the fasteners.

EMBLEMS AND BADGES

A thorough cleaning with a soft toothbrush and mild cleaner should remove accumulations of polish, wax, and dirt from tiny corners and impressions to make these items look like new. Be sure their fastening mechanisms are intact. Plastic emblems are not always easy to remove, and many times their plastic pins or supports crack during dismantling. If yours are damaged, you may have to replace them with new ones.

Chipped paint on emblems and badges does not necessarily mean you have to replace them. You can use an artist's paintbrush or lettering brush to repaint delicate emblem designs. Check with your auto body paint and supply professional to determine the correct

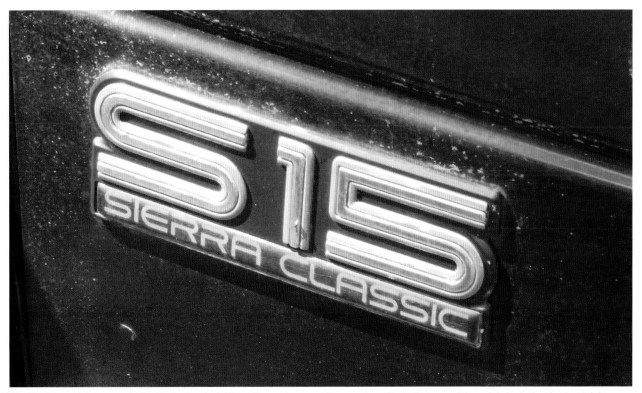

Trim like this used to be mounted to the fender, deck lid, or other body panel with a number of bolts that passed through holes in the sheet metal. As moisture penetrated behind the trim piece, the sheet metal began to rust. On a custom where all of the trim would be removed, the mounting holes would be welded shut prior to paint work. In the 1980s, auto manufacturers began using mostly plastic emblems that were simply glued in place by adhesive.

color. Unless your vehicle is a concours contender or other special classic, you might be able to match emblem colors closely with vials of auto body touch-up paint. However, for those vintage, classic, or concours needs, you may have to special order the perfect type and color paint to keep emblem and badge equipment in original condition.

New emblems, badges, and other decorative body items are normally available through dealership parts departments, even those for a lot of older cars and trucks. For parts unavailable at dealerships, you may have to look elsewhere for replacements. One of the best sources for locating companies that specialize in hard to find automobile parts is *Hemmings Motor News.*

This monthly publication is packed full of company-sponsored and individually supported advertisements that list just about every kind of automotive-related part, accessory, and service that any auto enthusiast could ask for. Since its hundreds of pages are broken down into a number of separate categories, you should be able to find a source for the

parts you need. Along with this publication, there are a lot of other magazines dedicated to auto enthusiasts, restorers, and do-it-yourself customizers. They also include sources for older car and truck parts.

VINYL TRIM

Unless you masked carefully along the edge of a vinyl stripe or decal for a spot paint job, chances are you removed the piece. Replacement vinyl stripes in all sorts of colors and widths, as well as decals, are available thorough dealership parts departments and auto body paint and supply stores.

If only one panel on your car was painted, leaving all of the rest of a vinyl stripe design intact, you might be able to purchase only the missing piece. Factory-installed stripes come in sections, while individual packets of custom striping just come in certain length rolls. Especially for newer cars, check with a dealership parts department when you need to buy a certain section of vinyl stripe tape. This saves you money over the purchase of an entire roll of matching, yet generic, stripe tape at the auto body paint and supply store.

Before attaching vinyl stripes or decals, make sure the fresh paint has cured according to label recommendations. Then, use a clean cloth dampened with wax and grease remover to clean those areas where you expect to attach them. Read any instructions provided with the vinyl material.

For vinyl pieces already cut to size, position them before peeling off any of the backing paper in order to match both ends equal distances from body panel edges, and also to be able to make adjustments to height as needed. One way to do this is by securing vinyl tape sections with a piece of masking tape. You can move the masking tape around as necessary until it is securing the vinyl tape exactly where you want it. Then, tilt the vinyl tape up from the masking tape— the masking tape acts as a hinge—remove the backing, and set the vinyl tape back down.

With thin stripes, you may be able to lightly lay a section down and lift it up again for repositioning. Wide stripes and decals are not so forgiving. Once their extra-strength adhesive makes contact with a body surface, they generally cannot be removed without suffering some sort of damage. So take your time, have patience, and ask someone to help you with large projects.

Match painted pinstripes using the proper kind of pinstripe paintbrush and slow-drying enamel paint, such as One-Shot Sign Painter's Enamel. Unless you have done this before, practice on an old hood or door before trying your hand on your favorite car. The Eastwood Company offers a full range of pinstripe and lettering paintbrushes for all kinds of uses. Eastwood also sells a variety of slow-drying lettering enamel most commonly used by professional pinstripers. Auto body paints and supply stores also sell these supplies.

Although practice with a pinstripe brush helps you learn how to put stripes on straight and symmetrically, you may have trouble matching the color of existing pinstripes. Professional pinstripers often mix different colors to arrive at new and exciting tints. Through trial and error, and some advice from a color expert at your auto body paint and supply store, you can match existing colors by following color charts and mixing drops of one color with drops of another.

In order to paint perfectly symmetrical and evenly spaced pinstripes, you might want to use stencil tape. Finesse Stencil Tape looks like pinstripe tape, except that all of the different sizes and designs are the same color. Apply it like vinyl pinstripe tape, but instead of staying on the car, use it only as a boundary for pinstripe paint. Paint attaches to the car body between tape sections in perfectly straight and even widths. Once the paint is dry, remove the tape for perfectly painted pinstripes. Finesse Stencil Tape is available at auto body paint and supply stores and artists' supply houses.

MISCELLANEOUS

Along with those parts already mentioned, you might have to install windshield wipers, license plates, side reflectors, trunk locks, radio antennae, luggage racks, door edge guards, mud flaps, running boards, ground effects, spoilers, weather stripping, hood bumpers, and so on. If you removed them in preparation for your car or truck's paint job, you should at least have some idea how to put them back on.

Use strips of masking tape to protect painted body areas adjacent to parts you're installing. Rest the doors atop crates or boxes while securing their hinges, and use large cotton towels to act as buffers between the doors and the crates. Think of new paint as your car's skin, and treat it as you would your own. Plan ahead while replacing parts and try to anticipate potential scratch or chip hazards. Use masking tape, towels, or cardboard to maximize the degree of protection offered newly painted parts so they do not incur scratches, chips, nicks, scrapes, gouges, or blemishes of any kind.

Chapter 10
Keeping the Shine

After spending considerable hours, and maybe even days, cleaning, polishing, painting, and waxing exterior body parts, you may think that your car is detailed to the highest degree. But have you looked at the vents on your car's dashboard? Are they dusty? If you spent any time at all sanding the body of your car or truck, chances are good that more sanding dust than you had imagined has infiltrated the interior, trunk, and engine compartment. That stuff is amazing. It seems to find its way into just about every nook and cranny possible.

CLEANING

Since the outside of your automobile looks so good, why not spend a little time on the interior? Your vacuum cleaner with a soft brush attachment will work well to remove large accumulations of dust on and around the dashboard. Use a soft cloth, toothbrush, or cotton swab to clean corners and confined spaces. The vacuum cleaner's crevice attachment fits into tight spaces around seats and center consoles to remove dust and debris.

Mix a small amount of a cleaner such as Simple Green in a bucket and dip cleaning cloths into it periodically to

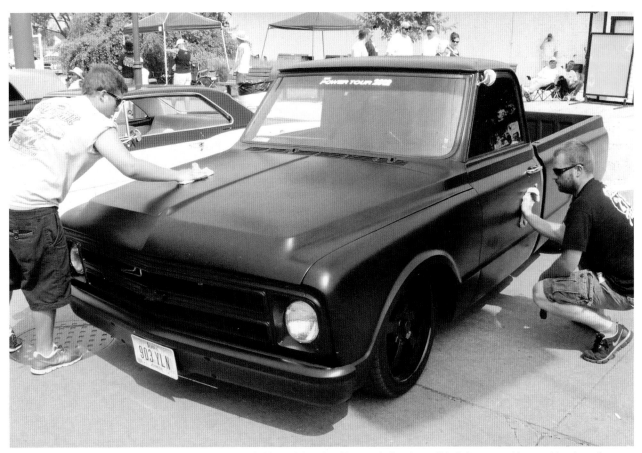

Who says the "primer look" is low maintenance? Even though this truck is painted in a semi-gloss form of black, to presumably resemble primer, these guys were quick to bring out the cleaning supplies to get rid of any road rash upon arrival at a major car event. Regardless of the quality of the bodywork or paint, any vehicle will look better if it is clean.

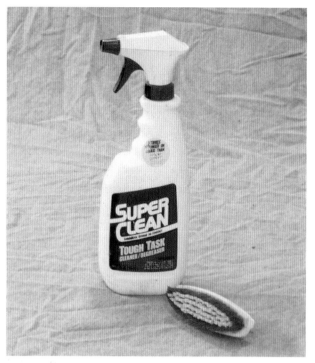

Your local auto parts store or discount store should have a wide variety of all-purpose cleaners in their car care section. While you are there, pick up a small scrub brush for scrubbing those stubborn stains. Remember that the hardest part of keeping a vehicle clean is just doing it. Once you get it clean and then properly maintain it, it will be easier to keep clean.

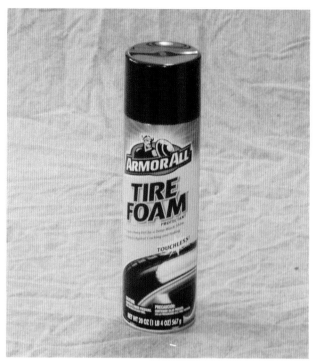

Armor-All and others have a large selection of products for cleaning, detailing, and protecting tires, hoses, and other surfaces. Avoid getting these products or any others that contain silicone on painted surfaces. Should the panel ever require repaint, an abundance of silicone on the surface can quickly cause paint defects; however, cleaning the surface with soap and water prior to paint application can help to minimize the damage.

Doesn't everyone know that a car runs better if the windows are clean? They certainly look better. A good glass cleaner, paper towels, and 10 minutes of your time will have your car's windows looking great. Just make sure that you do not get primer or paint on your vehicle's glass. Masking beforehand is much better than scraping with a razor blade later.

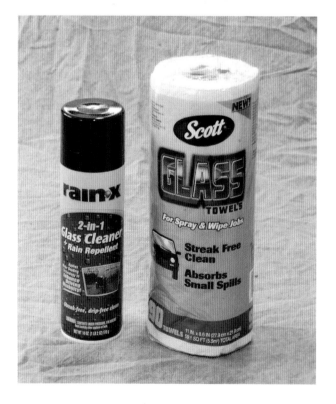

help clean sticky steering wheels, stained sun visors, dirty door panels, and vinyl seats. You will be amazed at how much dirt gathers on your cleaning cloth.

DETAILING

Next, vacuum the trunk thoroughly. If yours is an older American car that features an open metal space with no cardboard or carpet siding, and if it has been neglected for far too long, take the time to detail it. Remove scale, rust deposits, and other debris with a wire brush. Use a vacuum to remove residue. Then consider applying a couple of coats of a rust-inhibiting paint as a sealer. To really make the trunk space look new and original, apply a quality coat of trunk splatter paint. Two cans are generally enough for normal-sized 1950 to 1970 vintage American car trunks.

Trunk splatter paint comes in a few different colors. The unique part about splatter paint is that three colors are generally spit out. The base color might be gray, highlighted by spots of white and black, just like an original finish. Do not apply this material to the back of the rear seats, and make sure the entire space is clean before application.

Engine compartments can present detailers with more than just sanding dust. Cleaning the engine compartment may seem impossible after years of accumulated grease and oil buildup. An engine cleaner like Gunk, however, combined with the pressure from the wand of a self-serve car wash, easily removes the bulk of those accumulations. Be sure to cover newly painted fenders with large towels or other soft material, and keep the water wand away from the distributor and carburetor.

After that, some time with a stiff paintbrush and a cleaner such as Simple Green can make the engine compartment on your automobile look almost as good as the new paint job. You can take more time to make the engine compartment look better by painting the engine block and polishing all of those items that need it. The more you do, the better it will look.

LONG-TERM PAINT CARE

Although newer catalyzed paint products are much more durable and longer lasting than the materials used before them, you cannot expect their finish to shine forever without a minimal amount of routine maintenance. Routine maintenance entails washing, polishing, and periodic waxing as needed.

Even though some paint products may be advertised as never requiring wax, many auto enthusiasts and professionals believe that good coats of wax not only help provide great paint longevity, but also make washing car bodies a lot easier. It almost seems like dirt and road debris float off waxed surfaces.

Sooner or later, nicks and chips begin to appear on your vehicle (unless it's a show car that is seldom, if ever, driven). Along with regular maintenance, you must also repair these minor paint problems as soon as possible. If not, exposed metal will oxidize and that corrosion will spread under paint to affect adjacent metal areas.

Washing, Polishing, and Waxing

For years, farmers washed their tractors with kerosene. Not only did it do a good job of cleaning, but it also afforded a measure of rust protection by forming a film over the tractor body. This procedure might be good for farmer's tractors, but it is certainly not the way you should take care of your newly painted car or truck.

Auto parts stores, some variety outlets, and even a few supermarkets sell car wash soap products. For the most part, almost any brand should be well suited for the finish on your vehicle. Many auto enthusiasts prefer to use liquids, as opposed to granular types, because they believe that just one undissolved granule on a wash mitt could cause scratches. Be sure to follow the mixing directions on labels of any product that you use.

The best way to prevent minute scratches or other blemishes in the paint is to wash the car in sections. Wash the hood, roof, and trunk areas first. Then clean the vehicle sides. Finish up with the dirtiest parts, like rocker panels, fender well lips, and the lower front and rear end panels.

Anytime you notice that your wash mitt is dirty, or if it should fall to the ground, always rinse it off with clear water before dipping it into the wash bucket. This helps to keep the wash water clean and free of debris.

To clean inside tight spaces, like window molding edges and cowl louvers, use a soft, natural hair, floppy paintbrush. Do not use synthetic-bristled paintbrushes because they could cause minute scratches on paint surfaces. In addition, wrap a thick layer of heavy duct tape over the paintbrush's metal band. This will help to guard against paint scratches or nicks as you vigorously agitate the paintbrush in tight spaces, possibly knocking the brush into painted body parts such as those around headlights and grilles.

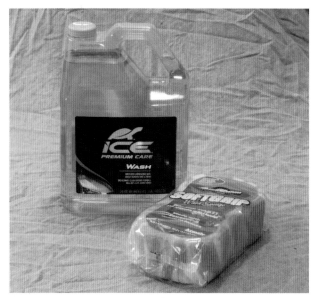

Your choice of car wash liquids, a large sponge (or car wash mitt,) a bucket, and a hose are all you really need to improve the looks of your car in as few as 30 minutes or so. While automatic car washes are good (some better than others), doing a good, old-fashioned hand wash on your vehicle will give you a better idea of the condition of your vehicle's paint and body condition.

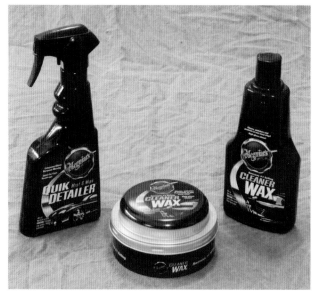

Several companies offer a wide variety of auto detailing products, but my personal favorite is Meguiars. Shown are their paste wax (center), liquid wax (right), and Quik Detailer (left). The latter is great for quick use after washing your vehicle, presuming that it already has a good coat of wax on it. This is great for shining up your vehicle for a show or special date, without building up too much wax that can begin to look dull.

Let's talk a moment about polish and wax. Although both products are designed as paint finish maintenance materials, each has its own separate purpose. Polishes clean paint finishes and remove oxidation and other contaminants. Wax, on the other hand, does no cleaning or shining. It does, however, protect those paint finishes that have already been cleaned and polished. Simply stated, polish cleans; wax protects.

Auto body paint and supply stores generally carry the largest selection of auto polishes and waxes, although many auto parts stores stock good assortments. Every polish should include a definitive label that explains what kind of paint finish it is designed for—heavily oxidized, mildly oxidized, and/or new finish glaze. Those designed for heavy oxidation problems contain much coarser grit than those for new car finishes.

The labels also note whether the product is intended for machine (buffer) use. Those with heavy concentrations of coarse grit are not recommended for machine use. Their polishing strength, combined with the power of a buffer, could cause large-scale paint burning problems.

Carnauba wax is perhaps the best product to use for protecting automobile paint finishes. Meguiar's, Eagle 1, and other cosmetic car-care product manufacturers offer auto enthusiasts an assortment of carnauba-based auto wax products. There are other paint protection products available that profess to work like wax, but contain different chemical bases react differently to your vehicle's finish. You must clearly understand this before applying them to your new paint job.

Some of these (typically, they have poly or polymer in the product name) are loaded with silicone materials. Although they may protect your car's finish for a long time, professional auto painters advise against them because the silicone can saturate the paint right down to the metal and create fish-eye problems if you need another repaint down the road. In some cases, silicones can even become embedded in the sheet metal itself.

If you find yourself in a quandary when it comes time to select a polish or wax product, seek advice from a knowledgeable auto body paint and supply professional. This person should be up-to-date on the latest product information from manufacturers and the view professional painters and detailers in the field have of the products.

When to Wash New Paint Finishes

Allow plenty of time for your paint's solvents to evaporate or chemically react before washing the vehicle. For uncatalyzed enamels, this may entail a few days or a week. You can generally wash newer paints with hardener additives after one or two days, as long as you use mild automotive soap products and a gentle approach.

Because auto painters have such a wide selection of paint products to choose from and since each brand or system may react differently from others, it is always best to confirm appropriate paint drying times with a professional auto body paint and supply professional before washing, polishing, or waxing any new finish.

How Long Before Waxing?

The rule of thumb is to wait 90 to 120 days before waxing your freshly painted vehicle. This length of time varies according to weather conditions. During summer months, while temperatures are warm and humidity low, 90 days should allow plenty of time for paint solvents to completely evaporate. Cool, wet weather reduces solvent evaporation activity and therefore requires a longer waiting period.

Light coats of quality auto wax actually form a protective seal on top of the paint finish. Even though it is quite thin and by no means permanent, this wax seal prevents solvent evaporation. When solvents evaporate, vapors that need to exit paint are trapped. As a result, they slowly build up pressure within the paint, which eventually damages it, frequently in the form of blistering.

So instead of protecting a paint surface, waxing too soon after new paint applications can actually cause unexpected damage. Remember, this is wax, not polish. Polish does not normally carry with it any long-lasting protective additives. Its main function is to clean and shine. Be aware that many new cosmetic paint finish products are advertised as cleaner-waxes. They do combine polish and wax ingredients.

Do not use combination polish/wax products until paint has cured for at least 90 to 120 days, because the wax ingredients in these products forms a light seal over surfaces and traps solvents, just like dedicated wax-only products. If you need to polish a new catalyzed or lacquer paint job, be absolutely certain it contains no wax ingredients. Read labels to be sure, and do not be afraid to consult with an auto body paint and supply store professional.

Repairing Small Nicks

No matter how hard you try to guard against them, small nicks or paint chips find their way onto new paint finishes much sooner than expected. For those vehicles driven on a daily basis, this dilemma is simply unavoidable. Along with rock chips that occur in traffic, parking lot door slammers are merciless. Add to that a long list of other accidental and careless mishaps and sooner or later your new paint job suffers some degree of minor damage. Fortunately you can repair small nicks with a minimal amount of work, providing they are small and the affected paint job is not exotic. You need some touch-up paint, a small artist's or lettering paintbrush, and masking tape.

Clean the damaged area with wax and grease remover and then closely mask off the nick, or nicks. Stir or shake the touch-up paint as needed. Now simply dab your paintbrush into paint and retrieve just a very small amount of paint on the tip of the bristles. Apply that drop of paint to the nick. Do not attempt to fill in the entire nick depth with the first paint dab. Wait for a while to let the first dab set up, and then apply a second small dab.

Continue the dabbing and setting up until paint has filled the nick to just over the surface. It should be obvious before you quit that you've applied touch-up paint above the height of the main finish; in other words, it should look as if you put on too much paint. Then let the new paint cure. Do not touch it for about a week to 10 days.

After a lengthy drying period, mask the nick again. This time, mask a wider area. Then use 1,200-grit sandpaper with water to gently smooth the nick area and bring the surface of the new paint down to the surrounding finish. The masking tape will prevent unnecessary sanding on the surface surrounding the repair area.

When you have smoothed the newly applied dabs of paint to the same level as the rest of the finish, remove the masking tape. Then, use polish to further blend the repair into its surroundings. If polishing scratches appear, graduate to a finer polish. Let the repair cure for a few weeks before waxing.

Other than vehicles that grow old sitting in a museum, all vehicles are going to be subjected to flying gravel or other road debris, accidental, or deliberate damage. While some of that damage will require professional help, minor rock chips or scratches can be repaired with a just a little bit of touch-up paint.

If just a little bit of paint has been separated from the vehicle's body, but there is no other damage to the sheet metal, some touch-up paint in the appropriate color and a small piece of 800-grit or finer sandpaper is all you need. Auto parts stores used to have a pretty good stock of touch-up paint, but with the ever increasing variety of colors, many have quit carrying touch-up paint. If this is the case with your local auto parts store, you may need to purchase touch-up paint from the dealer where you purchased your vehicle. While this might be slightly more expensive, it will be the best bet in getting the correct color. In either case, you may need to review the paint and options tag for your vehicle to find the correct color code.

Once you find the correct color, the rest is pretty easy. Most paint touch-up bottles include a small brush, built right into the cap. This makes the paint easy to apply, but like all great paint jobs, there is some amount of prep work to be completed first. Just as primer and paint

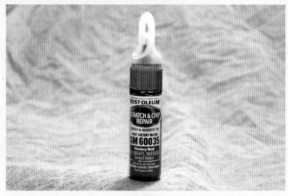

I was able to find this touch-up paint for my 2008 Chevrolet Silverado along with several other common colors at a local discount department store. This particular label includes the name of the color (Victory Red)—the same as my truck—and the numbers below the name match the numbers from the truck's paint and options tag. It is the correct touch up paint for my application.

being sprayed from a spray gun, touch-up paint will not properly adhere to wax, grease, or dirt. Saturate a paper towel with wax and grease remover and wipe off the area to be repaired. Then wipe the area dry with a clean paper towel. If you have a piece of 800-grit sandpaper of finer, use it to lightly scuff the surface where the touch-up paint is to be applied. Avoid scuffing undamaged paint. Clean the area again, then brush on a light coat of touch-up paint to the affected area and give it ample time to dry.

Chances are that this first brushed on coat will appear rough and uneven. Use the same extremely fine sandpaper that you used previously to sand down the new paint to a smooth surface. It is not your intent or desire to sand the touch-up paint off, just make it smooth. When it is smooth, clean away any sanding residue, then apply another light coat of touch-up paint, just as before. Let the touch-up paint dry and repeat the process until the rock chip or scratch is no longer noticeable.

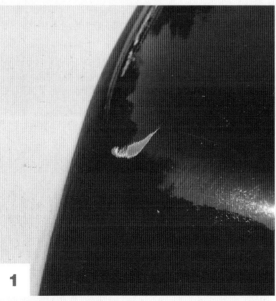

1 Large or small, clean any areas to be painted in order for the paint to adhere to the surface. Spray on some wax and grease remover, then wipe it off with a clean paper towel.

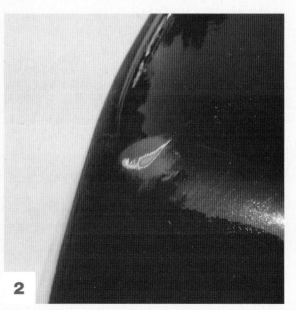

2 Use 1,000-grit or finer sandpaper to knock off the slick surface of the area so the paint has some tooth to grip to. Notice that the area to be touched up has a slightly cloudy look to it after being scuffed.

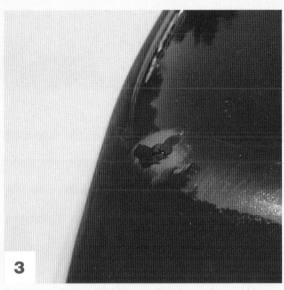

3 Shake the bottle of touch-up paint well prior to each use. Using the brush in the cap of the touch-up paint, apply a light coat to the affected area. Apply a light coat, so that it will dry quickly. Complete coverage may require several applications.

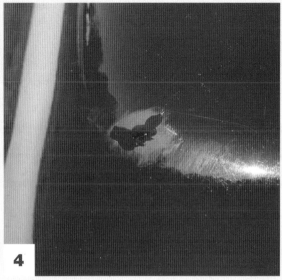

4 If there are any globs after the touch-up paint has dried, gently sand the surface again. Unlike a dent that may be filled with body filler, this type of repair is being filled with paint only.

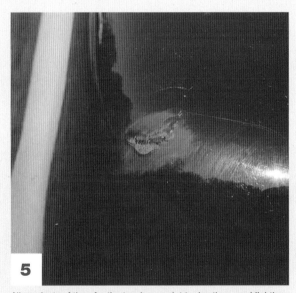

5 Allow plenty of time for the touch-up paint to dry, then sand lightly again, and apply more touch-up paint. Repeat the process until coverage is achieved and the surface finish is repaired.

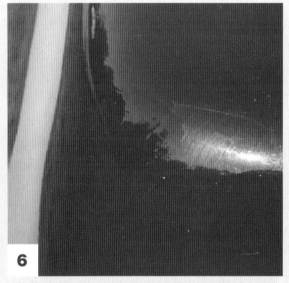

6 In this final photo, the repair is covered, but the paint doesn't match as well as I would like. However, it is not bad considering that the truck is red, close to five years old, and sits outside all the time. The OEM paint has faded somewhat, so matching it exactly may be difficult at best. After the paint is thoroughly dry and the paint touch-up is finished, wash the vehicle and apply a coat of high-quality wax.

OVERVIEW

As long as you have your automobile torn down for paint work, why not spend some extra time detailing the extras? Not only will the effort make your paint job look its best, but it will also do a lot to prolong the life of many accessory parts. Besides, everyone knows an automobile runs better when the windows are clean.

Automotive paint jobs can last for years as long as their finishes are maintained, protected, and not abused. Frequent washing, maintaining effective wax protection, and limiting exposure to ultraviolet rays will add greatly to almost any paint job's longevity. Although the new catalyzed paint systems are more durable than most paint products employed before them, gross neglect will cause their shine and luster to fade and oxidize over time. It is up to you to maintain them in clean condition and prevent the penetration of lingering dirt, tree sap, bird droppings, airborne pollution, and mildew.

Soft wash mitts, soft cotton towels, and soft waxing applicators and cloths go a long way toward keeping paint finishes in pristine condition. Operating any mitt or cloth on your car's surface in a straight back-and-forth movement also helps to greatly reduce the formation of swirls or spider-webbing. Always read the labels of any car wash soap, polish, or wax product to determine exactly what it is intended to do. If you still don't understand, ask for help.

Quality car covers made of materials that breathe provide an excellent means for overall paint protection, especially when your car has to sit out in the sun for days on end. The sun is your paint finish's enemy. The more you can do to prevent it from suffering through endless days of baking under harsh sunlight, the longer its shine will last. If a quality car cover is not within your budget now, try parking in the shadow of a building. Or park head-first in the parking lot on one day and then back in the next to alternate sunlight exposure between your car's body sides.

From beginning to end, automobile painting can be interesting, illuminating, fun, and rewarding. By the time you complete your project, you will have devoted a lot of time to sanding, masking, spraying, cleaning, and polishing. You will have spent a lot of time reading product information sheets and application guides, as well as conferring with your local auto body paint and supply professional. You will have spent hundreds of dollars on materials, chemicals, tools, and equipment. But you will have saved much more by doing the job yourself and will have also gained much more personal satisfaction than you ever could by simply dropping your favorite car off at the local paint shop.

With advances in chemical technology, automobile painting has become a high-tech profession. The multitude of material choices and their ability to blend or bond with similar yet unlike substances create tremendous potential—and also some risks—for the person seeking to apply his or her own paint. In this arena, you have to read labels and confirm product usage with your auto body paint and supply professional. And you absolutely must acknowledge, accept, understand, and incorporate all of the available safety recommendations set forth by paint manufacturers and the regulatory agencies responsible for overall worker safety. Your health, and that of those around you, is more important than any vehicle and any paint job. Protect yourself first, so you can enjoy the fruits of your labors for a good, long time.

After your job is complete, tools wiped off and put away, material carefully sealed and stored, your work place squared away and hands cleaned, stop and take a good long look at your achievement. Although it takes years of experience to become a professional automobile painter, conscientious auto enthusiasts with a keen do-it-yourself desire to learn can accomplish professional results, if they understand the basics and are not afraid to ask for help. I hope this book has given you the information and confidence to go out and give auto painting a try.

Chapter 11
Painting Other Parts and Components

Throughout most of this book, my advice to the novice painter has been to use base coat/clear coat for your automotive projects. The reason for this is quite simple . . . you can apply enough base coat to achieve coverage and then protect that color with clear. You can then wet sand, buff, and polish the clear to obtain a fantastic shine with relative ease. Many novice painters end up with more runs and drips while they try in vain to build up gloss with a single-stage paint. Additionally, fenders, doors, and other panels are fairly easy to buff and polish to a nice shine.

However, not everything is as easy to buff and polish, but you still want it to shine when you are done. For some of these instances, such as a chassis, wheels, and an engine block, single-stage acrylic urethane has proven to be a more appropriate choice for obtaining the desired results. If you are simply painting your car in order to make it look a little bit better until you can afford a different one, you will probably never paint these items. But if you have the slightest bit of

automotive enthusiast in your blood, the following will be good stuff to know.

PAINTING AN ENGINE BLOCK

Whether you are building a high-performance engine for your hot rod or swapping a rebuilt or junkyard engine into your daily driver, the engine should be painted before you install it. It simply is not any easier to clean, paint, and detail than it is while it is out of the vehicle. Besides looking much nicer whenever you open the hood, a clean and nicely painted engine will make it easier to spot small leaks before they become a big problem.

If the engine is covered with the slightest bit of oil and grease, load the engine into the back of a pickup truck or onto a trailer and haul it down to the local car wash. Make sure that the induction system and distributor are covered to protect them from moisture, then blast away with the "engine cleaner" setting of the car wash until the bulk of the oil and grease is gone or at least loosened from the engine. Then rinse everything off with the high-pressure rinse cycle. If this didn't get all of the grease and grime off the engine, you may need to spend some time with an assortment of putty knives and wire brushes, along with some engine cleaner from your favorite auto parts store. No matter what you have

The best way to paint an engine is to mount it on a rotatable engine stand. Remove any removable components that are not to be painted and mask any surfaces that should not be painted. Clean the surface thoroughly and apply the primer and paint of your choice. After the paint has had plenty of time to dry, remove any masking materials and verify that machined surfaces are free of paint. Use the proper size tap to chase any holes that may have received paint, prior to bolting on components.

As this book is being written, I am beginning the construction of a 1955 Chevrolet pickup (similar to the 1957 GMC pickup that I drove in high school). My wheels of choice for the project are a set of steel GM rally wheels. Although a valid argument could be made for painting them in a contrasting color to the vehicle's color, I am choosing to paint them the same color. In addition, since wheels are 1) susceptible to rock chips, and 2) difficult to sand and buff due to their contours, I'm going to paint them with a single-stage acrylic urethane. This type of paint lends itself to simple touch-up should the need arise and I feel that I can avoid runs in the paint, yet still obtain very glossy results. The brand of paint does not really matter, but for anyone who might ask, I'll be using PPG's Concept® Acrylic Urethane, paint code 60972 over light gray Epoxy Primer. The steel wheels are advertised as having a silver powder coat; however, close inspection shows some areas where that coating is not what I would describe as seamless.

To better prepare the surface, begin by washing the wheels with warm soap and water and rinsing them well to remove any soap. After drying the wheels with a lint free towel or having let them drip dry, blow any moisture out of the crooks and crevices with compressed air. Then finish cleaning the wheels by applying wax and grease remover by spraying directly onto the wheels or by using a saturated paper towel. Then wipe away any wax and grease with a clean towel. Use a red Scotch-Brite™ pad to scuff the surface and to featheredge any defects in the powdercoated surface. When you have scuffed the surface sufficiently, the existing surface will have a uniform dull finish to it. You should now use an air nozzle on your air hose to blow away any dust that you might have created. Repeat the final cleaning step with wax and grease remover as described previously.

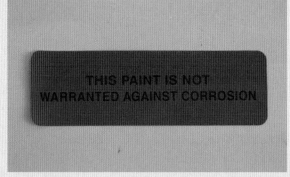

This is one of the stickers that was on the wheels as I received them. Although the wheels are advertised as having a silver powder coat (to give the same appearance as when they were OEM equipment), the wheels do come with this warning. I suppose the existing powder coat is to prevent them from rusting prior to reaching the customer.

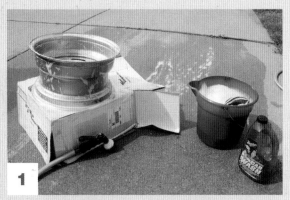

1 Using car wash soap, water, and a car wash mitt, wash off the wheels prior to doing anything else to them. While the wheels probably won't be dirty, this step is the first step toward removing any contaminants from causing a paint-related problem, as well as removing the aforementioned warning labels.

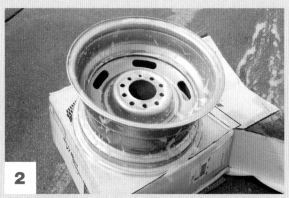

2 As well as removing any dirt or contaminants, be sure to rinse the wheels completely to get rid of the soap as well. No, I don't plan to use the cardboard box for anything now that it is soaked, but I did want to keep the wheels from scuffing on the concrete driveway.

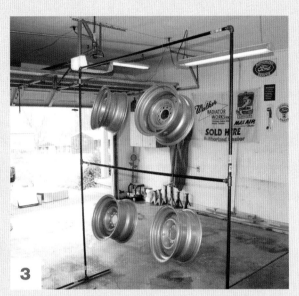

3 For this project, I built an easily assembled/disassembled rack out of ½ inch black iron pipe that is readily available at home repair centers, such as Lowe's or Home Depot. Having the wheels hanging made them much easier to paint than having to paint one side then flipping them over to paint the other side.

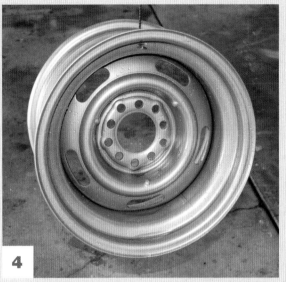

4 After rinsing the wheels and letting them drip dry for a while, use an air hose to blow them completely dry. Be sure to get all of the moisture out of the crevice between the outer wheel and the wheel center. This is a fairly tight crevice where water can hide and then drip out of at the least opportune time, just to ruin your paint job.

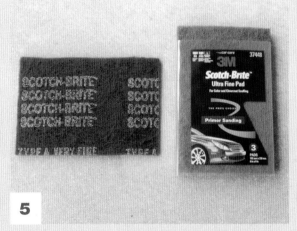

5 As mentioned in the text, you will need to use two different grades of Scotch-Brite™ for this type of project. Use the more coarse "red" pads to scuff the tough surface of the factory finish and later use the less coarse "gray" pad to lightly scuff the primer finish prior to painting.

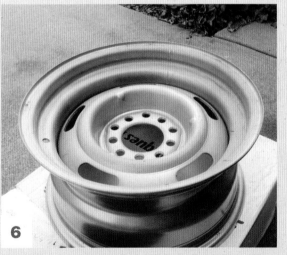

6 After scuffing the powdercoat finish with the "red" pad, there will be a bit of dust and the surface will now have a dull finish compared to the original shiny surface.

(continued)

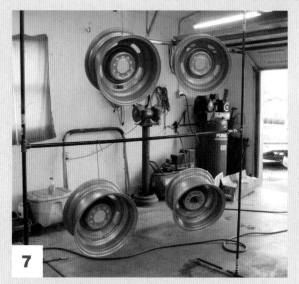

7

With all of the wheels hanging on the paint rack, spray them with wax and grease remover, or wipe them down with a folded paper towel saturated with wax and grease remover. I have found that spraying is much easier and ultimately uses less product.

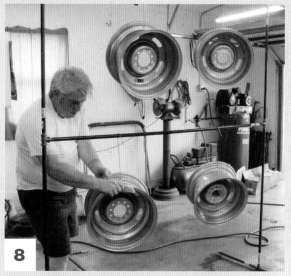

8

After applying the wax and grease remover by whichever method works best for you, wipe the wheels dry with a paper towel. Use a paper towel in each hand as you want to avoid getting oils from your hands on the surface as well. As you can see from this photo, this work is being done in my home garage, proving that a fancy spray booth is not really a must have.

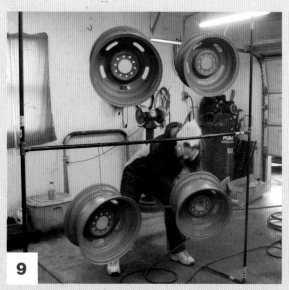

9

While you don't have to have a paint suit as I am wearing in this photo, you must keep your body protected when spraying epoxy primer or any paint product that contains isocyanates. Simply put, isocyanates are very bad for your health and can enter your bloodstream through your skin, nose, or even your eyes. Therefore, you must keep your body covered as well as using a filtered mask.

Stir the epoxy primer sufficiently until all clumps of solids at the bottom of the can are now liquid. Then mix the epoxy primer and catalyst following the mixing instructions and allow for any induction period if needed. Be sure to use a strainer as you pour the two parts of the epoxy primer into the mixing cup and use a clean strainer as you pour the mixture into the spray cup.

To make navigating around the undulating contour of the wheels, use a detail spray gun if you have one. Regardless of which type of spray gun that you use, verify that it has a large enough fluid tip for the epoxy primer to pass through. Using a piece of paper or cardboard as a target, adjust your spray gun to the correct spray pattern, and then apply two coats of epoxy primer to the wheels. Be sure to allow the proper flash time between coats.

If you are in a hurry, you could top coat the wheels with color within an hour or two. Your primer and paint information sheets lists the specific drying time. However, my choice is to allow the wheels and their new coats of epoxy primer to sit overnight. Regardless of when you paint, clean the wheels again with wax and grease remover, and scuff them slightly with a gray Scotch-Brite™ pad (slightly finer than the red pads). After cleaning one last time with wax and grease remover, mix the acrylic urethane, temperature appropriate reducer, and hardener and apply in accordance with the product's instruction sheet. Apply acrylic urethane in two coats (or until coverage). If you feel the need or desire to polish the wheels after painting them, you should apply an extra coat of color. After allowing the wheels to completely dry (refer to the information sheets for your specific products) tires can be mounted and balanced.

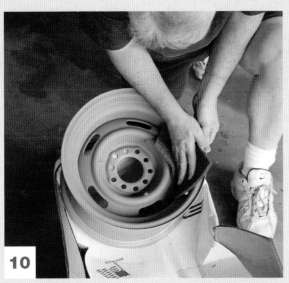

10

After waiting the required time (refer to the specific primer's instruction sheet), scuff the surface of the wheels slightly with a gray Scotch-Brite™ pad. This will assure that there is good adhesion between the primer and the top coat.

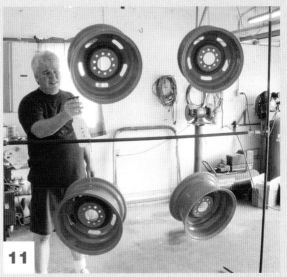

11

After scuffing the primed wheels with the gray pad and blowing any dust away with an air hose, I hung the wheels on my impromptu paint rack. Then I sprayed each wheel with wax and grease remover.

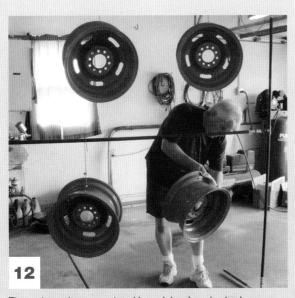

12

Then using a clean paper towel in each hand, each wheel was wiped down to remove any wax, grease, or other contaminant that might spoil the paint finish. Again, clean towels were used with each wheel. Otherwise, you are just spreading contaminants from one wheel to the next.

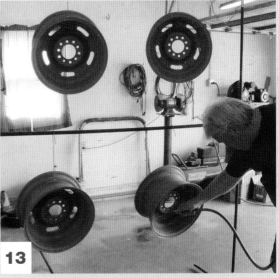

13

After wiping away any residue, use an air hose with nozzle to blow any dust or dirt out of the crevice between the wheel center and the outer wheel. Be sure to wipe off or blow dry any of the wax and grease remover.

(continued)

PAINTING OTHER PARTS AND COMPONENTS

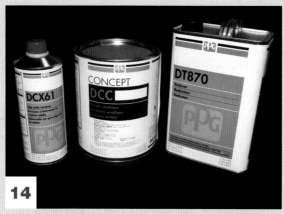

14

Most paint companies have multiple lines of products, with each having their own set of advantages. These wheels and the truck they are going on is intended to be a long-time keeper, so I felt justified in using PPG's top of the line acrylic urethane (single stage). Color is in the round can in the middle, temperature appropriate reducer is in the square can, with hardener in the smaller can. Mixing ratio for the three is 4:2:1, respectively.

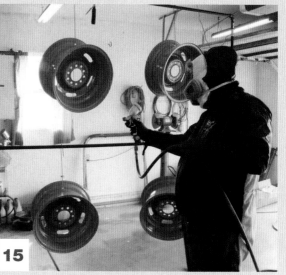

15

After suiting up with a Shoot Suit, rubber gloves, head sock, glasses, and filter mask, I could then get to spraying paint. Mix the paint, check the spray pattern, adjust gun as necessary, and then apply two wet coats with the proper amount of time between coats. Be sure to check the instructions for the specific products you are using, as there are many variables to doing it correctly. If necessary, apply additional coats to achieve full coverage.

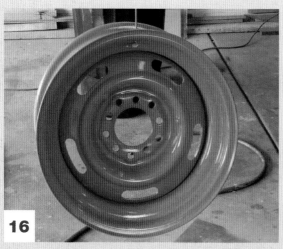

16

I didn't have a specific paint code to use when I ordered my paint. I just knew that I wanted a nice, clean, solid orange, so I was pleased to see that the color I chose based on a postage stamp–size sample ended up being what I was looking for. To match the paint now, I just have to refer to the number on the label of the can.

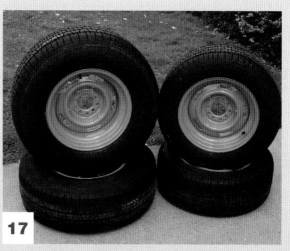

17

To put the wheels into a little better perspective, here they are mounted and balanced. With today's technology, wheel and tire assemblies can be balanced with all of the required weight being placed on the inside of the wheel. The benefit of that is that the tire technicians should not damage the outside of your wheels when they install the wheel weights.

PAINTING OTHER PARTS AND COMPONENTS

to do to get it done, remove all grease and oil from the engine block prior to painting it.

If you have not done so already, secure the engine block on an engine stand. After you have the engine degreased, remove any bolt-on items, such as the starter, exhaust, and carburetor. Plug or cap any holes that might allow moisture into the engine's internals. If you are going to do any grinding on the outside of the engine, now is the time to do it. Most engine blocks have a fair amount of "rough" casting that when removed goes a long ways toward improving the engine's appearance. However, be sure that you do not remove or obscure any of the engine's ID numbers, as that may lead to problems when you attempt to license the vehicle or sell it later. With all of the grinding done, you may want to use a strong magnet to help pick up any metal chips or shavings. When that is done, wash the block with some warm soapy water. Again, make sure you have capped any orifices before doing so. Remove the excess water with clean towels and an air hose. Anything that should not be painted, such as the carburetor mounting flange, should be masked off with masking tape. Finally, just as with every other pre-paint process, clean all of the surfaces to be painted with wax and grease remover.

Now you have the choice of spraying the engine with high temperature engine enamel from a spray can or using automotive grade paint to match or contrast with your vehicle's paint scheme. For some situations, a spray can (or two) will be adequate. If this is your choice, spray multiple light coats (allowing an appropriate flash time between coats), rather than one heavy coat.

If you choose to use automotive-grade paint, you should apply a couple of coats of epoxy primer first, again allowing proper flash time between coats, and then follow up with your choice of color. Unless you are working toward a custom show car, single-stage urethane will most likely be adequate for providing enough shine for the engine. You could use base coat/clear coat, but you will find that an engine block will be very time consuming to color sand, buff, and polish.

Whenever you are finished painting and detailing your engine block, let it set for a day or two prior to mounting any accessories, so that the paint has plenty of time to cure, and not lift when you remove bolt-on parts later.

SPRAY BOMBS, RATTLE CANS, AND GRAFFITI

Anyone who has ever *really* looked at a new vehicle on the showroom floor or at a well-detailed vehicle at a car show

quickly realizes that there are a wide variety of finishes on a vehicle. Some are glossy, some are not, and others are at different places between the two. Some are rough, some are smooth, while others go on clear. Your favorite ride is also subject to a wide variety of custom finishes.

Most of these specialty products are available in bulk for spray, roller, or spray gun application, but are also available in spray cans as well. Among these products are finishes specially designed for brake calipers, radiators, imitation cadmium plating, underhood, carburetors, aluminum, high temperature exhaust, gas tanks, and trunk spatter. Perhaps the best way to determine what you need is to look around at car shows to find vehicles detailed as you desire, and then ask the owner which products they used to obtain those results. Most car fanatics will gladly tell you how they improved anything on their vehicles.

Except for these and possibly other specialty coatings (such as touch-up paint), refrain from using spray cans when painting or detailing your vehicle. While buying a case of spray cans from the local discount store may seem like an inexpensive paint job, you will not be happy with the results in the not so long run. If you are serious about priming and/or painting your vehicle, borrow, rent, or buy the equipment to do it right if you want it to last.

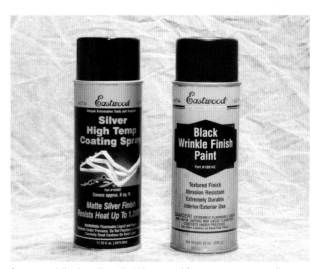

Some specialized coatings that I have used from a spray can are silver high temp coating spray and black wrinkle finish paint, both from Eastwood. The matte silver finish was an inexpensive finish that looked OK on the exhaust system on the Track T project seen elsewhere in this book. The black wrinkle finish was used on the valve covers of that same project to simulate Ford Cobra valve covers.

Although I don't know how old it (the truck) or he (my wife's grandfather) was when he bought this 1985 GMC S15 pickup, he drove it for several years after turning 90 years old. Although he managed to keep the sheet metal straight, he couldn't (or at least didn't) keep it from rusting. Fast forward several years and this same truck is being handed down four generations to our nephew. Alex, like most any other new driver, is looking forward to having his own set of wheels. As luck would have it, yours truly is working on a paint book and I simply couldn't stand the thought of Alex driving to school in an absolute rust bucket. Well, I needed something to take pictures of for the book anyway. . .

The following photos give a realistic glimpse of a complete paint job from start to finish. For the most part, they are in chronological order, rather than following one part or group of pieces through the entire process. Part of the reason for this is that I ended up subcontracting a body shop to weld the new bedsides, rocker panels, and cab corners in place. This resulted in a delay for most of the truck being finished, but ultimately worked out for the best. Most likely, you will be interrupted by some scheduling issues as well. Don't get discouraged—work around them and see the job through.

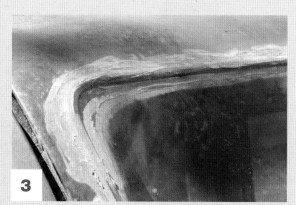

Prior to taking on any project (automotive painting or otherwise), it is a good idea to scope out the work required and determine what needs to be done, what you can do yourself, and what you may require help with. The hood is slightly misaligned with the fender, the front bumper is still usable, and the fender is straight but rusty. Reproduction fenders are available and affordable.

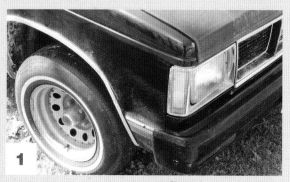

The bracketry for the outside rearview mirror needs to be refinished. It will be easy to remove from the door and will require only a minimum amount of prep and repaint work. Additionally, the doors themselves are pretty rusty at the bottom, so they will be replaced anyway. Reproduction doors will not include the door hardware, so that, including the mirrors, will be removed from the original and used on the new.

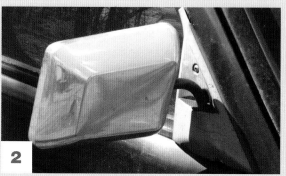

While rust has taken a toll on this truck, it has also allowed the stock windshield to leak at the top. Most likely, the sheetmetal flange to which the windshield is glued to is rusting away. To correct this, new sheet metal should be welded in place, but that is beyond the scope of this book. Various unsuccessful attempts to prevent leakage have included application of some unattractive caulking. For this project, I'll attempt to remove the caulking from the sheet metal and glass, then use some silicone sealant designed for this application.

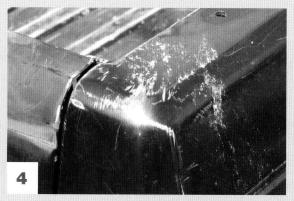

This truck was never babied, so its sheet metal includes lots of nicks, scrapes, and abrasions. This damage to the top of the bedsides would be easy to smooth out by filling and sanding. The holes drilled for bolting down a former camper shell could be welded shut. However due to large amounts of rust near the bottoms on both sides, the bedsides will be replaced too.

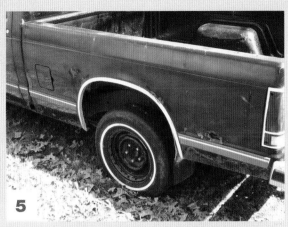

5

Patch panels for this vehicle are available for the area in front of, above, and behind the wheel well, as well as complete bedsides. For the amount of labor required to replace all of them on each bedsides, I chose to replace the entire bedside on both sides, rather than piece it together. The original taillights and gas filler door will be retained.

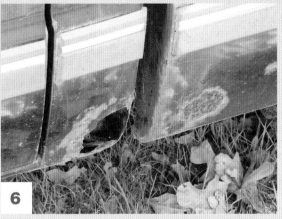

6

The rust on the front portion of the bedside is not as bad as the rust through at the cab corners. Cab corner replacement is a common need for pickup trucks, so the necessary panels for this repair are available and will be utilized. To gain access to the front of the bed and the rear of the cab, the bed will be removed.

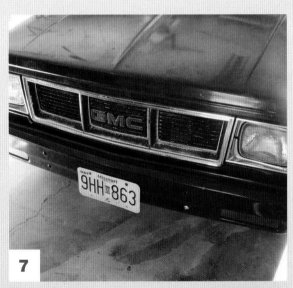

7

Disassembly might as well start in the front, but you can really start wherever you want. Just be sure to develop a system for storing and identifying the various nuts, bolts, and other fasteners that will be removed in the process. Remove the license plate and store it for safe keeping.

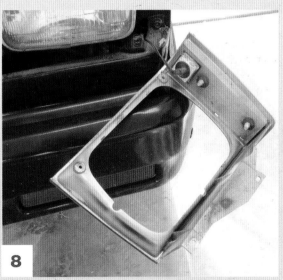

8

Since it would be more likely to remove a headlight bezel for maintenance than the grille, the headlight bezels were removed first. Depending on your vehicle, you will probably need to open the hood to gain access to some of the fasteners securing the grille and headlight trim. Removing one piece of trim will usually reveal fasteners that secure other pieces of trim.

(continued)

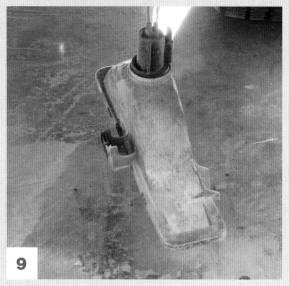

9

The bumper-mounted turn signal lights were secured by two screws in the top and one on the bottom. Some fasteners will be easier to find than others. The light socket can usually be disconnected from the fixture by twisting it one way or another.

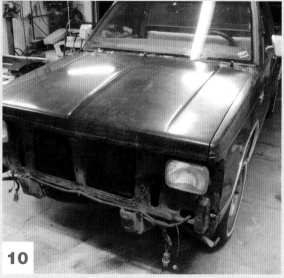

10

With the bumper removed, the front grille area is as disassembled as it will be during the entire repaint process. The headlights need some adjustment, as the one on the passenger side is slanted somewhat. The radiator support to which the grille and headlights mount will be repainted with some rattle can "satin black" later on in the process for a new look.

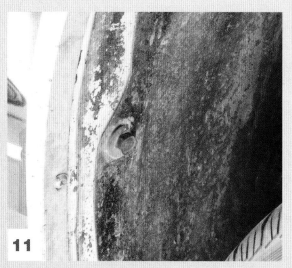

11

Front fenders are bolted on, so removing them is simply a matter of finding all of the required bolts. On this GMC S-15, several of them are inside the wheelwell. Others are commonly located in the radiator support, near the hood hinges, and near the bottom of the fender, somewhere behind the front wheel. Trim is not included on the reproduction fender, so it must be purchased separately, swapped over from the originals, or left off. I chose to go with the latter option.

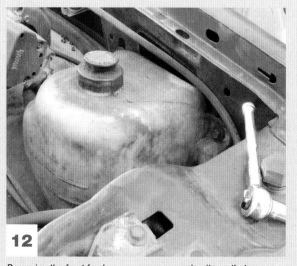

12

Removing the front fenders may mean removing items that are bolted to their "inner" sides. The radiator overflow tank had to be removed from the driver side fender, while the battery tray was removed from the passenger side. Fortunately, these are simply bolted on.

PAINTING OTHER PARTS AND COMPONENTS

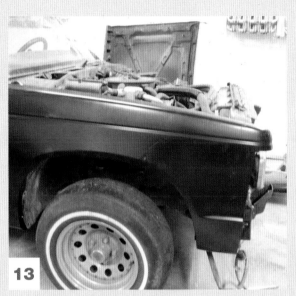

13

No, the new fender has not been painted yet. However, I did check it for proper fit before doing anything else to it. Obtaining a good fit between OEM, expensive reproduction parts, and inexpensive reproduction parts is always going to be a compromise. Surprisingly, the fender fit was better than I would have guessed.

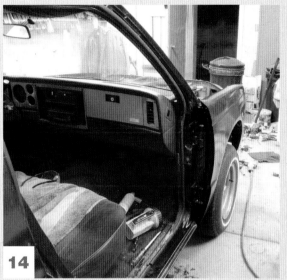

14

With both new front fenders installed, it was time to move back to the doors. Most passenger car and many trucks have hinges that bolt on to the body, allowing the doors to simply be bolted to the hinges. However, many GM trucks and presumably other makes utilize a hinge assembly that uses only a couple of pins to secure the door to the hinge. Using a hammer and punch, the pins were removed and the doors lifted off.

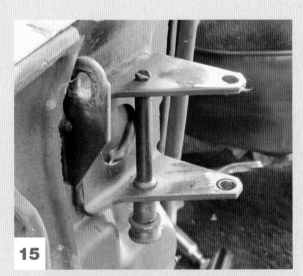

15

With the door out of the way, it is much easier to see the components of the body portion of the hinge. Shown is the top hinge for the driver side door, looking toward the rear of the truck. The door's portion of the hinge fits to the outside (above and below) the body portion on the top hinge. A hinge pin fits through the two holes shown and a corresponding hole in each of the other tines. The roller at the bottom end of the inner shaft is where a multi-position bracket on the door lands to hold the door open in a variety of positions.

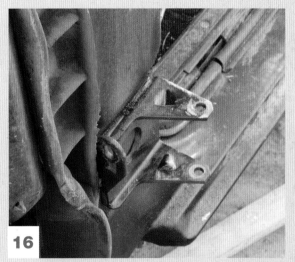

16

Shown is the lower hinge on the same side of the truck. Conversely of the top hinge, the door portion of the hinge fits between the tines on the lower hinge. New hinge pins include new bushings to provide a better fit for doors with worn hinges.

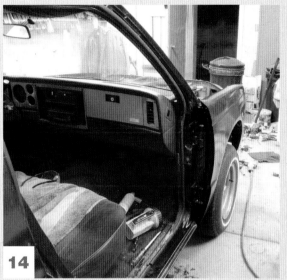

(continued)

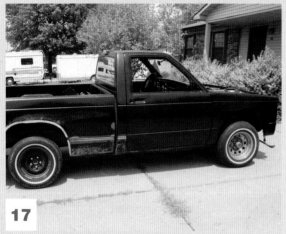

17

With new fenders and doors installed, the truck is already looking much better. Still need to work on panel alignment a bit. As shown in this photo, these new panels are coated with their EDP coating. This will provide protection from rusting while in the warehouse, but will not provide any protection from being out in the elements. These new panels and the remaining original sheet metal will all be sprayed with epoxy primer prior to being painted, to enhance their corrosion resistance.

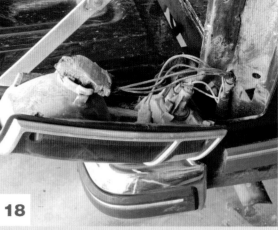

18

Taillights are much like the front turn signals in regards to disassembly. Remove four or five fasteners, pull them away from the body, and then twist the light sockets to disconnect them from the vehicle.

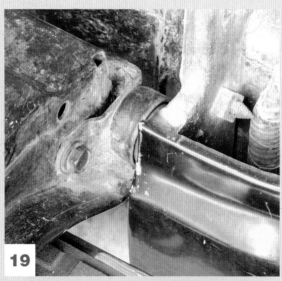

19

Pickup trucks offer the unique opportunity of dealing with a tailgate that passenger cars do not provide. On this style of tailgate, the round metal cap that rotates about the trunion is attached to the tailgate with an "L"-shaped bracket. Remove this bracket by removing two bolts. Removing this piece from either side will allow the tailgate to be removed.

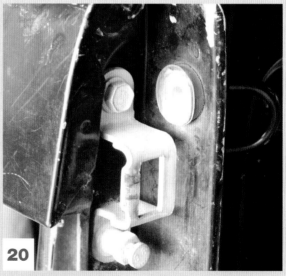

20

Tailgates also require a latch system. Originally designed as utilitarian vehicles, pickup trucks and their tailgate assemblies are usually pretty simple in design. Removing a total of four bolts removes this latch from both sides of the truck. Since I will be replacing the bedsides, all of this hardware must be removed and retained for use on the new bedsides.

PAINTING OTHER PARTS AND COMPONENTS

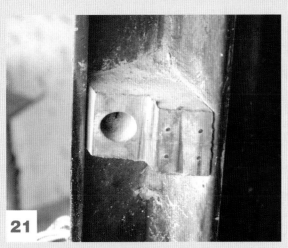

21 Anti-rattle bumpers for tailgates, doors, hoods, and other opening panels are usually held in place by just one screw or bolt. Again, salvaging from the old will eliminate the need to purchase new when replacing major parts.

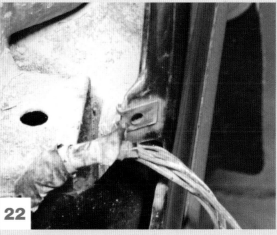

22 Even though "J" clips like this are common from one vehicle manufacture to another, and therefore available at most auto parts houses, they are still another expense that you can avoid by removing them from the original panels that will be removed.

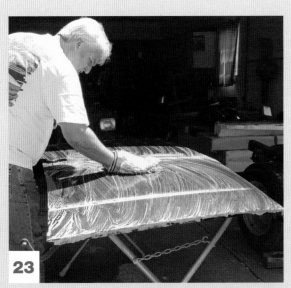

23 I know that this truck has been around for quite awhile and very little of its life has been spent in a garage. Therefore, to minimize any chances of contaminants wreaking havoc with my priming and painting procedures, all sheet metal will be washed with warm, soapy water prior to any sanding being done on them.

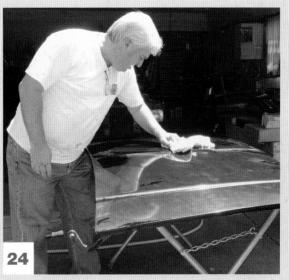

24 After washing and rinsing the hood, it was dried off with a hand towel. This procedure also provides a good opportunity to look for any potential trouble spots that you may have overlooked in the past.

(continued)

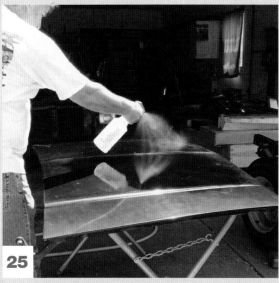

25

Now comes additional cleaning with wax and grease remover. This cleaning should be done on all panels that are to be painted, whether they are original to the vehicle, OEM replacement, salvage yard, or aftermarket. It is much easier to clean in the beginning than to sand off and redo the painting process.

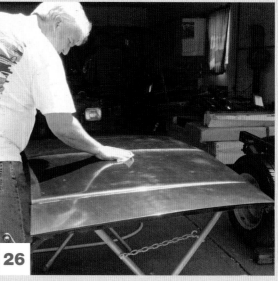

26

After applying the wax and degreaser, wipe the panel clean with a second paper towel.

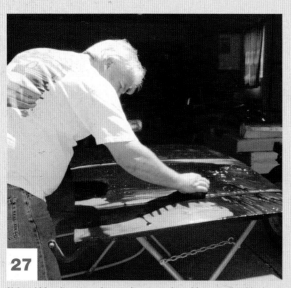

27

Using 180-grit wet-or-dry sandpaper and a rubber sanding block, I block sanded the hood. This is to scuff the existing surface for proper adhesion of the epoxy primer to be applied soon, to help smooth the surface, and to help find any paint defects or hail dents that require attention.

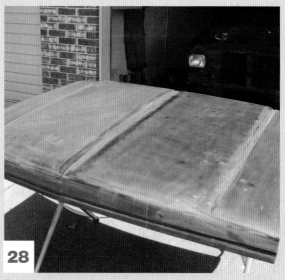

28

The passenger side of the hood (left side of photo) has been sanded adequately at this point. The opposite side still requires attention, as several somewhat shiny areas still exist (near the center ridge and the front).

PAINTING OTHER PARTS AND COMPONENTS

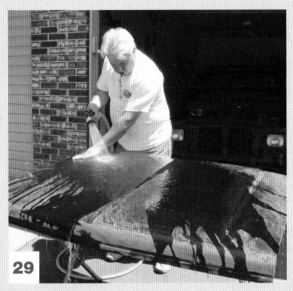

29

Running water helps to remove any sanding residue from the surface and helps you to feel irregularities in the surface. Many surface irregularities can be felt easier than they can be seen . . . until you put some nice shiny paint on them, that is. Because of this water, however, you must use an air hose to eliminate any water that might have pooled in cracks and crevices prior to applying any primer or paint products.

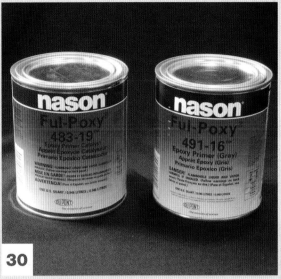

30

Unlike the wheels for my 1955 Chevrolet truck (painted elsewhere in this book), this S15 project is more of a limited budget project. For that reason, I chose to go with Nason products, which are one of DuPont's smaller (and less expensive) lines. The product is still good, just more budget friendly. As with all painting projects, you should use one line throughout, rather than playing chemist and mixing and matching on your own. Gray epoxy primer and catalyst will be mixed in accordance with the manufacturer's directions to provide good paint adhesion and corrosion resistance.

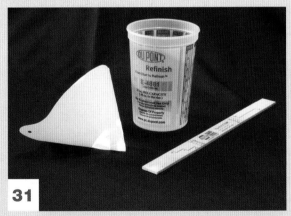

31

Epoxy primer, filler primer, sealer, color, or clear, it doesn't matter. They must all be mixed according to the manufacturer's directions, in a clean mixing cup. You should always use a strainer when you pour the materials into your paint gun.

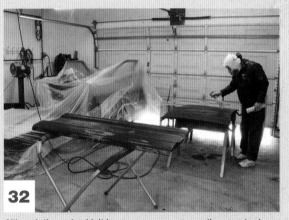

32

Although there shouldn't be any wax or grease on these parts since they were just cleaned and sanded, you should not assume that to be the case. A majority of paint defects are caused by contamination in one form or another, so taking time to reclean the surface should not be considered a waste.

(continued)

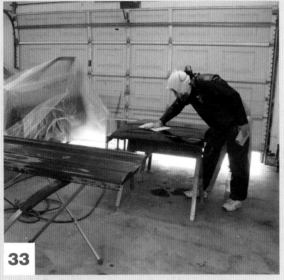

33

Always use a clean towel to wipe the wax and grease remover off, and then use an air hose to remove any remaining fluid out of nooks and crannies. Note that I am wearing a painting suit, head sock, and mask as I prepare to spray epoxy primer, which is full of isocyanates. Prior to spraying, I will also put on latex gloves and glasses.

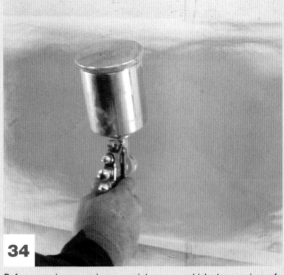

34

Before spraying any primer or paint on your vehicle, tape a piece of masking paper on the wall of your shop and test the pattern of your spray gun. If it is off, make adjustments now, and then retest. Better on the paper than on your car if it isn't right.

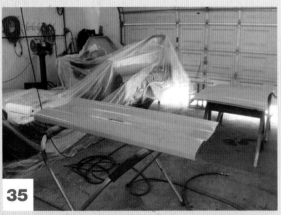

35

Epoxy primer can get just about everywhere if you let it, so I protected parts from various other projects with masking film. Then the hood and tailgate were sprayed with two coats of epoxy primer, with the proper amount of flash time in between coats. Notice that the garage door is opened slightly to allow for ventilation.

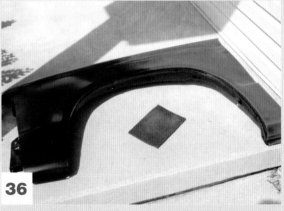

36

The front fenders, doors, rocker panels, cab corners, and bedsides comprise the new sheet metal that will be on this vehicle. From the factory, they are EDP coated to protect them from rust and corrosion while in a warehouse. However, this will not protect them from corrosion when put into use. Scuffing the surface with a red Scotch-Brite™ pad will be sufficient. Here we can see the back half of the fender has been scuffed, but the front is not completed yet.

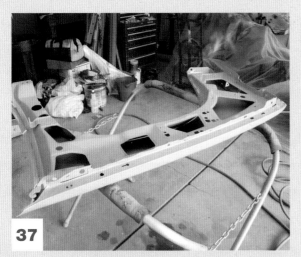

37

The insides of these components will need to be sprayed as well. Scuff with a Scotch-Brite™ pad, clean with wax and grease remover, and then apply epoxy primer. Priced at around $35, this folding work stand has certainly paid for itself.

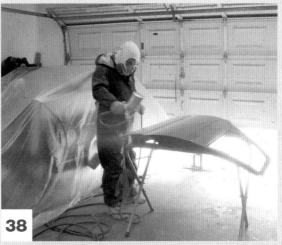

38

Having multiple work stands would have sped up the epoxy primer spraying process, but I didn't have another one available. Priming both front fenders inside and out, along with both doors (inside and out) took longer this way, but I had the time. Primers tend to dry reasonably quickly, so it didn't take all day.

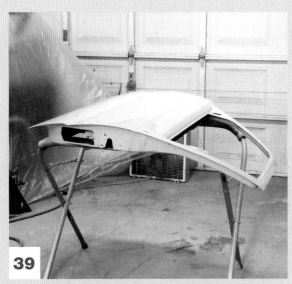

39

After the last coat on the outer side of the last door . . .

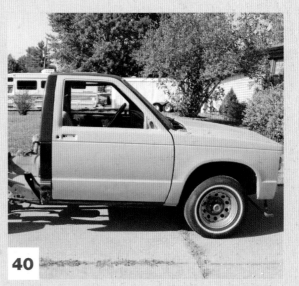

40

After giving the various panels now in epoxy primer ample time to dry, they were all reassembled on the truck, showing significant improvement. As this is written, the original bedsides still need to be removed from the bed and the new ones installed. Additionally, the replacement cab corners and rocker panels need to be welded in place. When that is done, the sanding, and epoxy primer application will be done on the rest of the truck.

(continued)

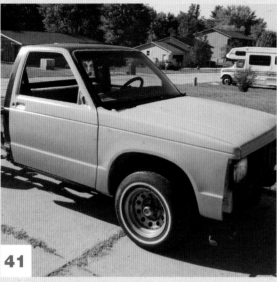

41

Not looking bad at this point, but still quite away to go. When all of the body painting is completed, the truck will go up on jack stands, have the stock steel wheels removed, and the tires dismounted. The steel wheels will then be media blasted, painted, and new tires installed. The plan for the truck is to be painted silver below the upper bodyline, black above it, with a red pinstripe separating the two. The wheels will be black with chrome lug nuts.

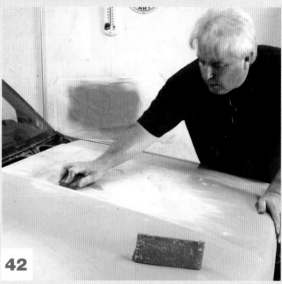

42

This truck had been caught in a hail storm somewhere along the line as the hood had several divots. Those were filled with body filler and then sanded with 80- and 220-grit sandpaper.

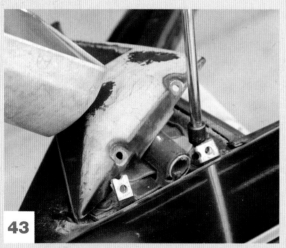

43

Prior to disposing of the discarded sheet metal, remove any parts that can be salvaged for immediate or future use. I'll be using the outside mirrors, although their cover plates need to be refinished. Removing two screws from the bottom allow access to the bolts that actually secure the mirror assembly to the door.

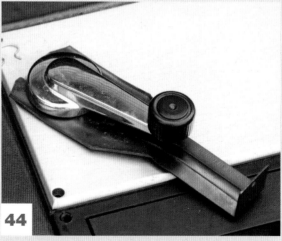

44

Some interior door handles are secured to a shaft with set screws, while others use a retaining clip. A very small screwdriver is required to loosen set screws, with a tool such as this required to remove the retaining clip. The retaining clip (shown at the upper left) is removed by sliding the tool between the handle and the interior door panel, pushing the retaining clip out of its installed position.

PAINTING OTHER PARTS AND COMPONENTS

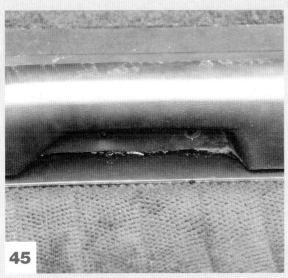

45

Interior armrests are often secured to the interior door panel with one or two screws located out of clear sight in the door pull area. On this vehicle, these two screws should be removed, and then the armrest slides in one direction and can then be pulled off. Quite simple, once you figure it out.

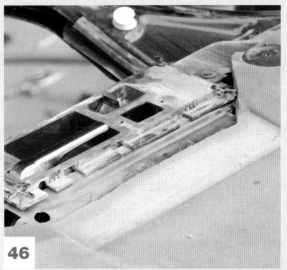

46

After removing the interior door panel, you will now have access to the door latch mechanism. Disconnect the actuator rods between the latch and handle, then the handle can be removed from the door. This portion of the disassembly is not required if you are retaining your existing doors.

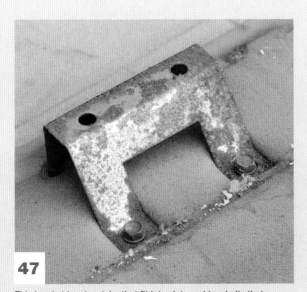

47

This bracket has two tabs that fit into slots and two bolts that secure it to the inside of the door. It is what the armrest (door pull) mounting screws attach to. This is somewhat important in this application, as the required slots and bolt holes do not exist in the replacement doors. To use the stock door panels, slots will need to be cut into the new doors and bolt holes drilled. Not a big deal, just another step along the way.

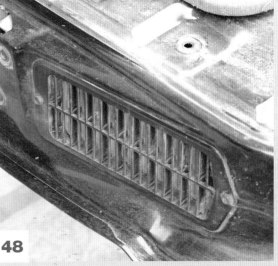

48

Vents like this help are designed to help moisture that finds its way into the inside of the door to evaporate, rather than cause rust. On the other door, this vent was missing and had been replaced with a piece of thin sheet metal. Consequently, that door had substantially more rust.

(continued)

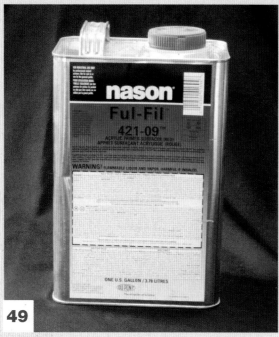

49

Staying with the Nason line, this is the primer-surfacer that I'll use to prep the body prior to paint. Most of this will be sanded off with each phase of block sanding, applied again, then sanded of yet again. All part of the necessary process toward getting a good paint job.

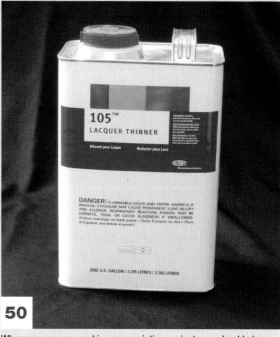

50

Whenever you are working on a painting project, you should always have plenty of paint thinner on hand. This particular thinner is compatible with most of the Nason products that I am using. You will also need it to clean your spray gun.

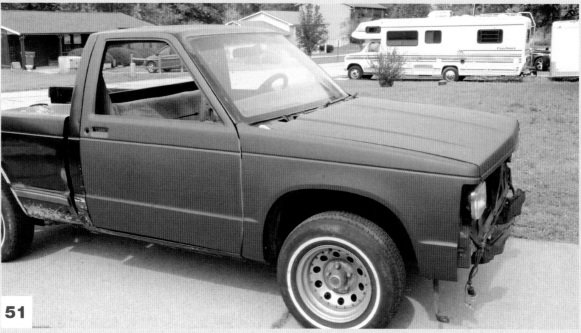

51

With a couple of coats of epoxy primer, followed by primer-surfacer, the new panels (fenders and doors) are looking pretty good. They will need to be block sanded with 220-, 320-, and 400-grit sandpaper before being ready for paint. The existing wheels and tires will be replaced, so I'm not concerned about getting primer or paint on them.

PAINTING OTHER PARTS AND COMPONENTS

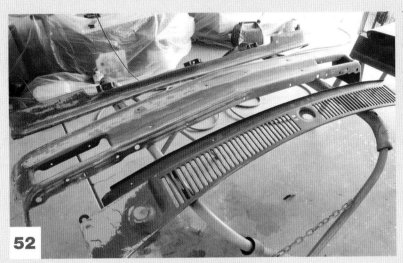

The cowl panel, front bumper, and gravel pan are some small parts that I could work on while waiting for the welding work to be done on the rest of the truck. After spraying them with epoxy primer and primer-surfacer, they were block sanded multiple times.

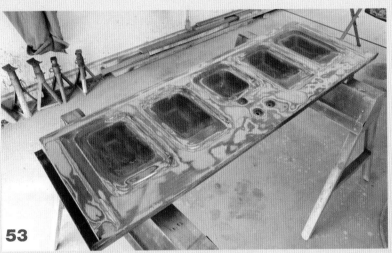

Same with the tailgate. The inside of it proved that this truck has been used as a truck, as it was rather rough. At this point, it has epoxy primer, primer-surfacer, and some spots of body filler. It still isn't perfect, but it is better than it was. The outside of the tailgate will look much better, however.

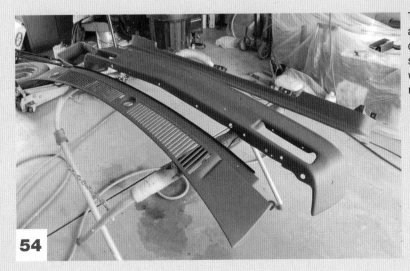

The cowl panel, front bumper, and gravel pan are looking pretty good after a fair amount of block sanding. A few dabs of spot putty in select places and some additional sanding with 400-grit sandpaper and they will be ready for sealer.

(continued)

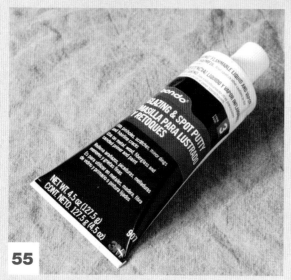

55

This spot putty is ready to use, dries quickly, and sand easily, making it easy for the beginner to use. Some brands require the user to mix the putty with a hardener, much like body filler. With either type, simply spread the filler into the required area and smoothing it out with a plastic spreader.

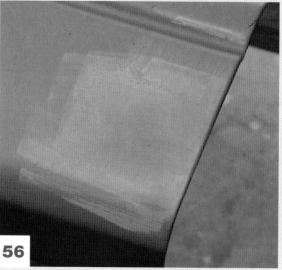

56

This is what the spot putty looks like after being spread and beginning to cure. Using 400-grit sandpaper will smooth this up real quick, hiding pinholes and other small imperfections in the process.

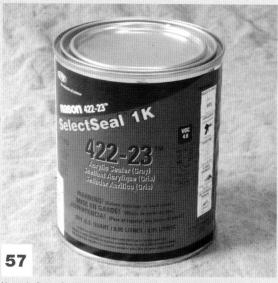

57

Nason's SelectSeal is a premixed, ready-to-spray sealer. Some epoxy primers can be used as a sealer by following prescribed mixing ratios with the primer and hardener. Regardless of which type of sealer you prefer, you should always use sealer between the undercoats and top coats.

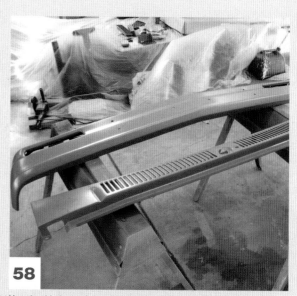

58

You should always follow the specific directions for any paint products for the best results, including drying time and time until the application of the next top coat. Specific times will vary among products, but most color coats are designed to be applied relatively soon after the sealer is applied.

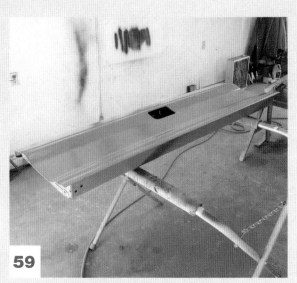

59

If you must wait longer than recommended to apply color coats, many sealers require a new coat of sealer prior to application of the top coat, so plan your time wisely. With the sealer applied to the tailgate, front bumper, cowl panel, and gravel pan, color will be applied soon.

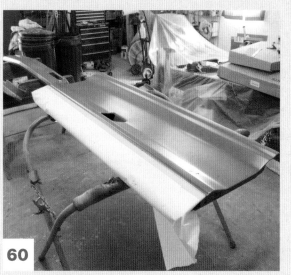

60

The final color for this truck will be silver below the body line that wraps around the entire truck and black above it. I figure that it will be easier to paint the lower areas first, then mask them off to paint the upper portions. I first laid down a ¼-inch strip of Fine Line tape just above the bodyline across the tailgate. I then followed that up with a piece of ¾-inch masking tape. Masking paper was then secured to the ¾-inch tape to cover the are that will eventually be black.

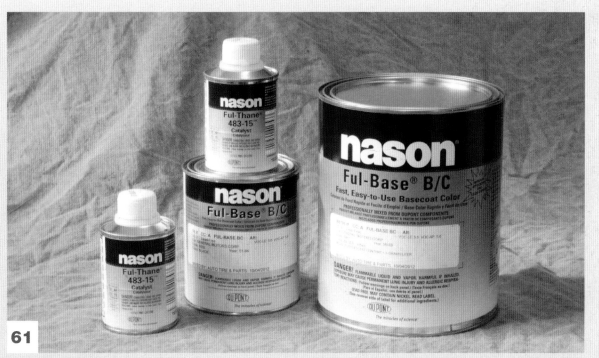

61

Based upon recommendations from the guys at the paint supply store, a quart of black base coat should be more than adequate for the top portion of the truck and two quarts enough for the bottom. Rather than two individual quarts of the silver base coat, I asked that it be combined into a one-gallon can. This will help to ensure that it is the same color throughout. The small cans are the activator (hardener) for the base coat.

(continued)

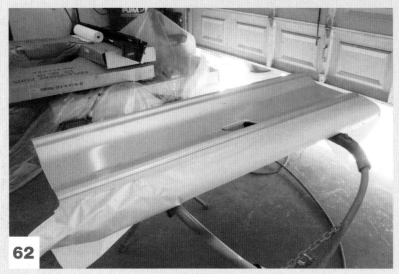

Three coats of silver have been applied. When using base coat/clear coat systems, you must always achieve coverage with the base coat, whether that requires one coat or several. Gloss will come from the clear coat, so you should not apply more coats of base than necessary attempting to achieve a glossy finish.

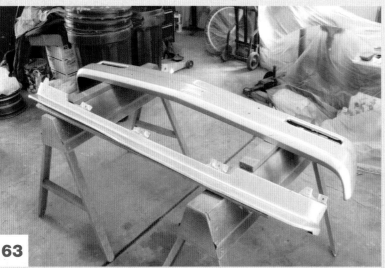

While the silver base coat is not shiny, it will show any imperfections in the prep work. Remember, a paint job is no better than the surface preparation.

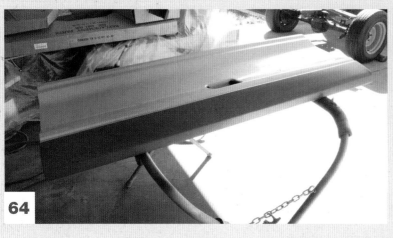

After allowing the silver ample time to dry (less than 15 minutes for most base coat systems), the masking can be removed from the upper portion of the tailgate. The dark area is the dark gray sealer, while the silver is the base coat.

PAINTING OTHER PARTS AND COMPONENTS

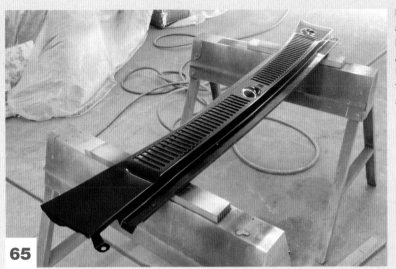

65

Unlike the bumper and gravel pan that are all silver, the cowl panel is above the paint break and will be all black in this case. Again, achieve coverage with the base coat. In a louvered panel such as this, verify that the edge of the openings are fully covered as well.

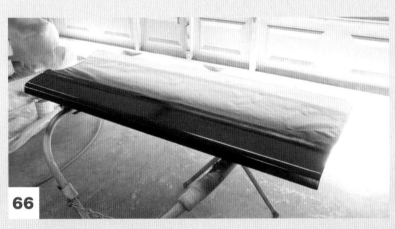

66

In similar fashion as before, the silver area was covered with masking paper. The black base coat was then applied. Have no fear, the top edge of the tailgate did receive ample amounts of paint. The nonblack color is just the reflections.

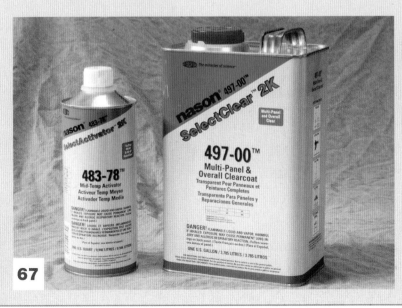

67

Most every professional painter you talk to will have a strong opinion about which clear they think is the absolute best. With this being a budget paint job, I continued to steer away from the high-priced products, but stayed within one paint system. This Nason SelectClear is economical and seems to work well. The 2K designation simply means that it requires an activator.

PAINTING OTHER PARTS AND COMPONENTS

(continued)

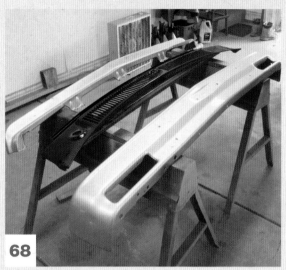

68

The Nason SelectClear will be used on all of the panels that are painted with base coat/clear coat, regardless of what color they are painted. The clear is applied fairly soon after application of the base coat. In most instances, by the time you finish cleaning your spray gun after applying the base coat, it will be time to apply the clear.

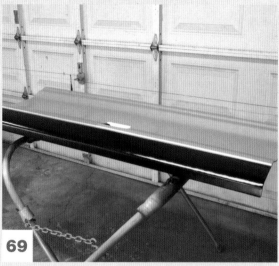

69

Other than applying a red pinstripe over the paint seam, the tailgate is ready for wet sanding and buffing. Rather than actually applying pinstripes with a striping brush, I will mask both the black and the silver, and then apply a red stripe. Then I'll remove the masking and apply two more coats of clear to the entire tailgate.

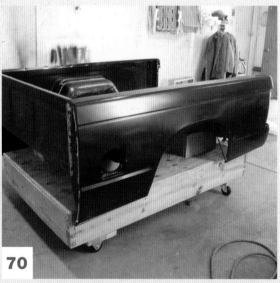

70

After getting the truck back with the bedsides, cab corners, and rocker panels installed, the bed was removed from the truck again and placed on this universal roll-around body dolly. To raise the bed up a little bit so that it will be easier to prime and paint the lower portion, four concrete blocks were used as spacers to lift the bed upward.

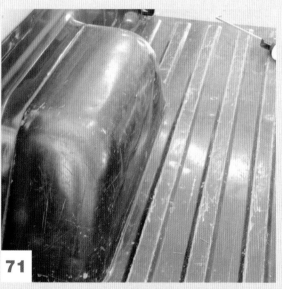

71

The first order of business is to sweep all of the dirt and debris out of the bed. Then use a shop vacuum to verify that the crevice between the mating edge of the bedside and the mating edge of the bed floor is clean.

PAINTING OTHER PARTS AND COMPONENTS

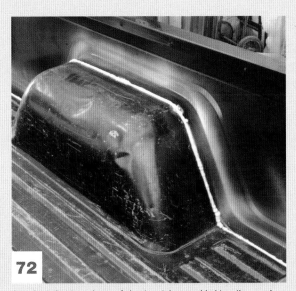

72

Anywhere that two pieces of sheet metal are welded together, apply seam sealer to prevent moisture from finding its way between the two pieces of metal and forming rust. Some seam sealers are designed to be brushed on, while others are applied with a caulking gun.

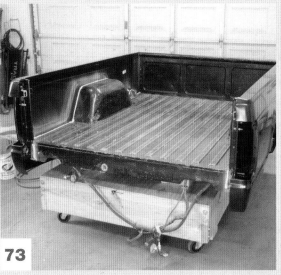

73

Apply seam sealer prior to epoxy primer; seam sealer is designed to be painted over. The wires in the foreground connect to the main wiring harness on one end and to the taillights on the other; they need to be tucked up under the bed to avoid being covered with overspray.

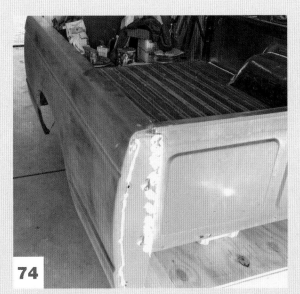

74

Scuff the reproduction bedsides with a red Scotch-Brite™ pad before applying epoxy primer. The fenders and doors also need to be scuffed. Here, the original sheet metal (front bed panel and rear cross sill in this case) was scuffed with 180-grit sandpaper after being cleaned with wax and grease remover.

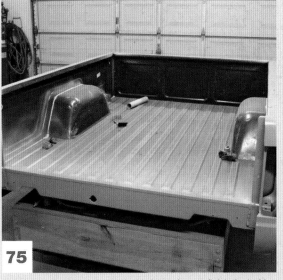

75

At this time, I'm somewhat undecided as to how to finish the inside of the bed. In my next project (a 1955 Chevrolet pickup), the metal will all be new, so it will be finished just as the rest of the sheet metal. For this S15, I'm considering a textured finish or most likely just leaving it as it is.

(continued)

PAINTING OTHER PARTS AND COMPONENTS

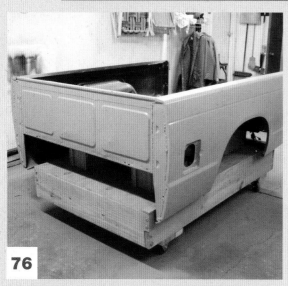

76

The new bedsides already look much better than the rusty ones they replaced. The front bed panel is far from pristine, but no one will notice the dings in it after it is in place behind the truck cab.

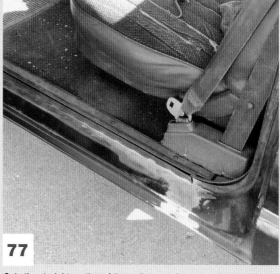

77

Only the straight portion of the rocker panels was replaced, rather than the entire panel. When dealing with patch panels, it is often better to purchase more panel than you need.

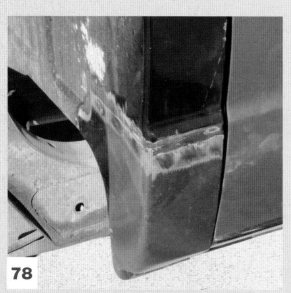

78

The cab corners are now in place as well. They were both welded and glued in place. The welds have been ground smooth, but will most likely require a bit of body filler prior to paint (at least no critters can crawl into the truck now).

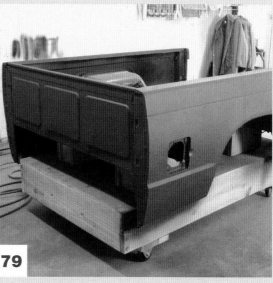

79

Filler primer was applied after giving the epoxy primer on the bed plenty of time to dry. I applied three medium coats of epoxy primer because much of it will be sanded off during block sanding in order to smooth the sheet metal.

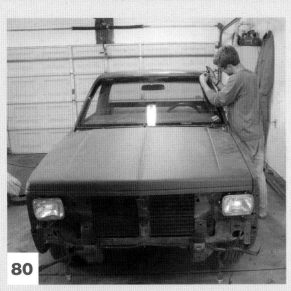

80

After my nephew Alex discovered I was repainting his truck for him (it was supposed to be a surprise), he was eager to come over and help out after school. Here he is sanding the original black paint of the cab's A-pillar prior to applying the epoxy primer.

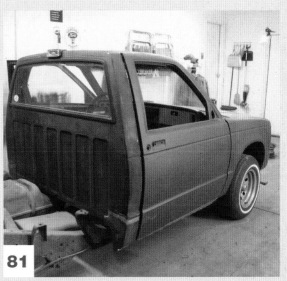

81

Thanks to Alex's help, the surface of the cab was finally sanded and ready for epoxy primer. Still, some masking is required.

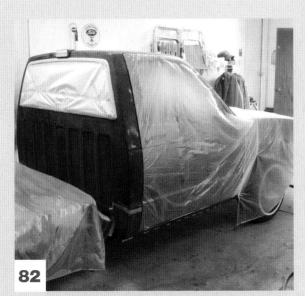

82

Since we are going to be spraying epoxy primer on the entire cab, the rear window was masked with masking paper and masking tape. The front fenders and doors have already been primed with epoxy primer and filler primer, so they were covered with masking film. The rear portion of the truck's frame was also covered with masking film so that it would not look sloppy.

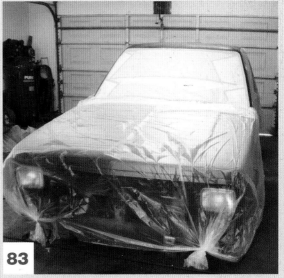

83

The front windshield was also masked with masking paper and masking tape. Most of this masking could have been done with one larger piece of masking film, had it not been for the A-pillars that still need to have epoxy primer applied to them.

(continued)

PAINTING OTHER PARTS AND COMPONENTS

175

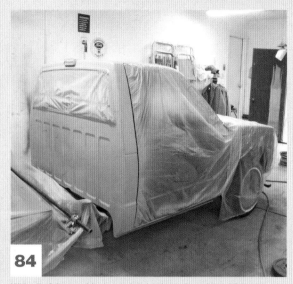

84

With all of the masking materials in place, the cab's roof, back panel, rocker panels, and A-pillars were all treated to a couple of coats of epoxy primer.

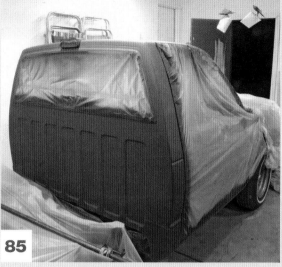

85

After the epoxy primer had enough time to dry, but before removing the masking materials, three coats of filler primer were applied to the same panels. At this point, it is finally starting to look like we are getting somewhere.

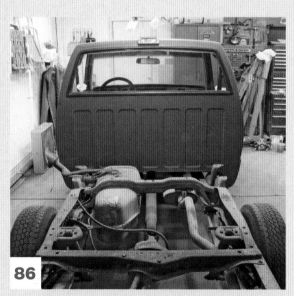

86

The masking materials can be removed after giving the primer enough time to become tack-free. You should not leave masking materials on for too long after the primer or paint is applied, as the masking tape will begin to break down slightly and become difficult to remove easily. You do not want to remove it too soon however, as you risk marring the primer or paint.

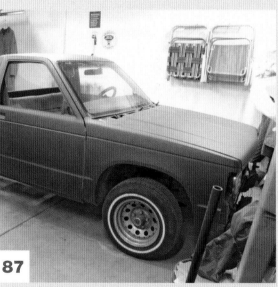

87

The front fender still needs to be moved outward slightly at the front to provide better hood clearance. This will also improve the gap between fender and door. The hood itself may need to be moved back slightly.

PAINTING OTHER PARTS AND COMPONENTS

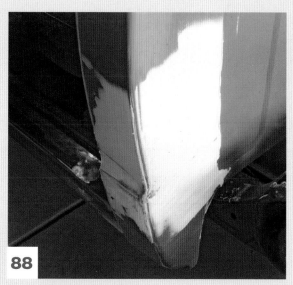

88

The first layer of plastic body filler has now been applied to the cab corners. The goal with body filler is to use the least amount as required, sand until smooth, and then fill any remaining low spots with a second layer if necessary.

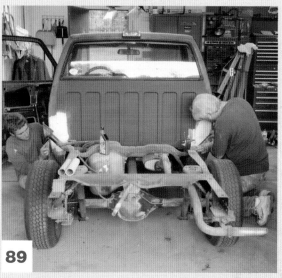

89

Alex getting his first experience with a sanding block and auto body repair. Yours truly is on the other side of the truck shaping some body filler with a cheese grater file.

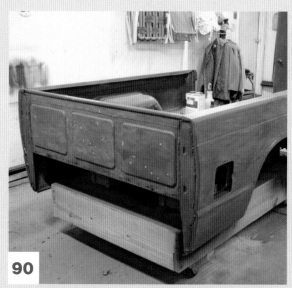

90

The replacement bedsides have been sanded with 220-grit, 320-grit, and finally 400-grit sandpaper, in preparation for paint. The original front bed panel was also sanded with 180-grit sandpaper to prep the original surface for epoxy primer. The next steps of sealer and paint will need to be done within certain time frames, so the bed is good for now.

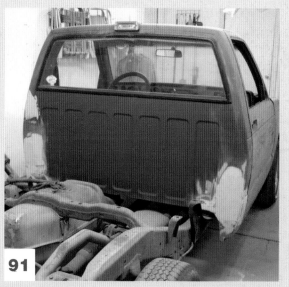

91

Prior to stopping for the night, some additional body filler was added to the cab corners and to a couple of other places that I had overlooked previously.

(continued)

Finally it is time to begin painting the bed. After cleaning the bed with wax and grease remover to promote good adhesion of the top coats, the dark gray sealer was applied. Sealer can be in any of a variety of ready to spray colors, but many brands can also be tinted to more closely match the final color of the paint. This would require fewer coats of paint to achieve coverage.

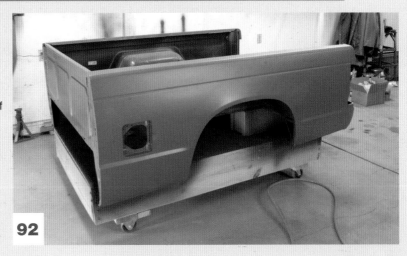

Time spent cleaning the spray gun after applying sealer will often times be long enough to wait prior to doing any necessary masking prior to applying color top coats. Just as with the tailgate previously and the cab eventually, the area above the yellow masking tape will be black. The area below it will be silver and will be applied first, as it will be easier to mask later.

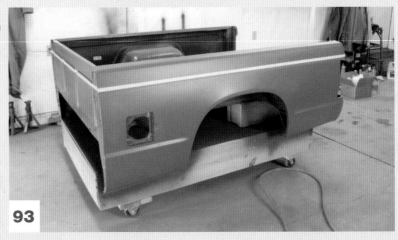

A piece of masking paper long enough to cover most of the front bed panel was cut from a roll and taped in place. When you do not have access to a masking paper rack, it often takes several small pieces of masking tape to hold the paper in place. You can then come back and add longer strips along the entire edge.

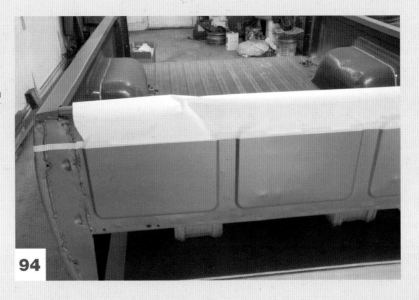

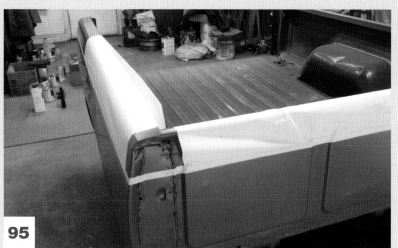

The bedsides were covered in much the same way. I figured that it was easier to cover them with two smaller pieces of paper, rather than one large one. This does leave the corner of the bedside and front bed panel exposed, but that can be addressed easily enough.

95

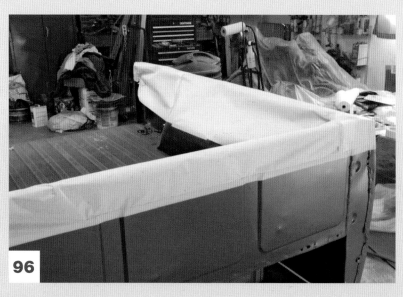

The actual corner of the bedsides and front bed panel were then covered with a third, much smaller piece of masking paper. Verify that all seams in masking paper are covered with masking tape and that all edges of masking tape are firmly pressed down.

96

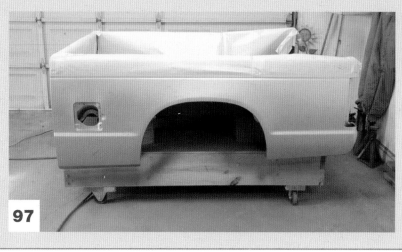

Full and complete coverage required three coats of the silver paint. With base coat/clear coat systems, the base coat's purpose is to obtain complete coverage. The clear coat (to be applied later) is what will provide the gloss.

97

(continued)

If this were a single-color job, any masking would be removed and clear applied next. However, in this two-tone application, the first color applied (silver) must be allowed to dry (spray gun cleaning time) and covered before applying the second color (black).

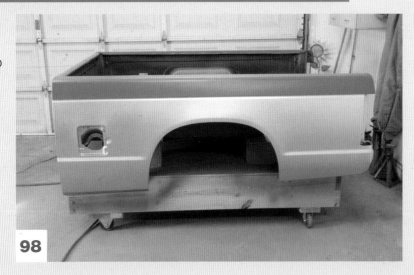

98

Masking tape is applied so that its top edge is at the top of the silver color. Masking paper is then secured to that first line of tape. This 18-inch-wide masking paper does not cover the entire bedside, but it covers adequately since paint will now be applied only at its top edge.

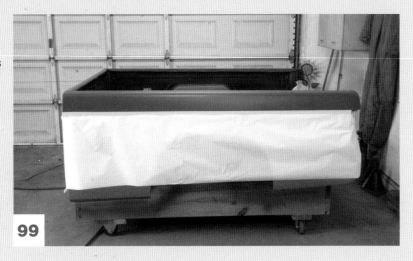

99

Again, like any other color coat, the black paint is applied to achieve complete coverage. The white area near the top of the nearer bedside is merely a reflection of an overhead light.

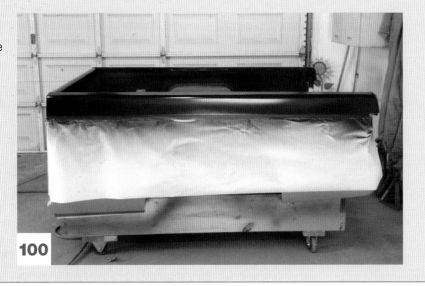

100

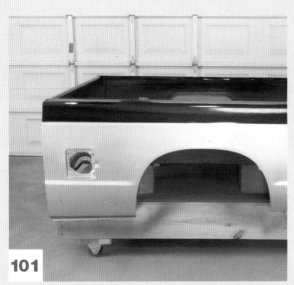

101

After ample drying time, the masking paper is removed and two coats of clear are applied. To provide ample clear to avoid wet sanding through the clear, three or four coats of clears are commonly applied. For this project, a red stripe is going to be applied over the seam of the two major colors, with two additional coats of clear added overall.

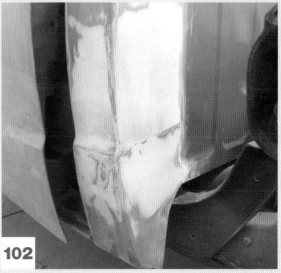

102

A little more sanding and the new cab corners will blend in nicely with the rest of the truck. Where body filler is used, shape the filler with a cheese grater file or 80-grit sandpaper as required, then sand smooth with 100-, 240-, 320-, and finally 400-grit sandpaper.

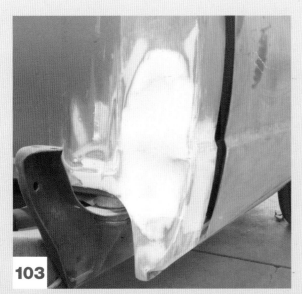

103

Just as with any other places where there is bodywork, you should sand until the area is feathered out so that you do not feel any differences between the various layers of primers.

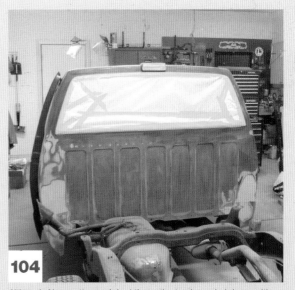

104

Although Alex pretty much had the entire truck sanded down with 320- and 400-grit sandpaper, I chose to spray on another coat of filler primer. The main reason for this is around the cab corners where there is some body filler, but an extra round of sanding won't hurt anything.

(continued)

PAINTING OTHER PARTS AND COMPONENTS

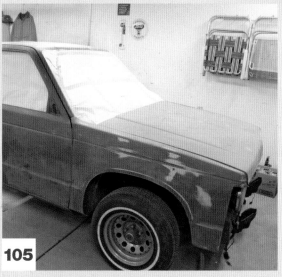

105

Of course, another coat of primer means masking the windows and door openings again.

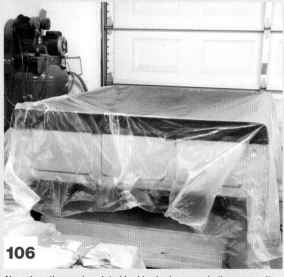

106

Also, since the newly painted bed is sharing room in the garage, it needs to be covered as well. Masking film designed to cover large areas during automotive painting works wonders for this.

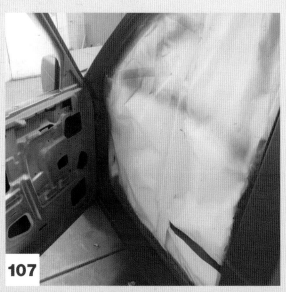

107

Be sure to sand, prime, and paint the doorjambs and the perimeters of the doors. If you have not removed the interior components, such as seat and carpeting, you will need to mask off the door openings with masking paper and masking tape.

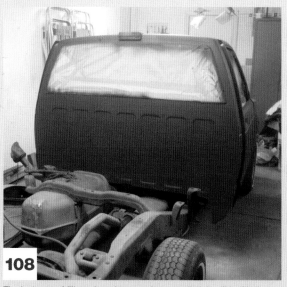

108

The last coat of filler primer has now been applied. It will be black sanded one last time with 320- and 400-grit sandpaper, and then carefully inspected for any flaws. If it passes muster, the next step will be to apply sealer.

PAINTING OTHER PARTS AND COMPONENTS

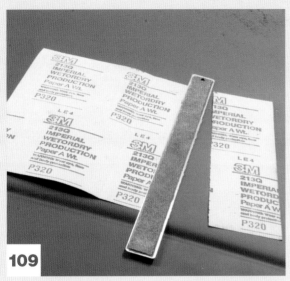

109

Should have told you this sooner, but when tearing sandpaper, first fold the paper in half and then half again (or as required if this does not fit your particular sanding block). Then tear the sandpaper against a straightedge along the fold for a near perfect tear.

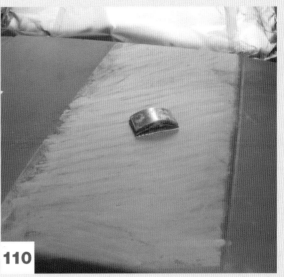

110

Also, when you are sanding large flat panels, sand in an alternating x-pattern. As you can see from the sanding block and the resultant sand dust, this middle portion of the hood has been sanded in one direction . . .

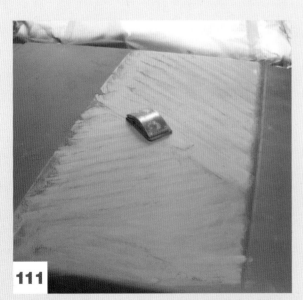

111

. . . and then sanded in a direction roughly 90 degrees to it. This helps to get the panel flat, without sanding a rut into any area of it.

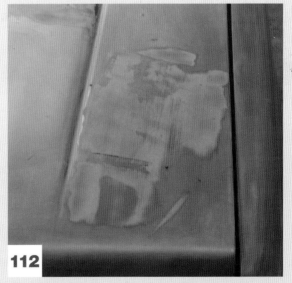

112

Some sanding with 320-grit sandpaper yielded some random scratches that I believe were beneath the original paint. To clarify, I believe this hood (original) and perhaps a salvage yard right front fender had been refinished previously with those random scratches simply covered with paint. To fill these scratches, apply some spot filler, then sand the area smooth.

(continued)

PAINTING OTHER PARTS AND COMPONENTS

183

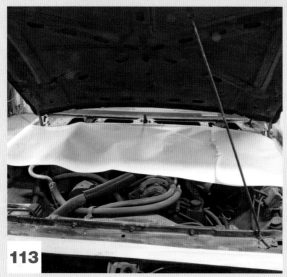

113

Unlike the bed, the cab and rest of the truck required substantial masking prior to spraying any paint. I wanted to paint the inside tops of the new front fenders, but didn't want overspray going all over the engine, so multiple pieces of masking paper were taped in place between the fenders.

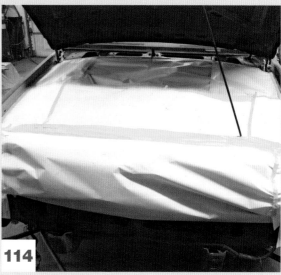

114

For vehicles that use prop rods to secure the hood in the open position, be sure to leave that prop rod accessible and masking it if necessary. Also, be sure to leave the hood latch mechanism accessible as well.

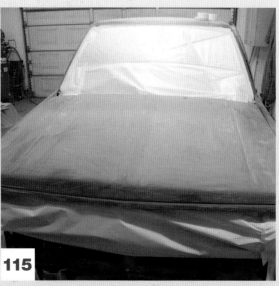

115

The engine is protected from overspray while the hood is open, yet I can still access the hood to paint it. This also allows access to the sides of the hood so that they can be painted as well.

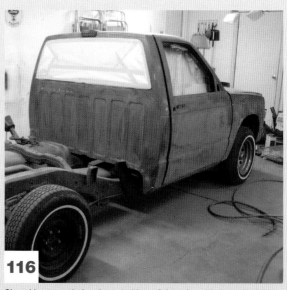

116

Since I have sanded and created lots of dust since I last masked the front and rear glass, that paper was removed and those areas masked again. Sanding dust can collect in creases and crevices of masking paper and fall into wet paint at the least opportune time, so it is best to eliminate that threat.

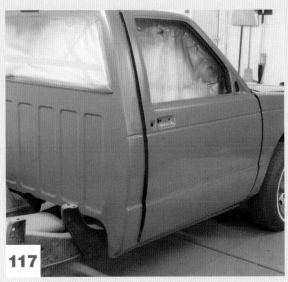

117

The masking between the inside of the doorjamb area and the passenger compartment is still in place. It will remain until the doorjambs have been painted with both base coat and clear. Dark gray sealer was now applied to seal any body filler so that it does not permeate the top coats and to provide a uniform base for color coats.

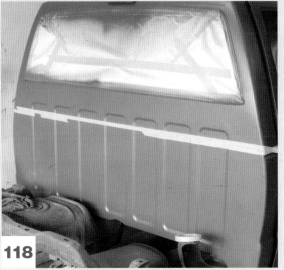

118

As with the bed, there will be a red stripe just above the body's character line. Since I will paint the lower color first, the area above the proposed stripe will be masked first. This requires the lower edge of the tape to be at the uppermost line of the lower (silver) color. Since the rear bed panel includes recessed areas, a second piece of tape was stretched across to provide a baseline. Multiple pieces of masking tape were then aligned to cover the high portions and the recessed portions independently, in hopes of the tape not pulling loose between the two.

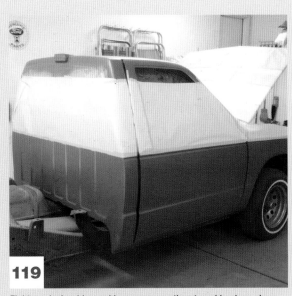

119

Eighteen-inch-wide masking paper was then taped in place above the color break line. Presumably, my aim with a spray gun is good enough that I won't send any overspray up over the top of the masking paper. Remember that if the doorjamb area is to be painted, the doors have to be operational and the insides of the door masked for this two-tone paint job.

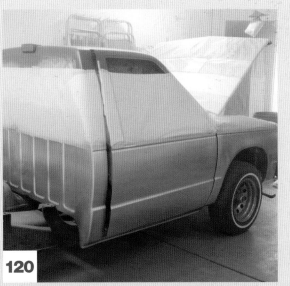

120

Along with the upper portion of the cab and doors, the hood was also masked to prevent it from being covered with silver overspray. This required several pieces of masking paper and masking tape.

(continued)

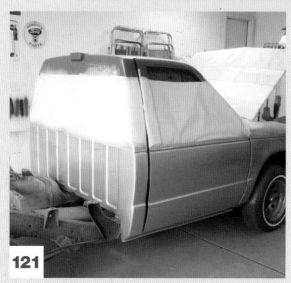

121

Two coats of base coat silver were applied to achieve coverage. Be sure to allow the proper amount of flash time between coats. Some colors cover better than others, while some colors may require three or four coats. Verify that you achieve coverage with the base coat.

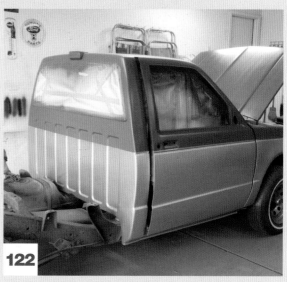

122

Satisfied with the coverage of the silver, the masking was then removed from the top of the vehicle.

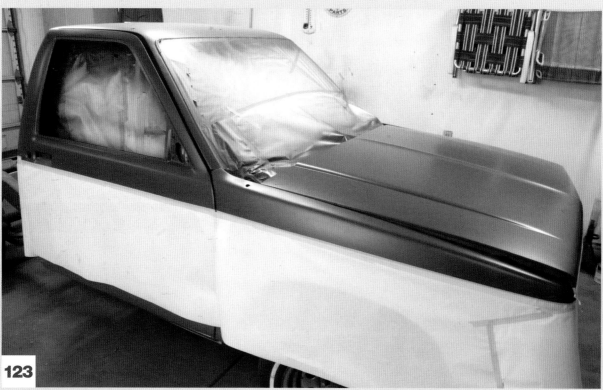

123

Had my timing been better, I could have proceeded directly with masking off the lower portion of the truck and painting the top. However, scheduling required me to stop for the day. That required that the sealer for the upper portion of the truck needed to be scuffed and a new coat of sealer applied prior to top coats. Therefore, after taping off the bottom portion of the truck, the sealer applied the previous day was scuffed with a gray Scotch-Brite™ pad, and another coat of sealer applied.

The sealer dries fairly quickly. So, by the time I had the primer spray gun cleaned and put away, the sealer was dry, allowing me to go ahead and begin mixing the black base coat and hardener for the upper portion of the truck.

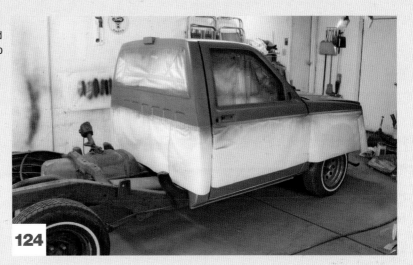

First coat of black on the truck and it is looking pretty good. Be sure to let the first coat flash and look closely again to verify that you have not missed any spots. Don't hesitate to add a second coat if necessary. Keeping the tip of the spray gun about 8 inches away from the surface and moving just fast enough to avoid runs seems to work best.

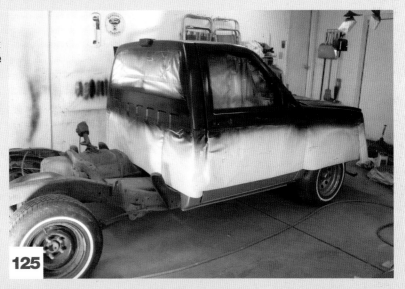

After the base coat is applied to achieve coverage, remove what masking can be removed and add a two or three coats of clear to the entire vehicle. I have applied two coats, but will apply two more coats overall after the red stripe is added to cover the seam between the black and silver paint.

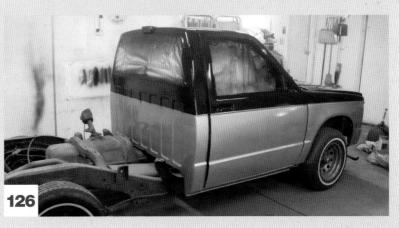

(continued)

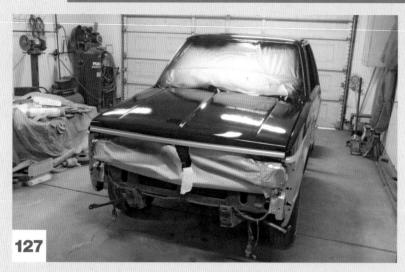

Certainly not perfect, but not bad for a home garage paint job. The clear calls for overnight drying time prior to taping, so that is all for now.

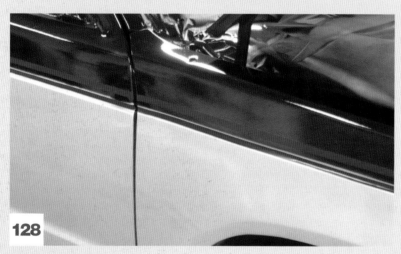

The next step will be to add masking tape where the stripe is to be, then mask off both sides of that. Then remove the masking from the area to be striped, spray the stripe on with a touch-up gun, then two coats of overall clear to be applied.

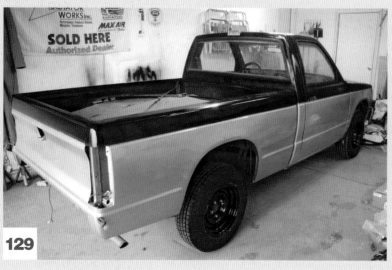

With the red stripe added, about all that is left to do is to wet-sand the clear to remove any imperfections. This is done by using 1,000-, 1,500-, and 2,000-grit sandpaper with lots of water and a light touch. Do not sand through the clear—just smooth it so that it is as smooth as can be. Then buff and polish with your favorite buffing and polishing compounds. After buffing and polishing, reinstall everything that was removed prior to painting. This will included bumpers, door windows, rearview mirrors, gas filler doors, and tailgate hardware. After about 30 days, wash the vehicle and apply a high-quality wax.

PAINTING OTHER PARTS AND COMPONENTS

VEHICLE PAINTING CHECKLIST

The following checklist gives the basic steps to follow when repainting a vehicle, whether it is a complete repaint or only a few panels. For the purpose of this checklist, the term "sheetmetal" will refer to any body panel, regardless of material.

NOTE: Always mask the vehicle appropriately before spraying any material. Always allow the appropriate flash and dry times before advancing to the next step.

1. Assess body damage (if any) and determine if chassis repair is necessary. Address chassis repairs prior to bodywork to ensure that body panel fit is correct.
2. Thoroughly wash the vehicle, using car wash soap. This will help eliminate adhesion problems later on, as body filler and paint products will not adhere to dirty or contaminated surfaces.
3. Remove all bumpers, trim accessories, mirrors, door handles, etc., that can be removed. Removing these items will usually be easier than masking around them. Removal will also make bodywork and painting more accessible.
4. Scuff metal surfaces with 180–220-grit sandpaper.
5. Apply epoxy primer.
6. Apply primer-surfacer directly to the epoxy primer if less than 72 hours have passed. If more than 72 hours, scuff epoxy primer with a Scotch-Brite™ pad before applying primer-surfacer.
7. After applying primer-surfacer, block sand with 320-, 400-, and 600-grit sandpaper.
8. Apply base coat. Remove nibs of dirt and debris with 1,200-grit sandpaper. Apply additional base coat as necessary for coverage.
9. Apply clear coat. Remove nibs of dirt and debris with 1,200-grit sandpaper.
10. Final sand with 2,000–2,500-grit before buffing.

FIBERGLASS BODY/BODY COMPONENT PREPARATION CHECKLIST

With the large number of companies reproducing complete bodies and countless body components out of fiberglass, it is likely that at one time or another, you will need to prepare fiberglass for paint.

Check with the manufacturer of your particular components to verify what they recommend for their product. Each company has its own special blend of components (resins, hardeners, etc.) for producing fiberglass parts. They should be able to tell you what method of surface preparation works best with their products.

If you cannot find specific instructions for your particular fiberglass products, the following should give you satisfactory results:

NOTE: Always mask the vehicle appropriately before spraying any material. Always allow the appropriate flash (dry) times before advancing to the next step.

1. Scuff the entire fiberglass surface with 80- to 100-grit sandpaper.
2. Take the fiberglass components to a body shop, and run the components through a bake cycle at 140 degrees.
3. Block sand the entire fiberglass surface with 120-grit sandpaper.
4. Perform bodywork as required.
5. Apply epoxy primer.
6. Block sand with 180-grit sandpaper.
7. Apply primer-surfacer. If primer-surfacer is applied within 72 hours, it can be applied directly to the epoxy primer. If more than 72 hours, epoxy primer must be scuffed using a Scotch-Brite™ pad before applying primer-surfacer.
8. Block sand with 180- and 220-grit sandpaper.
9. After applying primer-surfacer, block sand with 400- to 600-grit sandpaper.
10. Apply base coat. Remove nibs of dirt and debris with 1,200-grit sandpaper. Apply additional base coat as necessary for coverage.
11. Apply clear coat. Remove nibs of dirt and debris with 1,200-grit sandpaper.
12. Final sand with 2,000- to 2,500-grit before buffing.

Resources

3M/Speedway Automotive
5320 W. Washington Street
Indianapolis, IN 46241
www.speedwayautoparts.com
317-243-6696
Masking tape, paper, and other products

Automotive Technology, Inc.
544 Mae Court
Fenton, MO 63026
www.automotivetechnology.com
800-875-8101, 636-343-8101
Paint booths, equipment, and supplies

Badger Air-Brush Company
9128 W. Belmont Avenue
Franklin Park, IL 60131
www.badger-airbrush.com
800-247-2787, 847-678-3104
Airbrushes and accessories

BASF/Automotive Finish
26701 Telegraph Road
Southfield, MI 48034-2442
www.basf.com
800-080-0347, 248-948-2088
Paint products

California Car Cover Company
9525 DeSoto Avenue
Chatsworth, CA 91311-5011
www.calcarcover.com
800-423-5525, 818-998-2100
Car covers

Campbell Hausfeld
100 Production Drive
Harrison, OH 45030
www.chpower.com
888-247-6937, 513-367-4811
Air compressors and pneumatic tools

CASTAIR of Minnesota
550 Flying Cloud Drive #1B
Chaska, MN 55317
www.castair.net, acplus@aol.com
888-445-9251, 952-445-9251
Air compressors

Dupli-Color Products
101 Prospect Avenue NW500 Republic
Cleveland, OH 44115
www.duplicolor.com
800-247-3270, 216-515-7765
Paint products

DuPont
11215 Brower Road
North Bend, OH 45052
www.info@dupont.com, www1.dupont.com
800-441-7515, 513-941-4121
Paint products

Eastwood Company
263 Shoemaker Road
Pottstown, PA 19464
www.eastwoodcompany.com
800-345-1178
Automotive restoration tools, equipment,
and supplies

Finesse Pinstriping, Inc.
P.O. Box 541428
Linden Hill Station
Flushing, NY 11354
www.finessepinstriping.com
800-228-1258
Striping tape

Hemmings Motor News
P.O. Box 100
Bennington, VT 05201
www.hemmings.com
800-227-4373
Classified ads for vehicles, products,
and services

High Ridge NAPA
2707 High Ridge Boulevard
High Ridge, MO 63049
636-677-6400
Automotive parts, DuPont paint products

HTP America
3200 Nordic Road
Arlington Heights, IL 60005-4729
www.usaweld.com
800-872-9353, 847-357-0700
Welders, plasma cutters, tools,
and accessories

Imperial Restoration/POR-15
7550 E. Rice Road
Gardner, IL 60424
www.getrust.com
800-576-5822, 815-237-8678
Rust removal and restoration products

Jerry's Auto Body, Inc.
1399 Church Street
Union, MO 63084
636-583-4757
Auto body repair

Licari Auto Body Supply, Inc.
2800 High Ridge Boulevard
High Ridge, MO 63049
636-677-1566
PPG paint products and supplies

Meguiars
17991 Mitchell South
Irvine, CA 92614-6015
www.meguiars.com
800-854-8073, 949-752-8000
Car care products

Metro Moulded Parts, Inc.
11610 Jay Street
P.O. Box 48130
Minneapolis, MN 55448
MetroSales@metrommp.com
800-878-2237
Trim and molding products

Miller Electric Manufacturing Company
1635 W. Spencer Street
Appleton, WI 54914-4911
www.millerwelds.com
800-426-4553, 920-734-9821
Welders, plasma cutters, tools,
and accessories

Morfab Customs, Inc.
506 Suite C, Terry Street
Washington, MO 63090
www.morfabcustoms.com
636-262-1268
Hot rod fabrication and assembly,
welding, painting

Mothers Polish Company
5456 Industrial Drive
Huntington Beach, CA 92649-1519
www.mothers.com
800-221-8257, 714-891-3364
Polishes, waxes, and cleaners

PPG Refinish Group
19699 Progress Drive
Strongsville, OH 44149
www.ppgrefinish.com
440-572-6880 fax
Paint products

Sharpe Manufacturing Company
8750 Pioneer Boulevard
Santa Fe Springs, CA 90670
www.sharpe.com
800-742-7731
Paint spray guns and equipment

Sherwin-Williams Automotive Finishes
4440 Warrensville Center Road
Warrensville, OH 44128
www.sherwin-automotive.com
800-798-5872, 800-247-3268
Paint products

Stencils & Stripes Unlimited
1108 S. Crescent Avenue #38
Park Ridge, IL 60068
www.stencilsandstripes.com
847-692-6893
Reproduction paint stencils, stripes, and decals

Stilmore Designs
11458 Lucerne
Redford, MI 48239
www.stilmoredesigns.com
Concept drawings

Trim Parts
2175 Deer Field Road
Lebanon, OH 45036
www.trimparts.com, sales@trimparts.com
513-934-0815
GM Restoration Parts

Trim-Lok
6855 Hermosa Circle
Buena Park, CA 90620
www.trimlok.com
888-874-6565, 714-562-0500
Plastic and rubber trim and seals

Valspar Refinish
210 Crosby Street
Picayune, MS 39466
www.houseofkolor.com
601-798-4229
Paint products

Wyoming Technical Institute (Wyotech)
4373 N. 3rd Street
Laramie, WY 82072
www.wyomingtech.com
800-521-7158, 307-742-3776
Automotive technical school

Year One
P.O. Box 129
Tucker, GA 30085-0129
www.yearone.com
800-932-7663, 800-950-7663
Automotive restoration parts

Index